LIVING WITH
DECORATIVE TEXTILES
TRIBAL ART FROM AFRICA, ASIA AND THE AMERICAS

Nicholas Barnard

LIVING WITH
DECORATIVE TEXTILES

TRIBAL ART FROM AFRICA, ASIA AND THE AMERICAS

Photographs by James Merrell

With 267 illustrations, 190 in colour and 5 maps

Thames and Hudson

Frontispiece: Turkoman patchwork camel decoration

Right: Balouch woman's bag

Line drawings by Judith Blake

© 1989 Thames and Hudson Ltd, London

First published in paperback in the United States of America in 1995 by Thames and Hudson Inc., 500 Fifth Avenue, New York, New York 10110

Library of Congress Catalog Card Number 94-61397

ISBN 0-500-27821-0

Printed and bound in Italy.

Contents

Acknowledgments   6

Introduction   7

Chapter One   **Origins**   25

The Americas · Africa · Asia Minor to Central Asia · the Indian subcontinent · Indonesia

Chapter Two   **Function**   73

Utility and trade · decoration and symbolism

Chapter Three   **Raw materials and techniques**   81

Raw materials · spinning · dyestuffs and dyeing · looms · techniques

Chapter Four   **Decorative hangings**   89

Size and shape · scale · colour and pattern · formal and informal styles · durability · lighting · hanging methods

Chapter Five   **Unusually decorative**   121

Unusual yet traditional · upholstery · unusually casual

Chapter Six   **Decorative floor covers**   153

Floor surfaces · size and shape · colour and pattern · durability

Chapter Seven   **Collector's guide to sources and services**   177

Collecting textiles · care, repair and cleaning · further reading · international textile collections · international auction houses · dealers, importers and services · glossary

Index   190

Acknowledgments

James and I visited many homes in Europe and America over a twelve-month period in order to complete a selection of photographs for this book; for the patience, assistance and warm hospitality given freely by these textile collectors, we extend our thanks.

When in Santa Fé we were assisted in so many ways by Mary Hunt Kahlenberg, Judy Margolis, Bob and Charlotte Kornstein and De Wayne Youts. Valerie Justin was the key to the success of our trip to California and New Mexico. On the east coast, Peter-Ayers Tarantino shepherded us with great kindness around Philadelphia and in New York Robert and Marjorie Lawrence were generous and good-natured hosts at all times. Gail Martin made our work in New York a pleasure and Jack Larsen kindly recommended a fine location.

An expedition to France was organized by Jacqueline Daumas, and the Neutrogena Corporation kindly let us photograph their Paris collection of textiles. In the United Kingdom, Christopher Farr and Joss Graham assisted by introducing clients and friends, Sally Liddell successfully chased picture sources and Amanda Harcourt processed the list of dealers. José Luczyc-Wyhowska, John Gillow, Paul Hughes, Alastair Hull and Tim and Ferelith Ashfield freely lent textiles for studio photography.

We thank the following textile dealers and collectors for the use of their photographs: Peter Davies pp. 65 (old Kurdish kilim), 67 (Konya kilim, Erzurum kilim, Sivas kilim); Gail Martin and Vladimir Haustov pp. 59 (Toradja hanging), 62 (susani), 67 (Ottoman curtain), 68 (tunic decoration), 70 poncho; Valerie Justin pp. 65 (Kuba kilim), 68 (flatweave, hanbel), 71 (serape, mola), 72 (flatweave); Paul Hughes pp. 69 (raphia textile), 70 (Huari tunic), p. 126; Jonathan Hope pp. 58, 59 (hinggi); Steve Berger p. 70 (iscayo, llacota); De Wayne Youts p. 71 (flatwoven rug); Geert Keppens p. 66 (Thracian kilim); Christopher Farr pp. 60 (dhurrie), 61 (dhurrie); Pip Rau p. 62 (pardah); and Alastair Hull p. 63 (Maimana kilim).

Acknowledgments and thanks are due also to the following for permission to reproduce photographs: in England, the Hutchison Library p. 57; the India Office Library pp. 26, 29, 44, 154, and the Royal Commonwealth Society Library pp. 41, 54, 55; in America, the Textile Museum pp. 69 (Fulani blanket), 70 (Guatemalan Indian skirt); the National Gallery of Art, Washington (Collection of Mr and Mrs Paul Mellon) p. 122; the Philadelphia Museum of Art (The A.E. Gallatin Collection) p. 122; the Millicent A. Rogers Memorial Museum of Taos, New Mexico p. 72 (pictorial blanket); and the School of American Research, Santa Fé p. 72 (chief blanket).

Judith Blake patiently drew the illustrations.

This book is for Amanda, Tom and Lucy, and to thank Alastair and Jennie.

Introduction

In recent years I have been responsible for organizing and supervising many exhibitions of tribal and folk textiles from all over the world. One of my simple yet essential pleasures in running these events comes from observing the reactions of many first-time visitors to a show of ethnic art. Their obvious excitement and stimulation are perhaps aroused by two facts: that the textiles may be highly decorative, and yet utilitarian; and also that their inherent imperfections, individual charm and labour-intensive workmanship inspire an appreciation of a way of life that was once evident in our own pre-industrial past.

An investigation of contemporary tribal weaving communities shows that, on the whole, the art of traditional weaving is surviving and developing. Indeed, it is reassuring to find that, in the midst of our new world of instant communications, rapid travel and consumer ephemera, the ancient tradition of tapestry weaving is still flourishing amongst many tribal peoples. From the vertical looms of Anatolia to the backstrap weaving of the Andes, the painstaking work continues, whether for trade or for family use. Today, these weavers are entering a new era of rapid and unprecedented change in the development of their vibrant, energetic and largely naive folk art. Inspired by market forces and all kinds of cultural influences – from philanthropic collectors to peace corps volunteers, local merchants and tourists – the weavers are adapting, copying and replicating old work and inventing new styles and compositions. I find that it is impossible to determine whether any of these directions should be actively discouraged or encouraged, for so long as the melting pot of creative and technical influences continues to be stirred, so much the better. It is enough that the looms are still being worked by hand, producing textiles to give both pleasure and use to someone, somewhere.

This book is about flatwoven, resist dyed and woven, and embroidery-decorated weaves, made on simple looms by tribespeople all over the world. Certainly, *Living with Decorative Textiles* is not an all-embracing companion to world textile art. I have decided that textiles from Japan, China, Europe and European North America and White Russia do not fall under the loosely defined title of 'tribal' and are not represented. On the whole, workshop production and the processes of mass production are ignored. The hand-printing and painting of textiles, although a tribal occupation in West Africa and India, and reaching a high art form in the batik of Indonesia, is a vast topic requiring thorough treatment in a volume of its own.

Living with Decorative Textiles shows how the work of tribal weavers of ancient through to recent times may be enjoyed by more than just the specialist collector. Now, more than ever before, the availability of folk and tribal textiles is increasing as ethnic art galleries proliferate and enlightened department and speciality stores expand their horizons. This book will serve as your guide, from origins and techniques to methods of hanging and design considerations, right through to a survey of international dealers and retailers. The range of opportunities for an individual style of decoration is enormous. Old appliqué ceiling hangings from north-west India used as colourful bed covers in an English country manor house, dazzling new kilims from Kurdistan that look spectacular in a modern Paris apartment, and cushions covered in antique Bolivian shawl cloth on a sofa in Santa Fé – all are photographed here in an appreciation of a great creative tradition.

Antique, old and new tribal flatweaves and embroideries are examined regionally. The types of textiles represented here span a broad cross-section of what is available in the countries of origin, galleries and auction houses, as well as what can be seen in ethnographic museums throughout the world. There is a detailed summary of these sources within Chapter Seven and, of course, the glossary of weaving terms and the extensive bibliography will guide those seeking further information or a more detailed analysis of a particular textile or tribal weaving technique. The historical spelling of tribal place names, tribes and weaving techniques has been used, for which there is no internationally recognized standard. Familiar terms and names in the text with an unfamiliar spelling may be cross-referenced within the glossary and index for the alternative renditions.

(Opposite) In the living room of this North London apartment, European furnishings blend in complete sympathy with silk, wool and cotton textiles from Central Asia. Over the oak chest from the North-West Frontier is pinned a splendid mid-nineteenth-century silk and cotton ikat piece from Bokhara. A Sanchouli Balouch prayer kilim hangs on the wall, framed by Greek and Turkish icons; over the polished boards is a large sutrangi, a tapestry-woven cotton rug from Afghanistan made for use as a mosque floor covering. The embroidered cushions are from the Balkans.

(Left) Sewn onto a black cotton ground and stretched on a wooden frame is half of a pre-Columbian parrot feather poncho, a striking and textural blaze of colour. The woven cotton ground and the fragile birds' feathers have survived for over seven hundred years, by virtue of their being stored in the desiccated climate of the Peruvian coastal desert. Other pre-Columbian antiquities from Mexico are lined up alongside the more modern basket from the Amazon.

·(Right) Parts of this small adobe peasant house are over one hundred years of age. It has been lovingly renovated and decorated with tribal textiles by two avid collectors of ethnic and folk art. The rough whitewashed walls and simple furnishings are a minimalist match for the rich weaves. Here in the dining room, an embroidered raphia Kuba cloth from the Congo has been framed and hung on the wall; its four-panelled construction and eccentric composition has great vitality and charm. The modern American basket stands on a Spanish chest with two pre-Columbian Mexican pottery pieces – a study in shape, texture and pattern.

(Left) Tribal textiles have all manner of decorative uses. A pair of Turkoman kilims has been protectively lined and hung as curtains, tied back with lengths of tasselled hair decorations from *Afghanistan*. A tailor's dummy is clothed in a North-West Frontier patchwork dress and an ornate mirror is flanked by a framed Sindi embroidery and an Uzbek tent decoration.

(Opposite) In this, the London home of a writer on fine food and textiles, no corner is neglected, for there are either interesting embroideries and weavings decorating the walls, floor and furniture, or painted reproductions of Ottoman fabric designs stencilled on the walls. Costumes, framed fragments and loosely draped textiles create contrasts between different textures of cloth, and between formal and informal presentation.

(Below) The toran from Gujarat has been suspended, quite correctly, over the doorway to bring luck and good fortune to the owner of this house, while another Indian hanging, a square chakla, has been framed on a stretcher without needing a decorative border. Aside from the usual place for a kilim — on the floor — kilims such as this fine Senna example may be hung on the wall. The floral-patterned slitweave work is displayed most unusually and effectively in a landscape format.

(Below) *A light and spacious Californian house, in which the modern art of the Western world and primitive art meet in stimulating harmony. Over the sofa is draped a wonderfully simple Navajo Ute chief blanket. All about, statues and dolls of ancestors and spirits vie with the metal collages, the painting and the sculpture.*

(Above) *Woven as a palace decoration, this Indian cotton dhurrie is chequerboard patterned in mimicry of tiled floors, and forms the centrepiece to an English country house living room.*

(Left) *Similar colours and patterns of textiles from disparate cultures have come together in this bedroom. Around the bedside, a multi-mihrab dhurrie is matched by the dhurrie on the floor, and complemented by a West African Ewe stripwoven cloth on the bed.*

14

(Right) On a spacious landing, a new and harmoniously decorative Indian dhurrie may be seen and enjoyed from many levels. Laid over tiles on non-slip underlay, this large cotton flatweave will last well and be safe to walk on without risk of sliding.

(Right) In the Philadelphia home of a designer and textile collector, the decorative theme of chrome, black, and wood tones for the dining-room furniture is enriched by the wall display of powerfully individual, yet subtly decorated ceremonial textiles from the Congo and the Bolivian altiplano.

(Left) The decorated wrought-iron pole, from which a North African Berber flatweave is suspended, combines with the Indonesian theatrical masks to create a dramatic frame.

As one descends these gallery stairs the fine workmanship of an old Senna kilim may be appreciated, and from a distance the full impact of the central 'herati' medallion and mosque design may be enjoyed. Resting on another kilim, the sofa has been luxuriantly draped with an Ottoman embroidered bed cover.

16

(Opposite) In this Parisian home of a collector of Orientalist art, a table – covered by a Turkoman silk textile and set with a collection of Islamic glass and metalware – is surmounted by an Algerian scene, by Marius de Buzon.

Wall spaces compete to be filled by either books or textiles. A stairwell is an ideal location for a large textile that deserves to be seen from many vantage points. Framed with a narrow cloth border, the blaze-reds of the West African Ewe cloth complement the fine and bright embroidery of the adjacent Guatemalan huipil, or blouse.

Looking out over the Palisades, this section of a Santa Monican living room combines old and new in metal, wood and woven wool in a delightful panoply of incongruity. Behind the Rockola and draped over the piano bench are Mexican bridge serapes, made for use as card table cloths, and on the floor is a large crystal rug, adjacent to which lies a Teec Nos Pos rug – both are Navajo.

A beautifully carved marble fireplace provides a perfect setting for a fine collection of ancient pots and textiles from the Old World and the New. Hanging over an acid-free cardboard tube is a classic Huari tapestry decorated with abstract and feline creatures, and resting against the wall behind the gourd-like pots from ancient Peru are two framed Coptic tapestry fragments.

(Right) The dazzling centrepiece of this wall is an early nineteenth-century Bokhara silk and cotton ikat hanging, simply and effectively positioned with pushpins. The North-West Frontier furniture is bedecked with a fine assembly of hats and donkey bags from Central Asia, while an impressive collection of ikat cloth forms a jumble of silken colours and patterns.

Beneath a painted beam, an appliqué door hanging from north-west India mixes with a collection of china and pottery. Many of these wall hangings may be found complete with their original cotton loops for fixing to a wall with pins.

(Left) Pugin-influenced dining furniture is surrounded by Indonesian crafts. On the wall a Javanese batik hangs by a keris board and the table is richly covered by a twentieth-century Sumban man's ikat mantle. The bust of Hypnos calmly eyes a carved wooden box containing a useful Balinese accessory – a set of cock-fighting spurs.

Seen from the hallway of this large Santa Fé house, tribal textiles and objects form an underlying theme amongst the traditional furnishings. On the brick floor, safely anchored and protected by an underlay, is an *Afghan gypsy kilim*, in good company with the Navajo flatweaves in the adjacent den.

Chapter One   **Origins**

Origins

The production of fabrics woven by man has played a central role in the evolution of civilization; indeed, as man colonized the globe north and south of the tropics, weaving developed concurrently with the domestication of wild animals and the cultivation of fibrous plants. No doubt the primary function of the earliest woven fabrics was to provide insulation from the elements; their secondary role as objects of identification and decoration was a natural progression. Certainly both the art and craft of weaving are so ancient and important that every culture has oral or written records that link textiles with gods, goddesses, myths and legends. Every stage of cloth production, from the act of weaving to the textile itself, has inspired fables all over the world. The Dogon people of West Africa see weaving as an expression of order from formlessness, many Muslim weavers hang talismans and amulets from the loom to ward off the evil eye, and the Batak of Indonesia weave a circular cloth for a birth rite that represents the continuity of life from generation to generation.

The process of weaving, the interlacing of strands of vegetable or animal fibres to form a cloth, is thought to have been developed by many cultures on different continents. The scale of the cultural and technical dissemination that may have occurred between peoples in prehistoric times will probably never be divined. Textiles, by their very nature, will not survive for long periods unless preserved in extraordinary circumstances. Likewise, the tools of the weaver – wooden looms, spindles and combs – have rotted away, leaving at times only the metal or stone weaving implements to provide the archaeologist with some indication of the level of past weaving skills and activities at a particular site. It is ironic that the fruits of the successful excavations have proved so rich and exotic, for these discoveries tend to reinforce a romantic appreciation of the splendour of the past. Frozen tombs and desiccated burial mounds have given up their treasures as a tantalizing and often confusing glimpse of the scale and distribution of the textile production of ancient times.

Loom-woven textiles have been excavated from burial chambers in Egypt, coastal Ecuador and Peru that have survived for over one thousand years, entombed with their owners as a palliative to the gods and a passport to a new life after death. The dry atmosphere and the security of the tombs ensured their survival. Another well-known find from ancient times occurred in the frozen lands of Siberia in the tombs of Pazyryk. In a sarcophagus of ice lay the earliest known knotted rug, almost intact, as well as tapestries that were woven in the fourth or fifth century BC. In comparison to this rather limited assortment, the excavations at Fostat, near Cairo, have yielded an embarrassment of riches. Thousands of textile fragments dating from the seventh to the eleventh century and later have been excavated from what became, after the founding of Cairo in AD 969, the city dump.

Further evidence of the origins and importance of textiles in antiquity may be found in the records of the day. The engraved tablets of Babylon, Greece and Rome detail, as early as the seventh century BC, the sophisticated trade networks that existed along the caravan and coastal shipping routes between East and West. The Greeks and Romans developed a passion for the brilliant dyes and the diaphanous muslins, known as 'woven winds', of the Indian subcontinent. The decline of the northern Mediterranean empires and the speed with which Islam drove a cultural barrier and political wedge between the Southern Asian trade routes all but terminated this thriving trade in textiles.

The Islamic empires of the Seljuks, Ottomans, Mongols, Mughals and Safavids, which dominated life beyond the Mediterranean to the borders of the Orient between the seventh

and eighteenth centuries, shared a common appreciation of textiles. If the Roman and Byzantine Empires encouraged a trade in the weavings from the East, then the patronage of succeeding Muslim kingdoms created a new and golden era of decorative textiles. Enlightened rulers established workshops and gathered the finest weavers from throughout Asia to satisfy the affluent desires of the court and the ruling elite. The formal yet very ornate nature of Islamic art was enriched by influences from the fringes of their world through links with India, China and sub-Saharan Africa. The Indian sensitivity for colour, the finest Chinese silks and the power of the African abstract combined with the existing pre-Islamic tribal heritage in an amalgam of technical and artistic excellence. Centuries later a new trade and relationship between the looms of the East and the rich market in the West was established, the ramifications of which persist to this day. The knotted rugs from the Levant and beyond were imported as luxury goods to satisfy the opulent tastes of the church and gentry of a civilizing Europe.

The Spanish and Portuguese empire-building in the Americas and the East from the sixteenth century onwards opened new and direct sea trading links between textile producers and consumers. Whereas the Spanish adventurers marvelled at, and documented, the textile riches of the Mayan and Incan Empires and temporarily but forcefully reorganized the Indian weavers to meet the Iberian demand for tapestries, the Portuguese seized on the opportunity to be the first to control the export of cotton cloth to Europe. Calicut was their trading port on the Malabar coast of India, and the source of the word 'calico', denoting printed cotton. Until the Industrial Revolution the Indian sub-continent was the largest exporter of textiles in the world, whence came the names for types of textiles that are in familiar use today, such as 'chintz', 'shawl' and 'sash'.

Aside from the trade in 'Turkey' and 'Persian' carpets and the mass production of Indian cottons, there has been little mercantile exchange with the West to disturb the activities of the tribal weavers in parts known and unknown throughout the world until relatively recently. Tribes and peoples local to centres of power and wealth would have woven textiles in an environment of patronage or trade, and other utilitarian and decorative textiles would always have been made for family and personal use by many weavers. This parochial environment began to be disturbed irreversibly by the tumultuous

changes brought about by invasion and control by the European and Islamic powers, for whatever motives, and by social and economic revolutions. The subsequent disruption of social and religious behaviour impinged upon the types and styles of weaves produced. Muslim domination directly affected the elements of design in textiles, and Hispanic religious influence tampered with native styles of clothing, and with the ritual procedures of the death-cult ceremonies that had often involved the interment of thousands of beautiful textiles. These influences were a positive embellishment to an ancient weaving tradition by comparison with the consequences of the scale and pace of change that has occurred over the past two hundred years. The revolutionary processes of industrialization have irrevocably, whether directly or indirectly, transformed the way of life of the village and nomadic tribal weaver.

It is the rate of this change that is unprecedented in weaving history. At first the new powerloom production of Europe replaced the handloomed work of India. Manmade dyestuffs were accepted immediately because of their brilliant colours, ease of use and low cost. Tribal identity was challenged by political and social revolutions, and the flight to the cities and towns for work accelerated. The process of weaving in primitive circumstances, from unprepared yarn to a completed textile, is immensely labour-intensive and time-consuming; handloomed textiles as garments could not compete in price or style with the increasingly popular imported Western-style clothing, and the traditional uses for flatweaves and embroideries have become unfashionable and often irrelevant in a rapidly 'modernizing' society. These developments are, ironically, at odds with the established and exponentially growing demand for ethnic textiles by enlightened Western consumers since the Second World War. Textiles that were once seen to be worthy of collection by ethnographic museums and dedicated specialists are ever increasingly being used as decorations and utilitarian floor covers in every type and style of home in the Western world.

This combination of burgeoning exports, the acquisitive habits and cultural influences of the growing numbers of international travellers, and a general decline in traditional weaving standards and practices has proved to be a godsend for the income and lifestyle of weavers and merchants alike. Not so delighted are traditionalist Western collectors and dealers, and those tribespeople concerned about their

Mexican serape eye-dazzler pattern

disintegrating religious, social and cultural values. Of late, however, a coincidental combination of effort from domestic as well as Western sources is working to reverse this trend. Tribal leaders keen to save the identity of their people have encouraged a return to traditionalism in religious and social behaviour, if not in lifestyle. This will affect the weavers' work directly by the reintroduction of the ceremonial use and exchange of textiles and the rigorous reinforcement of control over symbolism and colour in weaving compositions. The Western emphasis on the importance of traditionalism is motivated by many factors, from philanthropy to sophisticated exploitation. The shocking results from the introduction of the first chemical dyes and the use of manmade yarn, and the perception that design influences were becoming too Western-orientated, have encouraged scholarly and commercial involvement in the tribal weaving process. From New Mexico to Turkey and from Ecuador to Persia, chemists have instructed weavers and dyers in the processes and use of natural dyestuffs and collectors have attempted, with photographs and examples, to inspire a return to atavistic designs and compositions. The reintroduction of hand-spun natural fibres and an awareness of quality rather than quantity have been encouraged.

Theoretically, the higher prices achieved for the new traditional weaves should compensate for the extra work involved. It is as if the weavers have come full circle, again, in their relationship with their work and their patrons. In many societies work that would have been controlled by courtly patronage is now, through merchant and dealer, inspired by an increasingly enlightened and discerning Western market. As ever, the textiles from the tribal looms reflect in some part the good, bad and indifferent skills of the weaver. But renewed availability of the high quality traditional weaves from many tribal weaving societies must be the healthy sign of a new appreciation and respect for the ancient and painstaking skills of the weaver and the beauty of his or her art. One hopes that the work of these born-again craftsmen will prove, as in the past, a rich source of inspiration and a catalyst for the inter-cultural dissemination of creative ideas with fellow weavers and artists throughout the world.

The inmates and jailers of Poona jail in British India display their dhurries, spinning wheels and weft-beating combs.

The Americas

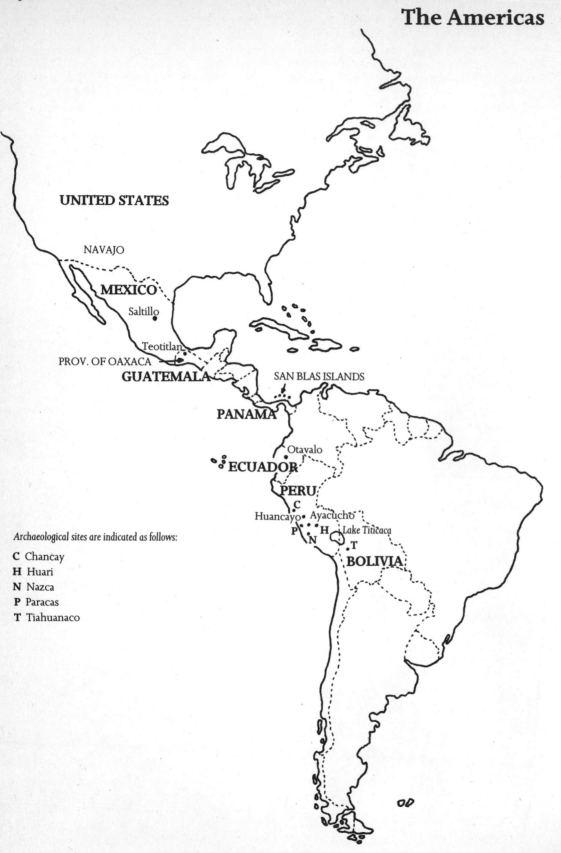

UNITED STATES

NAVAJO

MEXICO

Saltillo

Teotitlan

PROV. OF OAXACA

GUATEMALA

SAN BLAS ISLANDS

PANAMA

Otavalo

ECUADOR

PERU

C

Huancayo   Ayacucho

P   H   Lake Titicaca

N   T

BOLIVIA

Archaeological sites are indicated as follows:

C Chancay

H Huari

N Nazca

P Paracas

T Tiahuanaco

Textiles from the Americas were originally made by the weavers of various Indian tribes and kingdoms that, since the sixteenth century, have been subject to Spanish influence. Until the twentieth century, the Indians of the Americas wove textiles for use as garments, blankets, hangings and covers. Market forces have, more recently, been dictated by Western consumers, which has resulted in the weaving of many non-traditional flatwoven floor rugs.

North America

The Indian tribes of North America have been weaving cloth for garments and covers for thousands of years. From the relatively scant archaeological evidence available, it appears that true loom weaving in North America is a recent phenomenon. In ancient times the simplest techniques such as braiding, plaiting and finger weaving would have been widespread, and it was as late as AD 500 that the first belt or backstrap looms were in use and perhaps not until AD 1000 that the rigid loom was commonly found in the South-West. Considering that cultivated cotton was not introduced until between AD 700 and 1000 and that sheep were an alien species until the Spanish ventured north from Mexico at the end of the sixteenth century, it is probable that early raw materials must have consisted of vegetable fibres and animal hair.

The production of textiles and the development of weaving techniques in pre-Columbian times was dependent on relatively local inter-tribal communications and trade. The Indian tribes from areas along what is now the North Mexican borders are known to have influenced the work of neighbouring weavers, and the use and possible cultivation of cotton spread slowly northwards from this region; fragments of Pueblo Indian work from the fourteenth century show a mastery of sophisticated weaving techniques, such as weft-faced patterning and brocading and the use of vegetable dyes for tie-and-dye work, as well as simple striped decoration and colouring on a plainweave ground. These crafts, and the more rudimentary weaving of the Indians to the north and east, continued until the arrival of the white man from Europe in the sixteenth century.

This foreign influence was both direct and dramatic in its effects. Hispanic activity in the south and the invasions from the east transformed the distribution and nature of native weaving. The rolling back of the frontiers westwards by the white settlers and their large-scale import of machine-made European 'trade cloth' caused an almost universal cessation of domestic weaving in the north and east by the mid-eighteenth century. From that time, the tribal weaving 'tradition' of North America was to be found in the work of the Indian peoples of South-West America.

Pueblo Indian textiles Pueblo and Navajo Indian textiles have an intimately interrelated historical background that is part Indian, part Hispanic in origin. The pueblos of the South-West are compact villages of stone or mud-walled houses originally inhabited by the Hopi, Zuni and Pima people in what are now the States of Arizona and New Mexico. Although the Spaniards travelled into Pueblo Indian territory as early as 1540, it was in 1598 that their first colonists attempted to settle in the pueblo of San Juan. The weaving tradition that they encountered was male dominated, the looms vertical and cotton the predominant raw material. After documenting the scale, wealth and technical excellence of the textiles they found, the Spaniards changed the face of native weaving forever by introducing the Andalusian churro breed of sheep, new dyestuffs and new styles of dress. They alienated themselves from the Indians by implementing a custom of forced labour at the newly erected European treadle looms and by exacting tributes in cloth.

By 1650 woollen as well as cotton blankets were being produced on the traditional vertical looms that remain in use to this day. Spanish taste inspired the weaving of serapes, the rectangular cloth long in warp and narrow in weft, in which patterning was confined to simple weft stripes, techniques were simplified and weft-faced weave replaced plainweave. The Pueblo Revolt of 1680 returned the region to local rule, disrupted again twelve years later by the Spanish invasion of 1692. It was not until 1848 that the area was won by the Union, and it is from this time that most of the Spanish-influenced Pueblo Indian textiles were collected and have been preserved. As with the Navajo work, the original Spanish and Mexican influences on the scale of the textile and the designs used can be comprehensively traced from the early part of the nineteenth century, but sadly, unlike Navajo textile production, Pueblo Indian weaving has, in the last eighty years, declined to near obscurity.

Navajo Indian weaving Despite being late arrivals in the South-West and relative newcomers to weaving the Navajos have dominated an appreciation of North American Indian textiles with their exciting harmonies of colour and space, best exemplified by the classic Navajo blanket of the nineteenth century, the zenith of their creative achievement. The roots of Navajo weaving are firmly Pueblo Indian in provenance, for after the wars with the Spanish in the seventeenth century many of the Pueblo Indians settled in Navajo territory, cementing an existing cultural relationship between the farmer and hunter-gatherer. Navajo weavers adopted Pueblo weaving techniques and patterning with alacrity and energy so that by the eighteenth century their blankets were highly prized by their Pueblo Indian and Plains Indian compatriots and the Spanish alike. Unlike Pueblo work, Navajo weaving was exclusively the domain of the women, who worked on simple vertical looms with woollen thread. Until the seventeenth century the colour of woven thread was limited to the tonal variations found in sheep's wool from white to brown. The Spanish imported Mexican indigo blue dye and until the late nineteenth century, red threads were obtained from unravelled trade cloth, or baize ('bayeta' in Spanish).

The fine quality of the work and the dry climate of the South-West have ensured that there are sufficient quantities of Navajo textiles extant to enable the development of Navajo weaving to be charted with accuracy from the nineteenth century on. Two types of textiles were tapestry woven in the last century. The short-warped, wide-wefted textiles are called 'chief blankets' and are an indigenous American Indian weaving style inherited from the Pueblo people. Until about 1850 the striped work directly followed the Pueblo tradition of shimmering bands of white, blue, brown and red, and is known as the First Phase. This banded effect was partly broken and the shape of the blanket accentuated by the introduction of nine or twelve blocks of contrasting or reversed out colour in a Second Phase that lasted some fifteen years. From 1865 these blocks turned into an overlay of diamonds on the striped ground with only the central diamond motif fully visible (the Third Phase). The early development of this rhomboidal theme coincided with the four-year incarceration of the troublesome Navajo at the settlement camp Bosque Redondo from 1864 to 1868. Finally, from about 1880 until the production of chief's blankets ceased completely, just before 1900,

Navajo blanket

the diamonds grew in size and merged at their corners in a Fourth Phase.

A second type of textile produced in quantity in the nineteenth century was the serape-style blanket, sometimes woven as a poncho. Unlike the chief blankets, this work is of Spanish Mexican inspiration. Early striped Navajo serapes were influenced from the end of the eighteenth century onwards by imported serapes from the Saltillo area in northern Mexico. Made in two pieces and sewn together with a hole at the centre of the spine for use as a poncho, the Saltillo serapes were made of fine and soft wool yarn, excellently and tightly woven with small zigzag patterning and a powerful central diamond motif. Worn over the head and falling gently from the focus of the diamond, these serapes were an almost formal contrast to the traditional Navajo blanket worn as a wrap. As before, the Navajo women proved to be masterful creators of a new combination-style of textile that blended the Navajo sensibilities of colour and space with the Mexican eye for detail and sense of practicality. Horizontal bands were overlaid by and contrasted with a multitude of wavy lines, zigzags and small lozenges that eventually focus on a greatly simplified central medallion. The central tension of the Saltillo serape composition is thus released into the whole cloth, bathing the viewer in visual pleasure. The golden era of Navajo serape weaving dates from 1840 to 1860, and, in particular, those textiles woven with the red and blue yarn unravelled from the bayeta trade cloth were highly sought after as luxury items of trade and prestige by all the inhabitants of the South-West – Mexicans, Americans, Pueblo and Plains Indians alike.

The Navajo confinement was a turning point in the development of their weaving tradition. Supplied with Mexican-influenced Rio Grande blankets that inspired the eye-dazzler compositions, tempted by the bright synthetic dyes and especially by the tightly spun yarn from Germanstown, Pennsylvania, and attracted by the financial rewards from trade brought by the new railroad, many of the Navajo weavers saw a decline in demand for traditional work from their neighbouring tribes and looked to the new White marketplace in the east. By 1900 the merchants and middlemen were established as key perpetrators of new textile compositions, techniques and formats. Floor rugs were more useful than blankets, oriental-style framed compositions were in demand from the White settlers in the east and the new frontier towns, and soft colours popular. Pictorial rugs, which

had, in the early nineteenth century, featured the American flag, and the animals, letters, and words that were true Navajo folk art were, by 1900, commercially inspired and featured non-traditional 'Indian' compositions of spirits and masked men.

Rugs, blankets, saddlecloths and serapes continue to be made by Navajo weavers today on traditional looms to satisfy a tourist market. Revivalist trends have ensured that original compositions and techniques are used and non-traditional but market-orientated vegetable-dyed weaves are available. Since the early part of this century blankets and rugs have been categorized by trading posts and in the name of the weaver, a personality cult that has greater affinity with modern European weaving than original tribal production.

Central America

From southern Mexico to Colombia stretches a rugged isthmus, whose legacy of traditions, political instabilities and ruins has been created by over two thousand years of empire-building – by pre-Columbian cultures, by the Spanish and, more recently, by Superpower filibustering. No examples of textiles from antiquity have survived to highlight the central role that woven cloth played in the pre-Columbian cultures. The sixteenth-century Spanish adventurers recorded that the Indians of the Aztec and Mayan Empires made tributes of thousands of the very finest textiles to their living and supernatural gods in burial and sacrificial rites and that taxes in those pre-Columbian days were exacted in cloth.

Spanish-imported sheep, new dyestuffs and the European treadle loom were added to the Indian tradition of backstrap weaving of cotton and fibrous cloths. The introduction of man-made dyes and fibres in recent history and the impact of a burgeoning tourist market has given yet more energy to this vibrant mix of Indian and Hispanic weaving skills and traditions. Weaving remains a key activity for the Indian groups and throughout the region the back-strap and treadle loom production of simple belts, bags, ponchos and blankets for a local domestic market continues; there is no doubt, however, that this more traditional work is on the decline by comparison with the expanding tourist and designer ethnic market.

Although loomed textiles are produced throughout the region, most of the Central American weaves found in the collections,

museums and galleries of Europe and North America are from Mexico, Guatemala and Panama.

Mexico All but three of Mexico's states lie in North America, yet the cultural roots of the people and their weaving are Central American. From about 200 BC there was a series of Indian empires that often overlapped without succeeding each other in direct chronological order, and so the direction and source of many pre-Columbian cultural influences is unclear. The Olmec, Zapotec, Mixtec and Aztec peoples dominated the centre and north of what is present-day Mexico, the Toltecs and the Maya the south. According to legend, the Aztecs originated north of the Gulf of California and travelled south, subjugating other Indian groups into an imperial and militarily supreme nation and establishing the site of Mexico City, only to be defeated by the Spanish conquistadors under Cortés in 1519.

Spanish influences on village weaving tend to follow a similar pattern throughout their former colonies in the Americas. Taxes were collected in cloth for export to Europe or for use by the settlers, and this exploitation of sweatshop labour was one of the early cultivators of the seeds of open revolt and the path to self-government. Indians were forced to wear European-style dress and many of the pagan ceremonies that consumed vast quantities of textiles were banned. Village weaving for domestic and family use continued – and continues to this day – but the driving force of tradition was and is seen to be slowing in the face of the pressures of modernization.

Mexico, as a state that has enjoyed considerable American and European cultural influences for a relatively long time, has fared well in adapting to the conflicting demands of the export market and the traditions and unity of a village or Indian group. Much of the credit for the process of ethnic reawakening goes to the educated Hispanic and mestizo middle classes of the 1920s, who saw Mexican art and culture trapped in a bourgeois limbo. Prior to this, pre-Columbian art was seen as barbaric and backward and contemporary popular village art was scorned as junk. (One of the leading advocates for the return of Indian art to the level of respectful appreciation and acceptance which is its due, was the muralist Diego Rivera.)

The fashion for ethnic art and the reawakening of pre-Columbian and peasant consciousness was soon apparent in the weaving. Aztec

Guatemalan woven bands

and Mayan motifs copied from stone carvings proliferated on blankets and serapes. One of the less fortunate aspects of this ethnic revolution, especially for the collector and researcher, is that many communities began to weave using designs and motifs of multivarious and disparate origins, so tending to diminish regional and local variations of 'traditional' textile work. Nevertheless, Mexican weaving remains a glorious aspect of a village folk art that is unashamedly rich and colourful, modern yet traditional.

Throughout Mexico the backstrap loom continues to be used for weaving narrow lengths of cloth for garments, bags and belts. The treadle loom tends to be found in the villages where rugs, ponchos, serapes and other textiles are made for export or for the tourist trade. Exended family groups prepare or buy the woollen or cotton yarn, and weave and sell the textiles as a cash business that is a welcome supplement to the farming of their smallholdings and agricultural wage labour.

In the north of Mexico, a predominating composition is based on the classic Saltillo serape with central diamond. These serapes that so influenced weaving north of the border date back to the seventeenth century. Nineteenth- and twentieth-century work from the area shows a simplification of the central medallion, a bordering of the ends with stripes and a regular decoration of simple diamond or arrow motifs onto an otherwise plain ground. The most valuable of these serapes have a central medallion woven of silk and the remaining weave is of the finest spun white wool.

Simple striped blankets and belts are made by the northern frontier tribes that are directly related to American Indian peoples. These are the Tarahumara, Mayo and Yaqui, and commercial influences from across the border have resulted in the production of floor rugs in traditional as well as imported designs. In the south the province of Oaxaca is one of the centres of large-scale weaving activity. The Zapotec weavers followed the early twentieth-century ethnic revolution by copying the geometric Mixteca architectural motifs found carved in stone near Teotitlan. More recently a surge of American interest in the weaving of reproduction rugs has generated an export industry of Navajo copies using vegetable dyes, and tight weaving required for floor use.

Guatemala The major roots of Guatemalan Indian culture are to be found in the glories of the Mayan civilization that flourished between AD 300 and 900. The collapse of this pre-Columbian empire in mysterious circumstances has left a legacy of grand ruins and a rich weaving tradition that has continued to develop relatively unspoilt by the often destructive forces of Western commercial influence. Although largely uncharted by archaeological remains, it is known that cotton textiles were woven as the fine raiment of the Mayan priests and nobility, and even now the Mayan influence is evident in the weaving of traditional everyday costume, ceremonial garments and by the abundance of pre-Columbian designs and motifs.

Guatemalan textiles are alive with unusual combinations of bright colours that mix well with busy motifs. Birds, figures, horses and flowers are clearly represented in realistic forms by way of embroidery or in a geometric style on flatwoven work with much brocade. Although the increased tourist trade of the past twenty years has encouraged the production of blankets woven to what are now almost standard 'Latin American' compositions, the majority of the weaving is traditional and exclusively for animal trappings or personal use and decoration. This is clearly evident throughout the country where village, town and city life alike is a bustle of Indians wearing traditional clothing full of colour, intricate patterns and textures.

Backstrap looms are in common use throughout Guatemala, primarily for weaving and decoratively brocading the two or three panels for the 'huipil' (a type of blouse) and for making belts or sashes. More often than not, men weave with the treadle loom, producing 'refajo', 'corte' and 'rodillera' blanket skirts, a poncho-like blanket called a 'capixay', as well as sashes and 'tzute' headscarves. Ikat work in cotton is found in Guatemala over a wide area of Totonicapan and Salcaja and the ikat process, or 'jaspeado' work, is so popular that the colourful blanket skirts with their tiny patterns and inscriptions are found all over the country.

The Guatemalan highland terrain is ideal sheep pasture and the wool is woven, in centres such as Momostenango, as warm blankets, ponchos and wraps. Cotton is woven throughout Guatemala and synthetic dyes are universal; bright synthetic yarns are used with unashamed abandon for brocade work and embroidery. A visit to a village on market day leaves no doubt that weaving in Guatemala is guided and inspired by a thoroughly traditional domestic market.

Panama *Kuna Indian Appliqué* As Turkey is seen as the linchpin between Europe and the East, so Panama could be regarded as the umbilical cord joining North and South America and, until relatively recently, an infuriating impasse between the Atlantic and the Pacific Oceans. A vassal of Colombia until 1903, Panama's population is a mix of Hispanic, Negro and Indian peoples of which the Kuna Indians of the San Blas Islands and the Antioquia district of Colombia are thought to be the last vestiges of an indigenous Carib strain. The Kuna have maintained their peace-loving and independent traditions right from their first contact with Europeans and other outsiders; the strength of their cultural and political disciplines and their unity have largely preserved Kuna tribal identity to this day. Living on some three thousand coral islands on the Caribbean coast of eastern Panama, the Kuna Indians have become justifiably famous for their colourful cotton reverse appliqué blouse panels.

It would seem that the Kuna have been practising this appliqué technique for no more than one hundred and twenty-five years. It is a development of an ancient tradition of body painting and, more recently, of cloth painting. 'Mola', the Kuna word for cloth, consists of appliqué work which is cut and sewn in panels as blouse decorations, mostly by the women. The lively colouring, and variety of pictorial content – which can range from aeroplanes to sea monsters – of the molas, represent an adaptation, absorption and rejection of foreign influences on Kuna society. Their quality remains, however, painstakingly high in the face of an inexorably rising demand for this work from tourists and dealers. This ability to use a textile craft as a 'cash crop' and yet to maintain standards of workmanship and originality of composition is a reflection of the strength of Kuna traditions, central to which is the revered and protected status of their women. In this matriarchal society, most Kuna women and girls continue to make and wear blouses with mola panels as a prized element of their dress and as a representation of their tribal identity.

Many molas depict animals, birds and people in an expression of vivid colour and life, others bear legends relating to events such as the arrival of piped water, or the slogan of a Panamanian political party; from these one may see the delight with which the Kuna women interpret their surroundings. Molas are still made, however, that are truly representational of ancient religious beliefs and practices; again, some clearly portray religious ceremonies whereas others may be concerned with protection from evil spirits that the Kuna believe may be at work in the souls of all animals and plants.

South America

The South American Indian peoples of the Central Andes and the adjacent Pacific coastal area have inherited one of the richest and oldest weaving traditions in the world; the last, most well-known and largest empire of all, the Incan Empire, was but a sixty-year finale to over three thousand years of cultural development. A central element in all these ancient civilizations was the craft of weaving. Textiles were an expression of wealth and status, they were imbued with a religious significance and in these cultures devoid of a written language, their designs were a means of communication. The tombs of the coastal desert of Peru have yielded a glorious abundance of textiles, for the sands, rich in saltpetre, and the desiccated climate, have preserved, often immaculately, a wealth of fragments and complete weaves that represent a pinnacle of achievement in world textile history. From graves that are over one thousand years old, superlative weavings abound, for every known type of weaving has been catalogued, the finest spun wool has been unravelled and over one hundred and ninety dye colours and shades have been analysed.

The Spanish invaders of the sixteenth century were at first astonished by the quantity and quality of textiles that they found throughout the newly subjugated Incan Empire, and then quick to reorientate the skilled weavers away from a life of service to a living god towards a life of forced labour and misery. The traditional backstrap loom and the horizontal loom were now joined by the more efficient European treadle loom, sheep were introduced as well as flax and silk, and the new religion of Roman Catholicism imposed alien styles of dress and behaviour that attempted to remove many of the Indians' links with their pagan past. Fortunately, the craft of weaving is so deeply rooted in the culture of the Indian of the altiplano that, despite this cultural hiatus, textiles were then and are still being made in a mixture of colonial and pre-Columbian styles. Textiles from South America are, traditionally, made as loose fitting garments, or for use as belts, wraps or bags; recently, however, a precedent has been established for the manufacture of flatwoven floor rugs for a tourist and export market. Such new developments are examined here along with the history of weaving in South America. We journey country by country, following the high ridges and valleys of the Andes from Ecuador to Bolivia by way of Peru, matching, ironically, the boundaries of the Incan Empire at its brief climax.

Ecuador Ecuador was the northern boundary of the expanding Incan Empire of the fifteenth century and although few ancient textiles survive, there is sufficient archaeological evidence to suggest that the pre-Incan Andean tribes were proficient weavers of cotton textiles on the backstrap loom. The tribes of the altiplano had developed a sophisticated trade network with the peoples of the ocean plain in one direction, and with the inhabitants of the Amazon jungle in the other; indeed, this relationship between the suppliers of cotton and foodstuffs and the weavers in the highlands is repeated throughout the Andean region.

Although the Incas controlled Ecuador for less than a century before the arrival of the Spanish, in that time they introduced new crops, domesticated cameloids, the Quechua language and the worship of the sun. They superimposed their ways on an existing culture rather than attempting to destroy the indigenous way of life, but a bellicose tribe would be annihilated or split and moved within the Empire and loyal Quechua-speaking subjects imported in their place. In this way considerable cultural cross-fertilization must have occurred. The production of textiles at a local family level continued, and has done to this day; but the taxation of the individual in a system known as 'mit'a' resulted in the formation of weaving workshops throughout the Empire, which produced 'cumpi' – ceremonial tapestry cloth of the highest quality. Large quantities of textiles were buried with the dead and burned each day as an offering to the sun, and a rigid class system ensured that only priests and nobles were adorned with the finest weaves.

Two years after Pizarro landed in Peru in 1532, Sebastian de Benalcazar decided to invade what is now Ecuador. Such was the speed of the conquest that by 1535 land was being allotted to Spanish settlers and by the mid-sixteenth century the mit'a system became forced labour within the 'obraje' workshop firmly under the settlers' control. The traditional Indian weaving communities of the Andes became the sweated workforce of the Spanish and the agrarian serfs to the large colonial estates, called 'encomiendas'. One of the most important obraje in Ecuador was to be found in the Cara Indian village of Otavalo. Situated north-east of Quito, Otavalo was well known in the colonial period for its prolific output of plain blankets, ponchos and cloaks. Today Otavalo is a famous and thriving textile market town and the Otavalenos well known for their trading skills throughout the Andes and beyond. Adapting to the tourist demand, floor rugs and pictorial textiles are woven on the treadle loom, whereas the backstrap loom is used for the neo-traditional poncho and belt work for the family and the local market.

Weaving is a domestic occupation and a tourist craft industry throughout most of the Andean Indian and highland villages of Ecuador; many have regional or local specializations that are pre-Columbian or of mixed colonial and pre-colonial origin. Weaving with resist-dyed yarn is common in the villages of the southern province of Azuay, especially around Sigsig, where warp ikat is woven on backstrap looms for sashes and ponchos; and the area is also well known for the production of the 'rebozo', the fringed shawl of very fine and lightweight ikat work. Throughout Ecuador cheerful and bright synthetic dyes are used extensively, as are manmade fibres; here, as in many weaving communities of the Americas, the full circle of raw material influences is about to be completed. From indigenous cotton to the spread in use of wool from the domesticated cameloids, the Indian weavers of the Americas were introduced to sheep's wool, flax, silk and synthetic fibres by the Europeans, only now to be reorientated by market forces to take up their pre-Columbian and 'traditional' raw materials again.

Peru and Bolivia Of all the ancient cultures of the Americas, those of the central Andean region have provided, by a perfect combination of climatic and social factors, the most fecund source of pre-Columbian textiles. The remote locations ensured the survival of the ruins of their magnificent cities and on the Pacific coast the ideal combination of soil structure and dry climate preserved the rich contents of their burial chambers. Nowhere else on earth has yielded so many perfectly preserved ancient textiles of such high quality that are such a delight to behold. The cloth-stuffed and shrouded corpses within the burial sites of the Peruvian coastal desert were the guardians of the ancient textile treasures of the New World.

The earliest textiles found are cotton and are at least four and a half thousand years old; many are dyed and decorated, an astonishing achievement for what was after all a stone-age society. Woollen cameloid fibres have been discovered in textiles from coastal sites dating from 1600 BC, proving that the extensive trading links that were to follow between the highland and lowland cultures of the region were already developing. From about 900 BC onwards there was a rapid development in backstrap loom weaving techniques and in the art of dyeing cameloid and cotton fibres, suggesting that there was more involved in the relationship between the coast and the altiplano than just commodities alone. The Paracas coastal culture (1000 BC – 200 BC) was followed by that of the Nazca (200 BC – AD 500), the Huari (AD 500 – 1000) and the Chancay and the Chimu (AD 1000 – 1476); developing concurrently were the highland civilizations, from the Chavin (1000 BC – 700 BC), to the Tiahuanaco cultures (600 BC – AD 1200). It was from out of the highlands of the Lake Titicaca region that the Incan Empire grew to unify the entire Andean region, from north Chile to Colombia. Short-lived (AD 1350–1532) and infamous, the Incan Empire is the least well-represented pre-Columbian culture in terms of textile remains.

Few textiles survive from the Chavin culture. The fragments found on the coast depict a civilization dominated by fearsome, many creatured deities. Textiles were ceremonial, symbolic to the last detail, and are decorated with paint and embroidery in a wealth of intertwining colours and figurative patterns. The Paracas culture on the other hand is particularly well documented by textile remains. The textiles exhumed from the graves of the Paracas civilization are testament to a highly developed death-cult. The dead were seen to be the mediators between the temporal and spiritual world and must therefore be buried with the finest cloth; this cult explains the religious fervour with which these textiles were woven. The huge quantity of textiles uncovered and the painstaking complexity of their weaving depicts a society working more for the dead that the living. The mummy-bundles of the grave sites contained layers of simple cloth interspersed with packets of folded textiles of every description.

Less cluttered and more relaxed in expression than the Chavin work, the textiles are unused and decorated in brocade with super-natural forms that show part man, part animal motifs in a mastery of colour and form. The cloth of the Paracas era is highly textural, as their unique use of the cross-knit loop stitch process gives the representations of many religious characters a raised and crocheted dimension. Embroidery in general reached the zeniths of perfection in this period. The Nazca coastal culture was very much more concerned with pottery than with textiles as an expression of religious faith and imagination. The culture is obsessed by ghoulish images of sacrificial trophy heads and the largely figurative work has a strong sense of movement in clearly defined spirit beings and deities. Slit tapestry-woven work is more common than in earlier finds and the patchworking of pieces of tie-and-dyed cloth is an unusual and highly attractive element in the weaving of the late Nazca culture.

The altiplano around Lake Titicaca was the source of the great Tiahuanaco culture that, with the Huari civilization to the north, directly influenced the art of the central Andes for nearly a millennia. Trading people by nature, the Tiahuanaco used textiles as a means of communication, as their llama caravans crisscrossed the Andes linking the Amazonian basin with the Pacific. The Tiahuanaco/Huari textiles are exquisite, for their guilds wove the very finest weft-faced tapestries, patterning the work with slitweave and the tightest single interlock technique imaginable. Figurative motifs are plentiful, compressed into rigidly geometric shapes that were to develop eventually into a form of abstract ornamentation. The patterning is reminiscent of Muslim weaving, where rigid Islamic doctrine forbidding the idolatrous portrayal of God's animal creations drove pagan pictorial expression into a plethora of geometric forms. The designs for this Indian work originated in their decorated stonework; geometric religious motifs abound as stone reliefs on the gateways and walls of the monumental cities of Tiahuanaco and Huari. The slit and interlocking tapestry technique also suits, or rather tends to dictate, decorative work in geometric terms. The complicated interaction between signs, motifs and colours in these tapestries suggests a complex form of writing, or a calendar for scholars to puzzle over.

The decline of the Tiahuanaco/Huari Empire by the thirteenth century resulted in a period of some two centuries when no culture can be singled out as especially influential. The region was split into local states and communities, of which the Chancay coastal confederation and the Chimu kingdom are well documented by

Bolivian coca bag

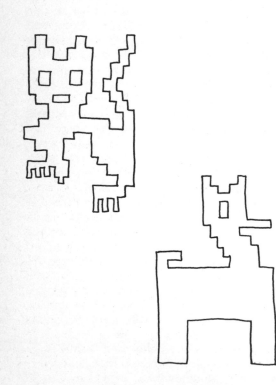

Contemporary Peruvian Indian textile motifs of pre-Columbian gods. The puma is the god of the High Plains; the llama is seen as a protector of their flocks of cameloids. Both have obvious everyday imagery.

textile finds. The Chancay era is best seen as a design rest period between the geometric dogma of the Tiahuanaco and the later Incan Empire. Chancay work is of fine quality and copious in quantity, and resist-dyed textiles have been found of both tie and dye as well as the more complicated ikat work, alongside tapestry and brocade techniques.

The rapid rise and precipitous fall of the Incan Empire ensured that only a relatively small quantity of textiles was buried for our retrieval, as a teasing taste of the greatness of their weaving. The Incas banished figurative forms and so created an era of textile production wherein geometric expression reached an artistic climax. By way of the mit'a system of taxation and from the specialist workshops of trained maidens and experienced male weavers, there came forth a powerfully standardized form of textile production.

The profoundly inhuman strength in design of some of the Incan textiles is a testament to the brittle ideology of an empire that a small number of Spaniards found so easy to topple. There was a strict class system, and the nobility and priests were dressed in, and their palaces decorated with, the finest weaves and tapestries, whereas the peasants wore warp-faced and patterned cloth, woven – much as today in Peru and Bolivia – on a village backstrap loom. The nobility of this region also commissioned the production of perhaps the most outlandish garments of the tribal world – composites of tropical birds' feathers attached to a cotton plainweave base, which have survived from the Incan, Nazca and Tiahuanaco eras. Their shimmering colours remain brilliant to this day.

Once the Spanish had harnessed the organized weaving skills of the Indians to serve their own purposes, tapestry weaving all but vanished without Incan patronage; only the remotest highland communities were able to maintain their weaving traditions linked to what became proto-pagan rites within the auspices of the Roman Catholic Church. Backstrap looms and small ground looms then, as now, continued the weaving of wraps, sashes and coca bags alongside the treadle loom production. The pattern of Spanish domination of Indian life is repeated throughout the Andes, although the final disintegration of tribal weaving traditions has been hastened at an exponential rate by the modernization and industrialization of these nations over the past century. What the Spanish failed to eradicate by coercion, the power of world commerce and trade is destroying by simple market forces.

In Peru today, Quechua-speaking Indians still weave their colonial and pre-colonial garments on ground and backstrap looms as part of their duties as farmers and workers of the land. Belts ('chumpis'), ceremonial wraps or mantles, ponchos and ponchitos, hats, purses and braid are made increasingly of manmade fibres. The techniques of warp-faced weaving and warp-float patterning continue to be handed down from generation to generation, almost unchanged for two millennia. Some Indian communities have continued the workshop tradition of weaving for the nobility from pre-Columbian and colonial times by satisfying the demands of the tourist and export market. In the villages round Huancayo and in Ayacucho and San Pedro de Cajas in central Peru, weaving has replaced farming as a full-time occupation. Treadle loom weaving and the use of the spinning wheel speed the production of contemporary art textiles, which vary from the pictorial representation of local scenes to an attempt at atavism. The export and selective tourist demand for quality textiles has ensured a minority return to the use of natural dyestuffs and the finest cameloid wools.

Weaving as a traditional Andean Indian craft continues to this day in Bolivia and, as elsewhere in the Spanish Americas, the European treadle loom production and the use of non-indigenous sheep's wool and synthetic yarn are corrupting a rich heritage. The textiles of the Aymara are of the greatest interest. The Aymara Indians inhabit the Lake Titicaca altiplano and are justifiably famous for their alpaca backstrap weaving of garments and capes; many examples survive from the late eighteenth and nineteenth centuries.

The Lake Titicaca area is known to have been the root of the great Tiahuanaco and Incan weaving cultures. As the Aymara were vassals of these regimes it is fitting that their textiles may be considered the last vestiges of a dying and nearly buried craft tradition. Too remote and and of too little consequence to the ruling classes, the Aymara communities survived relatively unscathed through the transition from Incan rule and the colonial era into an age of independence from 1825 onwards. The Spanish repression of Incan cultural mores during the late eighteenth century aided the survival of original textiles, as the pagan ceremonial garments were stored and so preserved, lasting through only occasional use and veneration. Handed down from generation to generation, worn infrequently by the head of the community and repaired and rewoven as necessary, these bundles of tunics, ponchitos, mantles and ancient headdresses known as 'q'epis', exist – but in ever-decreasing numbers – to this day.

For the Aymara, the nineteenth century seems to have been a golden era of warp-faced alpaca weaving. Striped mantles and tunics were woven with elaborate warp-faced patterning and sophisticated yet pleasing composi-tions, and the alpaca wool is finely spun and dyed in rich natural colours. Aymara mantles of this period with ostensibly simple composi-tions of colour bands exert a powerful impress-ion on the onlooker; their strength of character reaches out to stir up and innervate the spiritual subconscious.

Africa

The tribal weaving areas of the continent of Africa are divided by the desert and scrub of the Sahara. This impasse has acted as a filter to the rapid dissemination of the techniques, cultural influences and raw materials associated with textile production. The camel trade routes across the Sahara linked Egypt, and hence the Orient, with North and West Africa and the exchange of gold, salt and spices provided the notoriously independent Tuareg of the west and central desert with a livelihood from raiding and trading. The type and amount of the trade in cloth can never be accurately determined as there are no textile remains in North and West Africa; there is, however, a wealth of archaeological evidence from the tombs and dumps of Egypt that clearly points to an indigenous weaving tradition diffused with Hellenistic, Byzantine, Ottoman and Oriental influences rather than by West and Central African cultures.

If Egypt is well known for the quantities of ancient textiles that have survived there, then the North African states of Morocco, Algeria and Tunisia, the West African peoples and the tribes of Zaire are famous for their highly individual and regionally disparate styles of flatweaves, embroideries, patchwork and resist-dyed cloth. The geographical isolation of many of these tribes has provided a temporary buffer to the devastating influences of the modern world, so that the weaving of traditional textiles continues.

Ancient Egyptian textiles

The arid climate of Egypt and the predilection of the dynastic leaders for entombment in rather large mausoleums has allowed the sur-vival of ancient textile fragments on a scale comparable to that of the Peruvian coastal desert discoveries. The textiles and fragments of the earliest finds, dating from 4500 BC to 332 BC – when Egypt was incorporated into the Greek Empire – are primarily of exquisitely fine linen; wool may have been woven during this time but was considered impure and not suitable for burial. Mummy shrouds, girdles, tunics and hangings have been found that chart the de-velopment of weaving from plain to simple banded patterning, through to slit tapestry weave by about 1000 BC.

Most antiquarian textiles from Egypt date from the adoption of Christianity in AD 380 and the establishment of the Coptic Church. The Copts buried their dead fully clothed so that over an eight-hundred-year period many thousands of textiles were interred, to last and be exhumed by grave robbers and archaeolog-ists alike. Most of the surviving fragments, of the finest slitweave tapestry of linen and wool, would have been an integral part of clothing decoration; the free-flowing energy of their compositions is unmistakable. Cherubs cavort, Hellenistic figures smile and birds and animals glow with colour. The ability of the Coptic weavers to make the warps and wefts turn and flow and so express graceful movement, and their naturalistic representations using the medium of slit tapestry, are unexcelled in the history of weaving.

Egypt fell to the Arabs in AD 641 and their initial tolerance of Christians made certain that the Coptic weaving tradition continued, to be influenced, nourished and then dictated to by the succeeding Persian and Ottoman Empires. Textiles played a central role as objects of ornament, religious significance and wealth in medieval Islamic culture. Palaces must have been a riot of colour, decorated with the finest flaxen, silken, cotton and woollen weavings.

37

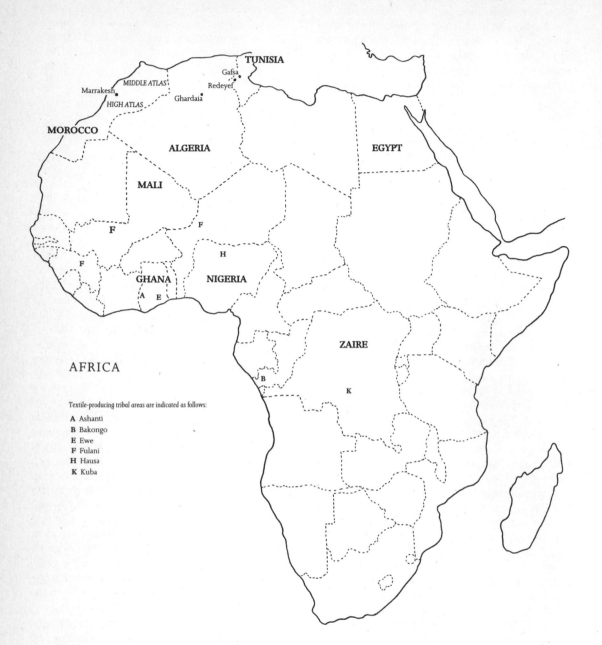

AFRICA

Textile-producing tribal areas are indicated as follows:

A Ashanti
B Bakongo
E Ewe
F Fulani
H Hausa
K Kuba

North Africa

The Muslim countries of Tunisia, Algeria and Morocco are and have been linked in culture and commerce by multivarious foreign empires and by the indigenous tribal peoples for at least two millennia. The short sea-crossing to southern Europe, especially by way of the Straits of Gibraltar, has resulted in the influences on the whole area rising and ebbing with the tides of Phoenician, Carthaginian, Roman, Vandal, Byzantine, Arab, Ottoman, Berber, Spanish and French cultures. To this day the traditional textile production within the area is linked largely with the descendants of the original inhabitants, the Berber tribespeople, whose migratory pastoralism from alpine to lowland habitats has necessitated the weaving of woollen and goat hair capes, tent cloth and floor coverings that insulate the owner from the extremes of heat and cold.

Over one thousand years of Muslim domination ensures that the patterning of the weaves is, for the most part, a blend of pagan and Islamic geometric designs. The dyestuffs which were used were, until the early part of this century, of natural origin. Two types of simple loom are in general use, producing weaves for family and commercial demands. Capes and flatwoven rugs are made on the vertical loom and the weft-faced patterning is woven semi-blind; the weaver sits and works on the reverse side of the rug, weaving the intricate designs from memory. Tent cloth, bands and sacks are woven on the ground loom, often from undyed goat hair and wool.

Tunisia and Algeria From as early as the twelth century BC the Phoenicians were trading along the north and west African coastline, establishing settlements, the most famous of which became the city of Carthage. It is thought that tapestry weaving and the use of the vertical loom were spawned from Phoenician influence, but the spread of this new technology from what was a coastal culture to the Berber tribes of the interior must have been a slow process. Roman weaving influences followed from 146 BC until the fifth century AD; and unfortunately the textile glories of this era, and the Vandal and Byzantine occupations that followed, have been lost forever.

From the seventh century to this day the area has remained Muslim in faith, a religion first introduced by the Arabs. Arts and crafts flourished within the succeeding empires of Moorish and Turkish rulers; fragments of Ottoman embroideries survive to hint at the skill of the weavers of the highly organized and male-dominated city and town crafts guilds. By contrast, the tribeswomen of the interior continued to weave for family use within the design auspices of the Faith.

The last seventy years have not been a memorable period for Tunisian and Algerian traditional weaving. The forces of industrialization, the struggle for independence and the pressures created by an expanding population on the land have, on the one hand, removed the demand for fine embroideries from the crafts guilds and on the other, disturbed the way of life of the Berber nomads and semi-nomadic peoples – perhaps forever. In general a Berber flatwoven rug or blanket (a 'hanbel' or 'hambel') made on a vertical loom from North Africa is traditionally all wool with stripes of weft-faced pattern work and small geometric motifs, often highlighted in cotton. Of the textile production of the nations, Tunisian flatweave work is perhaps the most interesting, for there are many variations in design and technique and weaving continues on a prolific basis to this day.

Around the oasis of Gafsa in central Tunisia there exists an Arabic tradition for the weaving of brightly coloured slit tapestry-woven rugs that are full of figurative, architectural and floral designs. In these flatweaves, caravans of camels and schools of fish mix in clear blues and yellows amidst a sea of geometric motifs. From Kairouan, more slit tapestry-woven rugs of the kilim type are to be found with bands of colour that clash, yet harmonize when the rug is viewed in its entirety. Near the Algerian border, west of Gafsa, Redeyev is known for tightly woven weft-faced patterned rugs with a field studded with diamond motifs, an intricate border and skirt decorated with deer designs.

Algeria's minority population of Berbers weave flatwoven rugs, blankets, clothing, tent cloth and bags in much the same style as those of Tunisia, with a similiar division of labour. These flatwoven blankets and rugs are very much in typical North African Berber tradition, with lines of tiny and tightly woven white motifs, especially diamonds and triangles, set against contrasting bands of colour, interspersed with stripes of white. Lacking a tourist trade on any scale and undergoing a breakneck modernization to their society that mixes urbanization with industrialization riding roughshod over their colonial and pre-colonial past alike, it is no wonder that the semi-nomadic Berber and Arab tribal peoples are being forced into a sedentary existence. The need and the desire to produce utilitarian and dowry textiles has diminished so that the availability of recently made traditional Berber weaves is limited, especially by comparison with the output of their Moroccan tribal cousins to the west.

Morocco This land of mountain, coastal plain and desert is the westernmost point of the spread of Islam, and is host to the largest and perhaps most dynamic population of Berber tribespeople in North Africa. It was the ancestors of these Berbers who continued the link of Arab and North African Islamic culture with that of Spain, for the Berber kingdoms of the Almoravids, succeeded by the Almohades, ruled Iberia for over two hundred years from the eleventh century. Their contribution to European history is clear, for these Berber dynasties brought with them the colour, the light and the excellence of Islamic art, philosophy and science that was to help to drag the Christian world from out of the mire of the Middle Ages and into the Renaissance. Morocco was peripheral to the interests of empire-builders such as the Ottomans and so the culture of the region developed over the centuries with links to the north in an unusual fusion of Hispanic, Jewish, Moorish and latterly, French influences. Secure and independent in their high mountains, it is the semi-nomadic Berber people who are famous for their traditional weaving skills. Scattered along the central spine of the country, the Atlas mountains, Berber tribes such as the Zaer, the Beni M'guild and the Zaiane move their flocks and their tents up to the high pastures in the summer and down to the valleys and their villages at the onset of winter.

The Middle Atlas is home to many Berber tribes, the most famous of which in weaving terms are the Zemmour, Beni M'tir, Beni M'guild and the Beni Ouarain. Using the wool from their flocks, the tribeswomen weave hanbels, capes, saddlebags and shawls for insulation from the extremes of heat and cold. The hanbel blankets are traditionally woven with bands of red plainweave alternating with bands of very intricate weft-faced patterning. The tightness of the weave, the size – ten feet by five feet – and the heavy nature of the weft-float technique will keep three or four people warm and snug at one time, as they lie asleep on knotted rugs laid over palm or grass mats. In the summer these hanbels are hung within the tents as protection against the heat, and are laid

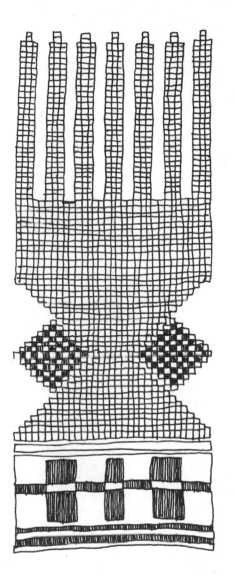

Ewe stripweave motif of a comb

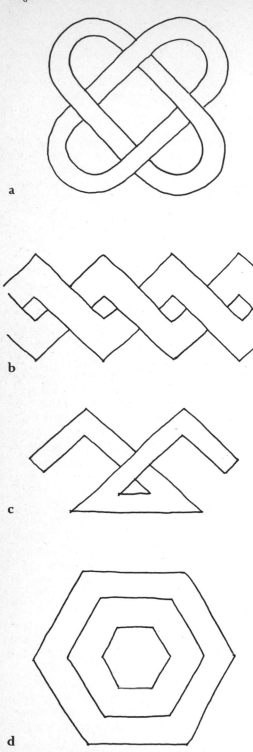

Kuba motifs from raphia cloths: **a** *basket work;* **b** *forest vines;* **c** *eyebrows;* **d** *tortoise*

underfoot on the rush matting; the predilection for incorporating sequins and beads in the weave must add a glittering decorative dimension to the hanging hanbel. Saddle rugs are similar in composition to the hanbels and roughly half the size.

The capes of the Beni Ouarain of the eastern Middle Atlas are runner-like in shape and exquisitely made, often of silk and wool, with restrained natural dye colours. Very finely worked with stripes of weft-faced patterning, these capes are instantly recognizable by their long strands of ivory wool that hang from the back as a thick and warm insulator. The Glaoua tribes of the High Atlas south of Marrakesh weave striking mixed technique rugs of knotted and flatweave work, again of a striped composition, often with stark and simple contrasts in pattern between dark and light bands. Some of the Berbers of the western High Atlas wear a most distinctive black hooded cloak emblazoned with a large and deep red eye motif that serves to ward off the evil in a covetous glance. Less well known are the flatweaves found to the west of Marrakesh and there is a curious parallel in designs and technique between the Arab-influenced Gafsa weaving of central Tunisia and these slit tapestry weaves. The Chiadma tribe of the Tennsift river basin are the sole producers in Morocco of simple flatwoven rugs with bands of colour alternating with areas of detailed slit tapestry designs and motifs.

Supported by a thriving tourist trade, many of the tribes of Morocco continue to weave some of the more useful yet traditional-style textiles in quantity. The story of the development of their work in recent history is a familiar one: the disintegration of their tribal lifestyle in the face of urbanization, the development of a leisure industry for tourists in the historic market towns and on the ski slopes of the Atlas Mountains, the use of unsophisticated aniline dyes and the lack of quality in the weaving, as short cuts are taken to finish an article of economic rather than family significance. In the short term, one might say that the weavers have never before known such financial prosperity from such simple requirements; one hopes for a resurgence of traditionalism to perpetuate the inheritance of the ancient skills.

West African weaving traditions

South of the Sahara Desert the traditional tribal societies of West Africa have been weaving textiles for ceremonial and utilitarian purposes

for at least a thousand years. Fibres from endemic plant species such as cotton and raphia palm predominate, woollen cloth is woven in the more temperate north and silk has been imported for luxury use since the Middle Ages or before. In the heat and damp of the tropics textiles last for a very short time, leaving few historical examples, yet providing a steady demand for the long-established commercial, yet traditional, weaving industry to satisfy.

In such a clime, garments of any description are largely superfluous and so it is no wonder that their use is status and ceremony orientated. The finest textiles are objects denoting rank and wealth, and their use is restricted by edict, custom and high cost. Today a good deal of the domestic and utilitarian weaving is in decline in the face of competition from Western-style garments and machine-made cloth; by contrast the commercial, mostly commissioned, weaving industry is as healthy as ever in quantity of output, if not in quality and originality. This distinct duality of production is a reflection of the types of looms used and the division of labour between men and women. Women, especially in Nigeria, work at home on a primitive, small, single heddled upright loom as part of their domestic duties, producing warp-faced cotton cloth. This domestic weaving has declined so that textiles are made as funeral wraps or for other ritual use, or as inexpensive handloomed cloth for sale to outsiders and tourists. Decorations are limited to warp-striping of colours, warp-float patterning and hand-picked extra weft-patterning of small figurative motifs. The majority of their production, and indeed the majority of all West African handloomed work, is of white cotton cloth.

Most of the highly decorative and fine textiles of West Africa have been made by men trained as full-time weaving specialists in a semi-luxury goods business, working individually to commission or for market sale, often in craft workshops. Their narrow strip looms with extended warps stretching away from the weaver at work present an unforgettable sight. The small double heddle loom (a primitive type of treadle loom) is a step towards the mechanization of the weaving process, allowing the weaver to speed up the production of cloth for commercial gain. The feet of the weaver manipulate the peddles that raise and lower the alternate or more complicated combinations of warps, leaving the hands free to throw the shuttle from side to side across the narrow strip of work. The long warps are held in tension by

A Soma cloth weaver of the Gold Coast, stripweaving on a drag loom, c.1905

a weight on a sled that is drawn to the weaver as the cloth is woven and wound onto the breast beam. Strips of cloth three to ten inches wide are woven, cut and joined selvedge to selvedge to make up toga-like men's robes, trousers, and hats, women's cloth and headscarves, blankets, wall hangings and floor covers. Between twenty and one hundred narrow strips are joined to make a cloth; matching the pattern from strip to strip is therefore a difficult job, requiring great experience, skill and a measuring stick. In this stripweave tradition that extends geographically from the Senegal River in the west to Lake Chad in the east, the Ashanti and Ewe work of Ghana is of legendary quality and of complex compositional variety.

The riches of the Ashanti kingdom of the seventeenth century afforded the commissioned weaving of exclusive cloth of the finest raw materials in the most complex techniques. Waste silk from the French and Italian processing mills arrived by caravan across the Sahara by way of Morocco, and was woven or combined with hand-spun cotton to make 'kente' and the finer 'asasia' cloth for royalty and courtiers, and the king of the Ashanti enjoyed the exclusive use of certain types of silk. This elitist and luxury tradition, centred at Bonwire and now in relative decline, has produced some of the most fabulously colourful and highly patterned African textiles in existence, and on close examination their warp-faced

41

weave with warp striping and elaborate weft patterning is a study in technical excellence. Narrow strip cloth from the neighbouring Ewe tribe is of similarly high quality and individual character.

The southernmost fringes of the Sahara are inhabited by Muslim tribespeople, of whom the widely scattered and nomadic pastoralists, the Fulani, are famous for their white woollen weft-faced stripweave, woven in fact by their more sedentary bretheren. Known as 'khasa' and used as blankets and saddle cloths, these textiles are in great demand during the cold mosquito season from November to January, after which they are often sold to the cloth dealers, so creating an active and unusual secondhand market.

In northern Nigeria, the Muslim Hausa people are known for their embroidered robes. Originating at the crossroads of sub-Saharan trade, the Hausa embroidery displays a fusion of Islamic and African tribal motifs, rather as if the stroke of a calligrapher's pen meets the cut of the woodcarver's adze, in complete harmony. Plain, often indigo blue, or simply striped robes are decorated with fine white cotton embroidery that focuses on the breast pocket and the collar, and although hidden by this voluminous gown, baggy trousers are also embellished with fine stitchwork. Essentially a dry-season activity, the work supplements a farming lifestyle, and, interestingly, the weavers specialize in producing elements of the composition drawn on the robe by an expert designer. In all, the embroidery may take two or three months to complete, and such fine robes are often commissioned by the ruling emirs to hold as a store of wealth then to dispense, munificently, as gifts to the worthies.

The Yoruba of southern Nigeria and the Baoule from the Ivory Coast are known for their imaginative use of resist-dyeing techniques. Stripwoven textiles are subtly patterned with warp ikat work; here, before weaving begins, the warps are bound in groups with fine cotton and dyed, then bound in different areas and dyed in another colour, the process continuing until the desired sequence of warp colouring is achieved. When woven, the cloth displays gentle and irregular variations in colour. Completed plain white cotton cloth, and with increasing frequency machine-made plain cotton, are also resist dyed by the simple method of folding and tie and dye. Known by the Yoruba as 'adire', these textiles are indigo dyed and patterned with small and large circles, often amidst geometric compositions.

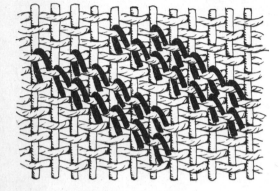

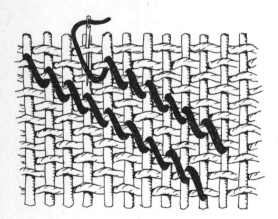

Plush stitching and overstitching

Raphia cloth from Zaire The weaving of cloth with fibres from the raphia palm leaf is practised throughout West Africa, Central Africa and Malagasy. Of this work, it is the finely decorated textiles of the Kuba people of central Zaire that have attracted the attention of European collectors for the past seventy years. A trade in raphia cloth is not a recent phenomenon, for from the earliest coastal colonialism of the Portuguese in Central Africa in the fifteenth and sixteenth centuries, fine palm leaf cloth was exchanged in the slave trade between Angola and South America. Today raphia textiles from Zaire remain a form of wealth that may be bartered or bought. Their decorative motifs are highly symbolic and personal, and the finest cloths are worn as dance skirts or as a mark of respect at funerals.

A branch of the great Bantu migration, the Kuba settled in the seventeenth century in the savannah plains between the Sankuru and Kasai rivers in what is now central Zaire. Of the Kuba people it is the Shoowa tribe who are justifiably famous for their raphia textiles. The Shoowa are utterly absorbed by the expression of geometric and rectilinear forms in all their craftwork. Wooden drums, chests, masks and cups are carved with interconnecting geometric motifs in an expression of imperfect orderliness. This venture into abstraction reaches a summit of decorative achievement in their embroidered and appliqué raphia textiles.

Unlike West African textile production, Shoowa men and women weave and decorate raphia cloth as an integral part of their lifestyle as farmers and part-time hunter-gatherers. Limited by the available length of the leaf fibres, the men weave the three to four feet squares and sections of the skirts and wraps in a balanced plainweave on a vertical or angled loom, and the women then decorate the textile with appliqué shapes or embroider the surface with either a velvet or an overstitch technique. Working in any spare time, the weaver may take months to complete the panels. Thus, a five-metre long appliqué and embroidered dance skirt of eight or nine panels is a labour both of tribal tradition and family and personal symbolism. The appliqué effect is said to have arisen out of the necessity to patch tears and holes in a cherished garment with raphia strips, roundels and small squares. This erstwhile repair work has developed into a method of textile decoration that, when the skirt is unfolded and complete in length, forms steadily and naturally developing panels of abstract designs.

By comparison, the overstitched or velvet-worked panels are regimented in composition with strong motifs that are often unsettling to the eye. Geometric and rectilinear shapes are known by name, such as 'tortoise', 'forest vine' and 'eyebrows'. Yet here, the seemingly naive and spontaneous compositional nature of these decorated raphia panels hides a brilliant interpretation of recurring geometric forms by reduction and distortion. These and other Shoowa panels were to prove fertile sources of inspiration for painters such as Klee and Matisse, and fortunately many thousands of raphia panels and skirts separated into panels have been collected from the Kuba peoples this century, documenting and preserving in public collections the glories of self-expression from a once self-sufficient tribe in the heart of a sorely abused land.

Asia Minor to Central Asia

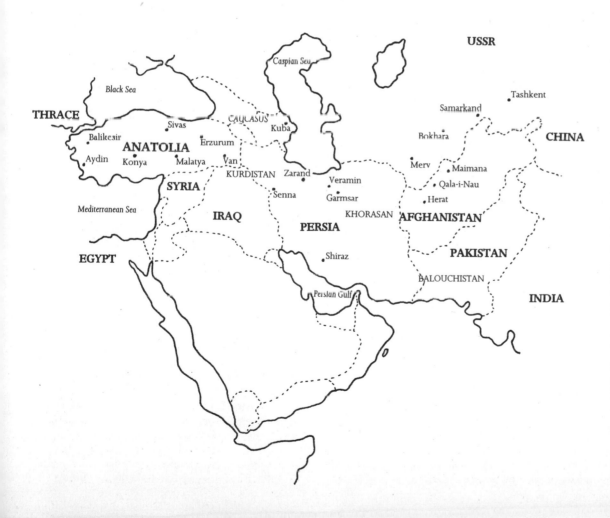

From Anatolia to Afghanistan there exists a multitude of diversely originated Muslim tribespeople living – often uneasily – within the boundaries of states created almost arbitrarily by the horse-trading of empires between the World Wars. The history of the region is brimful of tales of great empires and colourful cultures that, by way of trade and war, bound Western Europe with Asia in a web of commercial and political intrigue that lasted from the Middle Ages right through to the advent of the steamship. Indeed, there is a uniquely long-standing relationship between the wealthy consumers of Europe and the commercial weavers of the knotted carpet of the East; no other ethnic art in the world has been exported in such quantity, for so long and to so undiscerning a marketplace.

For over two millennia, whatever the origin and nature of the ruling empire or empires of the region, there has existed a flatweaving culture of great vigour and fecundity. Living in habitats as varied as the eastern Mediterranean shoreline and the slopes of the High Pamirs, groups of pastoral nomads have tended their flocks, herds and trains of sheep, goats and camels, using the animal's wool and hair to flatweave floor and wall coverings, tent cloth, blankets and trappings. For over a thousand years, this ancient domestic folk tradition has been developing within the rigorous design inspiration of Islam, so creating a range of textiles that sometimes almost perfectly balances utility with decoration.

Of greatest interest is the tapestry-woven rug, generally known throughout the region as a 'kilim'. This Turkish word means flatwoven, or rug without a knotted pile, and the linguistic variations range from 'chilim' in Rumania, 'kylym' in the Ukraine and 'gelim' or 'kelim' in

13

Afghanistan and Persia to 'palas' in the Caucasus and 'bsath' in Iraq, Syria and the Lebanon. Woven predominantly of wool on simple single heddle ground or vertical looms, kilims have developed in use over the centuries from a means of exchange – especially as part of a dowry – and objects of great domestic utility, of tribal identity and symbolism, to a commodity nowadays produced by a well-organized craft industry supplying the tourists, merchants and dealers with colourful floor rugs and wall decorations that are inexpensive, relatively hard-wearing and cheerful. Many of these new kilims, especially from Anatolia and Persia, are made to traditional specifications with natural dyes and the finest workmanship, and may best be compared with those flatweaves made, again for commercial gain, in organized weaving workshops for the discerning elite of the Ottoman and Safavid dynasties of the past.

The true nomadic and semi-nomadic production of kilims, with natural dyes and design compositions passed down from generation to generation, is without question, over. Pressured by governments to convert to a sedentary way of life, bewildered and delighted by the range of inexpensive chemical dyes and manmade fibres available, many of these nomadic groups such as the Koochi gypsies of Afghanistan continue to weave kilims with wonderfully garish colours and racy combinations of old and new motifs. Most of the previously nomadic tribes, such as the Qashqai of southern Persia, now live in permanent village dwellings throughout the winter, climbing to the high pastures with their flocks in the spring. It is these semi-nomadic peoples who are in the greatest danger of losing their weaving skills forever. They lack an organized export marketplace for their work and have less and less need for traditionally woven rugs, bags and trappings; although their standards of living have improved in a Western sense, their desire for further westernization alienates the children from the traditional work such as weaving and draws all but the eldest to that mirage of town and city lifestyle.

The kilim enjoys a long and varied history as a decorative object that may range in creative origin from naive folk art to courtly sophistication, and so is well suited to survive in production and use in this fast-developing world. By contrast, the weaving and manufacture in guild workshops of fine silk ikats, brocades, satins and embroideries within the towns of Anatolia, Syria, Persia and Central Asia have become a glory of the past. The refined and wealthy patrons of the arts of the pre-industrial Islamic

dynasties who enjoyed festooning their palaces and persons with the finest textiles are no more. The last remnants of this workmanship may be found in the silk ikat work of north Afghanistan.

Anatolia Anatolia reaches out from Asia to touch Europe as a bridge between the cultures of the East and West; no wonder, therefore, that the population of this mountainous land is so varied. Greeks, Kurds, Armenians, Assyrian and Turkic peoples mix as a reminder of past invaders and rulers. The Kurds are credited as the indigenous peoples of Asia Minor, whose central homeland inconviently straddles the modern borders of Turkey, Iraq and Persia. Fractious and necessarily mercenary in nature, the Kurds are well known for their fine kilim weaving. In general, Anatolian weaving is characterized and easily differentiated by village rather than by tribal area, and many kilims are made by Turkic peoples, descendants of the conquering tribes from Central Asia. Proud of the name 'Yoruk', meaning 'we who roam', they are now mostly village dwellers. A minority are semi-nomadic, and are found in the Taurus mountains and west-central Anatolia.

The longest running and most notorious of the Turkic empires was that of the Ottomans. Driven out of Central Asia by the Mongols, the Ottomans succeeded the Seljuk Turks in Asia Minor and began to expand their empire so that by 1566 their territory extended from the gates of Vienna to the central plains of Persia. The Ottomans presided over a highly organized colonial empire, the courtly traditions of which inspired the manufacture of the finest floral-decorated silks shimmering with bright colour. Examples of this work survive from the eighteenth and nineteenth century and the velvets, brocades and satins would have been used as curtains, hangings and robes. Made in guild workshops by craftsmen gathered from throughout the Empire, the intertwining labyrinths of carnations and tulips afford rich visual pleasure. Embroidered textiles used as clothing accessories and hangings were originally made in the home; their floral compositions are more liberated, and similar in patterning to Iznik ceramic tiles and vessels.

Ottoman floral silks and fine tapestries exerted their influence on the tribal village weavers, so that until the early twentieth century Anatolian kilims were patterned with a charming mix of courtly and parochial styles. This combination of stylized flowers within a

Professional Muslim cotton carders of eastern Bengal with their bows, c.1870

Anatolian prayer kilim

geometric framework is a hallmark of much Anatolian work today, but the radical change in inspiration from family duty to commercial zeal, and the use of chemically-dyed, machine-spun cottons and wool as yarn have removed much if not all of the natural naivety and textural quality so evident in earlier work. Today, Turkey leads the rug-producing world in the effort to reorientate the village weavers towards a return to their atavistic traditions, in order to supply a more discerning Western marketplace. A Turkish carpet research project has catalogued over three thousand traditional compositions from carpets and kilims, producing computer-generated cartoons of rugs for the weaver to copy to perfection.

From west to east, Anatolian kilims display diverse cultural influences. Greek and south-central European traditions are evident in the so-called Thracian kilims of north-west Anatolia and across the Bosporus around Sarkoy. The large kilims are predominantly full of simple floral motifs clustered about a tree of life. Balikesir kilims originate from an area in west Anatolia known for its enclave of semi-nomadic Yoruk peoples. The antique Balikesir rugs have distinctive and memorable compositions of a simple yet visually complex interlocking grid of blue and red patterns. Aydin, a town near the Aegean coast, is a fecund source of kilims that are small and busily patterned, often woven in two halves and joined together.

From central Anatolia there are found kilims named after the town of Konya and made in the surrounding villages. All-wool, often large and tapestry woven with much slitweave work, they bear strong Turkic medallions on a white or cream ground. Further to the east, the town of Malatya is in an area of Kurdish country rich in kilims woven by Turkic and Kurdish peoples. The rugs are narrow, woven with wool and cotton and made in two pieces; the join of the selvedges highlights by discontinuity the usual composition of three central medallions. East of Sivas there is a predominance of flatwoven prayer rugs and towards the Caucasus, the kilims from near Erzurum are well known for their ochre colouring and tiered central 'mihrabs', or arches, surrounded by stylized floral designs. To the east, the village of Bardiz is now known for producing most of the modern Bessarabian or Karabagh kilims. Here, as elsewhere, the Kurds prove excellent copyists, and since the early part of this century they have been weaving highly decorative rugs with large floral patterns, inspired by European tapestries that were themselves derived from Ottoman

45

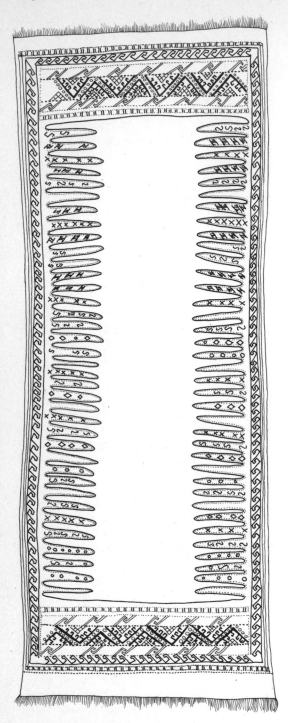

Persian eating-cloth kilim

textile design: yet another cultural circle of influences is completed. The Lake Van area is remote and mountainous. It is home to many Kurdish people who weave high quality kilims made in two pieces that are, unusually, square. The compositions of these woollen rugs are confusingly similar to the work of Kurdish peoples across the borders in the Caucasus and north-west Persia.

The Caucasus Sandwiched between the Middle East and West-Central Asia are the Soviet states of Azerbaijan, Armenia and Georgia. Through history the area has suffered the transient rule of many cultures – Greek, Persian, Arab, Turkic and Tartar – which have left in their wake isolated tribal groups, many languages and a reputation, now historic, for the weaving of energetically patterned fine kilims. The golden era of Caucasian weaving was the nineteenth century, a time of temporary stability brought to the region by Imperial Russia and the resultant increase of trans-Asian trade. The specialization of production is a familiar one: men wove in the workshops, and the women of the semi-nomadic tribes at portable looms when camped for any length of time.

The Avars, Samurs, Georgians, Armenians, Kurds, Persians, Turks and Arabs wove tightly spun woollen kilims until the 1920s and 1930s, and these are classified for convenience by the trade as either Kuba or Shirvan in origin. The large field of Kuba kilims is patterned with very colourful and bold geometric designs, bounded by a single, often crenellated, border. Shirvan flatweaves are more common and their simple compositions are distinctive: again, bold and geometric, but the medallions are set in bands on a borderless ground. A harmonious use of colour and the highest quality of slitweaving are the hallmarks of the Caucasian production.

Persia A country famous for its capacity to produce many fine knotted carpets, Persia's scattered minority of tribal groups of Turkic, Kurdish, Arabic and Balouch extraction are well known for their slitweaving of characterful and colourful kilims. Many of these tribal peoples are remnants and reminders of ruling invaders that have origins from Greece, Arabia and to the frontiers with China. In common

with the Ottoman Turks, the Persian Safavid dynasties of the seventeenth and eighteenth centuries encouraged and commissioned the weaving of intricate silk embroideries and kilims with silken yarn, the most famous of which came from the workshops of Senna. Woven by Kurdish weavers, these fine floral tapestries stimulated the establishment of a weaving tradition that is still alive today.

As well as acting as patrons of the Islamic arts, the Safavid monarchs had a predilection for moving ethnic minorities around the kingdom to act as demographic buffers to bandits and possible invaders. In the districts of Khorasan and the southern Caucasus the resulting ethnic mix is evident in the multivarious combinations of tribal motifs which decorate their flatweaves. Latterly, the non-Persian tribes have suffered territorial and cultural privations restricting their powers of independence. These political factors have combined with economic incentives to alter the lifestyle of the nomadic and semi-nomadic peoples such as the Qashqai and the Bakhtiari and the traditional skills of nomadic near self-sufficiency, such as flatweaving, are in decline.

Kilims from in or around Senna, now known as Sanandaj, the capital of Persian Kurdistan, are famous for their floral compositions. Inspired originally by the brocades and embroideries of the Safavid era, Senna kilims are small and woven of the very finest slit tapestry, depicting interlocking clusters of tiny flowers that are more reminiscent of a knotted carpet than a flatweave. Further to the east, Zarand kilims are woven by predominantly Turkic peoples from around the villages of Sava, Qazvin and Zarand. Densely woven of cotton and wool, their compositions are of small, stylized floral motifs that group to create many different scales of patterning, forming two or three central medallions.

South and east of Tehran, the region around the caravan-trading towns of Garmsar and Veramin is known for its distinctive kilims. Large and heavily woven of cotton and dark wool, these kilims are decorated with bands of diagonally arranged motifs or fields of interlocking designs coloured with brilliant reds, blues and, unusually, greens and yellows. In southern Persia the pastoral nomads of the Zagros mountains are the Turkic Qashquai. Their kilims are highly sought after, for their use of ancient Turkic motifs within parochial compositions gives rise to flatweaves that are a marvellous combination of strong designs balanced with subtle colours.

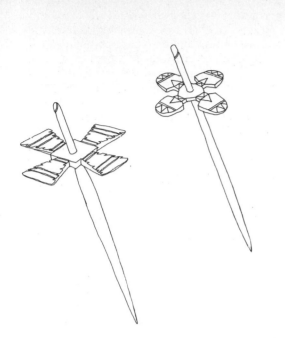

Wool spinning spindles of the Balouch weavers

Turkoman tent bag – a 'juval'

Afghanistan and Turkestan Used as a political and military buffer zone by the Superpowers for the past one hundred and fifty years, the area of South-Central Asia, now known as Afghanistan, has been a highly prized key communications route between Asia and India and the Ocean, and between Cathay and Persia. West of the impasse of the Himalayas, the mountain passes of the Hindhu Kush have been crossed by the Ancient Greeks, Mughals and British, and through history empire-builders have been thwarted by the fierce independence of the tribespeople fighting on their own terms in a terrain ideal for guerilla warfare. Afghanistan, with its frozen peaks and arid plains, is a land of sharp physical and demographic contrasts. Its people are of varied origin, some with Hellenistic features, others raven-haired and dark skinned. Their textiles are equally diverse and, unusually, little collected and appreciated. Tribes of Balouch and Uzbek, Tadjik and Turkic origin specialize in weaving distinctive kilims and, less commonly, fine embroideries.

For convenience, Afghanistan may be divided into two weaving regions, with the Balouch kilims to the south and west, the kilims and embroideries of the Turkic and Uzbek peoples to the north and, historically speaking, over the border into Turkestan, now a Soviet republic. The Balouch of west Afghanistan and Khorasan in Persia are the Rukhshani people, a nomadic and semi-nomadic group who are famous for their tightly woven and sombre coloured kilims. Balouch kilims are woven on simple, portable narrow ground looms for a distinct and traditional use – there is nothing superfluous about the life of a nomad. The largest of these kilims are the dowry rugs, often made in two sections and joined at the selvedge. Prayer mats, eating cloths and tent runners are decorated with compositions of small white motifs on a dark ground, woven with the finest weft-faced patterning and soumak.

In contrast, the kilims from the north are predominantly slitwoven with medallion patterning and bright colours. The town of Maimana has lent its name to a large-scale production of kilims, woven mostly by Uzbeks on vertical, continuous warped looms. Some of the largest and most robust flatweaves of the world are made in this area of north-west Afghanistan. The Uzbek Tartars weave large runners with a fine use of double interlocking technique that results in crisp motifs, always of a field of 'eight-legged spider' medallions in bright blues and reds. Uzbek nomads are well known for their stripwoven rugs and horse covers. Made on tiny ground looms that are easy to transport, the tent bands of warp-faced patterned work may be cut and sewn together to make a cover of any size. The tinkers and gypsies of Central Asia are the Koochi and their kilims, known as 'Mukkur', are always large runners with strong geometric patterning, made of coarsely spun wool with selvedge and elaborate fringe decorations of beads, shells and coins. Nearly all the kilims from this region are made of wool, often complemented with goat and camel hair, and the sole exception to the rule are the cotton rugs produced in the Mazar-i-Sharif area of north Afghanistan. Known as 'sutrangi', these cotton flatweaves are traditionally used on mosque floors and, like their Indian counterpart, the 'dhurrie', the weaving of these floor rugs by the local prison interns was established and encouraged, perhaps as an early form of useful occupational therapy.

North of Afghanistan the region of Uzbekistan is famous as an area of origin for highly decorative embroideries and ikat work of the nineteenth and early twentieth centuries. This land of oasis towns strung along the ancient Silk Route, of semi-desert hinterland and diversely originated population, is steeped in a history of violent invasions balanced by eras of creative munificence; the most famous of these was centred on Samarkand by Tamurlane in the fourteenth century. Ruled by the Uzbek princes from the sixteenth to the late nineteenth century, the region was then sequestered for the commercial gain of the Russian Empire. Arabs, Armenians, Jews, Sarts, Uzbeks, Tadjiks, Kirghiz and Kazaks have intermingled here for centuries, and the rich textile tradition is a medley of Turkic, Indian, Chinese and Persian influences. The sumptuous silk ikats and silk embroidered 'susanis' (from the Persian word for needle) are part of an organized weaving tradition of the town and village, whereas the colourful cotton embroidery and appliqué work of the region, and especially of the Uzbek Lakai, decorated the gloomy interiors of the nomads' circular wood and felted tents, called 'yurts', and gaily caparisoned their animals on festive occasions.

A susani was the most prized textile of a girl's dowry. These large floral embroideries were used as bed covers for newly weds, as curtains and as wall hangings at celebrations; the subtle irregularity of their patterns and colours belies their method of construction. At first the design composition of the susani was sketched onto the plain white cotton cloth by a professional draughtsman and the textile then divided into four, five or six strips to be embroidered with

Cotton Indian dhurrie

silk thread by a woman or women, often of the same family. The strips would then be sewn together to finish the cloth.

The old susanis from the town of Shakhrisyabz are highly prized for their colour range, excellence of embroidery and their sophisticated yet lyrical compositions. Samarkand work is similar, whereas from Bokhara the susanis tend to be simply decorated, and at times their use of large and powerful medallion designs overawes the floral theme that is the hallmark of these embroideries. By the turn of the century the golden era of susani production was over, destroyed by the twin evils of mechanization and excessive commercial exploitation. Machine-made cotton cloth, harsh synthetic dyes and repetitiveness in design are symptomatic of this more modern era.

Very much more widespread in use and availability in Turkestan and north Afghanistan was the colourful ikat cloth, known locally and appropriately as 'abr', the Persian for 'cloud'. These resist-dyed textiles of either silk or silk warps and cotton wefts were used as clothing, table cloths, curtains, bed covers and hangings. To this day the tradition of wearing ikat coats continues in north Afghanistan and printed cloth with ikat designs is common in Soviet Central Asia. In nineteenth-century Turkestan, the wearing of such luxury garb was strictly controlled to maintain a hierarchy of wealth and dignity and thus the finest silk robes, worn in layers, were the conspicuous preserve of the upper classes. Patterned with medallions, abstracted flowers and animals, and coloured with vivid reds, blues, greens and yellows, the ikat

clothing was a dazzling sight in the dusty streets and drab landscape of much of Turkestan.

Ikat production was a specialist affair, linking as many as nine different trades in the process, from domestic sericulture to the spinning of the yarn, the exact dyeing of the groups of warps, often by Jews, and the final weaving, performed by men and their assistants on harness looms. Production was prolific, for between 1840 and 1850 some 190,000 robes are recorded as having been exported from Turkestan into Russia. The domestic market for ikat was also very great, for ikat robes were not only items of rank but also important mediums of exchange for the rulers and the wealthy, to be given as gifts to visitors and courtesans, as wedding presents and to pay for services.

The textiles of the nomadic Turkmen are distinctively colourful and invariably made as tent or animal decorations. The dark interior of the round, felt-covered yurt was hung with ceremonial and utilitarian embroideries and appliqués whose rich and bright colours are a most cheering sight. Embroideries packed with brightly coloured and archaic geometric designs of stylized eagles and ram's horns are attributed to the Uzbek Lakai sub-tribe, and their small bags, fringed bedding decorations and square panels are miniature masterpieces of embroidery work. Larger tent hangings and animal trappings are found, invariably of appliqué and patchwork, wherein fragments of fine silk ikat are incongruously mixed with panels of printed Russian cottons and plain cloth. The resulting geometric mêlée of fine and base textiles is refreshingly original.

The Indian subcontinent

More than in any other part of the world, weaving is an integral part of the cultural heritage of the Indian subcontinent, the development of whose highly complex social and cultural infrastructure has been part of a mutual trade of influences with the Orient, the Levant and, latterly, Europe. The varying capacity of these Southern Asian cultures to absorb, disseminate and develop these inflows of creative and spiritual energy is reflected in the range of sharply contrasting textiles available, both regionally and inter-communally. The weaving of

diaphanous muslins is an unbreachable world apart from the coarse cotton produced on a tribal village loom and it is by virtue of these extremes that so rich and varied a textile culture has been developing to this day.

The free availability and use of two crucial resources has allowed the production of decorative textiles and the developments in the techniques of fine production to continue from prehistoric times. Firstly, India is one of the world centres where the cotton plant is endemic and secondly, from at least 3000 BC,

through the network of the Persian Empire to the Mediterranean and Greece, and the foray by Alexander the Great into the north-western region of the Subcontinent in 326 BC compounded the development of an east-to-west trade in the finest textiles, later inherited by the Romans. From the port of Broach in the Gulf of Cambay, indigenous cotton textiles and woven cloth of silk from China were exported to the Roman Empire, whose noblemen were ecstatic in their praise and appreciation of the fine muslins, giving them delightful names – 'woven winds', and 'nebula', or misty in nature.

This early long-distance trade was disturbed by the establishment and rapid growth of Islam, the influence of which reached north-west India by the eighth century AD. This separation of west and east by the middleground of the Muslim kingdoms was maintained until the Portuguese proved the efficacy of a sea route round the Cape of Good Hope in the sixteenth century. There seems, however, to have been no hiatus in the development and production of textiles from the Subcontinent. Trade networks of camel trains within the Muslim world extended the distribution of these textiles to West Africa, by way of Fostat in Egypt and northwards into Central Asia, and the ancient international trade within the Subcontinent itself and to China continued unabated. The return of Western visitors – including the peripatetic Marco Polo – from the thirteenth century onwards, and their descriptive eulogies on the quality and quantity of textile production, confirmed that the indigenous weaving traditions were vigorously alive and continuing to develop. The sea trade that began with the Portuguese soon brought to Europe much woven, painted and printed cloth, and so established a world primacy of cotton production centred on India that was to last until the Industrial Revolution.

At the same time as the reopening of links by sea with the West, the north and north-west areas of the Subcontinent were subjugated by the Mughal Empire, creating an amalgam of cultural influences that perfectly balanced technical expertise with decorative imagination. This Muslim courtly patronage of the arts was lavish in quality and quantity, fusing Central Asian, Persian and indigenous weaving and decorative skills. Thenceforth, textile production was a varied mix of the formality of Islamic designs with the delight in nature and colour for which the Hindu weavers were renowned.

The monopoly of the Portuguese traders was ended by the successful empire-building of the

mordant dyes were used, so creating fast colours; this process was not known in Europe until the seventeenth century. Few cloth fragments have survived from ancient times to chart this progress of weaving from the simplest techniques to the complex pinnacles of textile production for which the area is still notorious. It is certain, however, that the quality and decorative nature of Indian cloth was a legendary international trading commodity from at least 700 BC. There are records of textile commerce with Babylon, soon extended

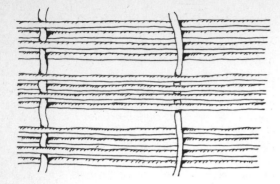

The ikat process
1   *Threads are grouped in bundles*

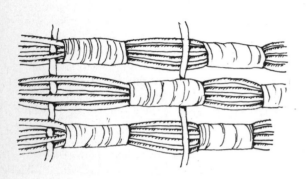

2   *Resist-binding with impermeable material*

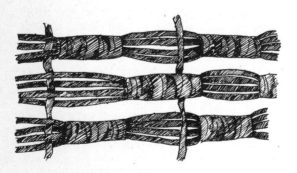

3   *The dyed result*

English and Dutch, so that by the seventeenth century Europe was more than familiar with the decorative qualities of Indian furnishing textiles. This outpouring of handloom production from Southern Asia was abruptly ended by the new mechanized mass production of printed cloth in Europe. By the nineteenth century the trading relationship had been reversed. Cheap cotton cloth printed with European interpretations and variations of Indian subcontinent and Asian designs flooded the colonies. The fall of the Mughal Empire and the subsequent decline in the patronage of the textile arts was a concurrent blow to the maintenance of a textile tradition that had been spearheaded by a striving for decorative perfection.

The textile crafts culture of the Subcontinent continues, however, to develop to this day. There has always existed a distinction between the organized production from the looms of the professional weavers for export, upper and middle class use, and the naive work from the looms and hands of the users themselves. The professional weavers – often male – continue to produce cloth and weavings for export and for the local demand for clothing and furnishing materials, but the family and domestic work is on the wane, under pressure from the economic and cultural forces of modernization and the inevitable westernization of aspects of a traditional society. Ceremonial family textiles continue to be made, however, and the lower castes weave and embroider these much as before.

The complex caste system and the religious disparities within the region have contributed much to the local and regional differences in textile production. A system wherein one is born, lives and dies as a member of a clearly defined community has obvious economic and cultural advantages for the production of textiles, at both workshop and family level. Different castes specialize in different processes fitting to their status and, within the same caste, members of an extended family group will each contribute an element to the production process. Most communities involved in the production of textiles are of lower castes, and generally speaking the coarser the cloth the lower the stratum; highly specialized weavers and decorators of silk and fine cloth enjoy the highest status possible.

The decorative textiles from the Indian subcontinent are best examined by type rather than by region, and aside from the flatweave tradition which uses the sheep's wool of the North-West Frontier area with Afghanistan and the work of the Brahui Balouch of west Pakistan, cotton remains the predominant natural fibre. Textiles from the Subcontinent are highly decorated using a variety of techniques, often on a pre-woven ground or by pattern dyeing the yarn before weaving. Most textiles are made as clothing and animal trappings and as ceremonial hangings within house and temple. The techniques discussed here are separated into three categories: flatweaving; decoration of a plain ground with embroidery, appliqué and quilting; and finally, decoration and weaving using the resist-dye techniques.

In recent years the production of flatwoven cotton floor rugs has become a major trading activity. Known as dhurries, these textiles are made on relatively simple ground looms and used throughout India, more commonly in the north. The weave is weft faced and the decorative techniques are much the same as in kilim weaving, such as slit work, dovetailing, double interlocking, eccentric wefts and weft-float patterning. Patterns can vary from nineteenth-century floral work inspired by Persian and Anatolian carpet motifs, to simple bands and blocks of colour on rugs found in chain stores throughout the Western world. Their uses are varied and as with the North African Berber hanbels, dhurries were often laid on the floor under carpets in the houses and palaces of the wealthy. The largest dhurries are still commissioned for palace decoration and may extend to over eighty feet in length and twenty-five feet in width. Smaller room dhurries are common, as are prayer dhurries with single or multiple niches. Bed dhurries are about six feet by three feet in size and used over a wooden framed bed, under the mattress and bedding. All these types of dhurrie were made to the highest standards in the jails of colonial India from the late nineteenth to the early twentieth century. Originally initiated by local rulers as a useful prison craft, the practice was encouraged by the British administration, and from the looms of the incarcerated came the finest dhurries in existence today. The high quality of the work was established and maintained by the jail governor and his supervisors. The dhurrie commissions – from the local gentry and the expatriates – for copies of carpets of diverse origin, traditional compositions and floor tiling patterns, ensured that this production of decorative floor rugs varied from simple to electric compositions in both colour and patterning. The inheritance of the dhurrie commissioning tradition has now passed to the Western decorator and designer and of all flatwoven

Appliqué hanging, from Gujarat, India

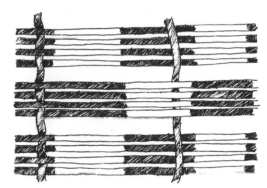

4   *The dyed result with bindings removed*

5   *The woven cloth*

floor rugs, the possible production of a dhurrie to individual requirements is certainly the most refined and highly organized.

The embroidered ornamentation of woven cloth with needle and thread is an ancient tradition in the Subcontinent and is particularly associated with the tribes and peoples of the North-West Frontier, the Sind desert of Pakistan and the Indian states of Gujarat, Rajasthan and the Punjab. Predominantly the work of the women in the villages and made for personal and family use, the embroidered skirts, blouses, veils, household and shrine hangings and animal trappings are colourfully patterned with a mixture of ancient and modern motifs. More often than not, the embroidered work almost completely covers the plain cotton ground in a range of figurative, floral and geometric designs according to religious observance. Mirror work is common, and colours that may seem harsh and visually unpalatable when alone are associated on a panel with harmony and skill beyond the imagination of the Western-trained mind. Each member of a caste and religious group declaims by way of dress their identity and status. Garments may be examined for colour, pattern and the richness of cloth from low wool to finest silk, for all contribute to the social labelling of the individual. The multiplicity of the caste system ensures that any gathering of people, especially in Gujarat, is an inspiringly colourful affair, which is brought to a climax at festivals, and especially marriages, with the caparisoning of animals, courtyards and houses and the creation of tented cities of embroidered and decorated awnings and panels.

Appliqué and quilted work is generally associated with village embroidery tradition and is also found further to the east in Bengal and Orissa. The attachment of pieces of cut cloth and other decorative objects to a plain ground in an appliqué technique and the joining together of layers of cloth with running stitches to make a quilted fabric are ancient methods of ornamentation. Such work is often combined with decorative embroidery stitches and the appliqué technique is used to greatest effect in large, many panelled ceremonial hangings and animal trappings such as ox covers. Gujarat is justifiably famous for the appliqué work of covers, hangings, trappings and household decorations, and the combinations of materials and motifs used may range increasingly from the charming to the bizarre.

The resist-dyeing techniques of 'bandhani' and 'bandha' are known elsewhere by their more familiar titles of tie and dye (or 'plangi'), and ikat work respectively. The decorating work is relatively simple for bandhana textiles, immensely complicated and time-consuming for the bandha technique. To tie and dye, selected parts of the plain coloured cloth – often folded once or twice to save time – are lifted and tied with wrapping thread and impermeable material in a selected pattern. The tied cloth is then dyed and this tie-and-dye process repeated again should more colours and patterns be needed. When the threads are removed the areas saved from the action of the dye or series of different coloured dyes will appear as circles, pinpricks, square patterns, rosettes and palmettes. The quality of decorative effect and cloth used varies from coarse wool with simple associations of colours to the finest silks with delicate floral motifs. Bandhana textiles are prized as veil cloths, saris, shoulder cloths and turbans and the tie-and-dye work is found throughout India, especially in Gujarat, Rajasthan, Orissa and Andhra Pradesh and is the monopoly of the Hindu and Muslim communities of professional weavers, dyers and printers.

Like bandhana work, the bandha technique has ancient roots in the history of weaving and textile decoration of the Indian subcontinent. The bandha or ikat process involves the resist wrapping of areas of bundles of warps, and sometimes of the weft as well, with tied thread, dyeing the tied yarn and continuing the process with more wrapping and dyeing until the desired combinations of colours and patterns are achieved. The warp yarn is then untied and arranged on the loom and the cloth woven with either plain or bandha-dyed wefts. Single bandha work is now practised in Gujarat, Andhra Pradesh and Orissa by professional weavers and dyers using silk, synthetic fibres and dyes and machine-spun cotton. The double bandha or

patola cloth of silk is exceedingly difficult and time-consuming to produce and is highly valued, not only within the Subcontinent but also as a trading commodity with South-East Asia. In Java, Sumatra and Bali the patola cloths have been imported from at least the fifteenth century onwards, treated with veneration and used for religious and court ceremonies. Historically a luxury commodity from Gujarat, the weaving of patola cloths has all but died out and old and antique examples are treasured as festive clothing and shrine decorations amongst the traditionalist upper class families of the region. By contrast the professional weavers and dyers of Orissa and Andhra Pradesh have, since the late nineteenth century and more recently, adopted and adapted bandha techniques most successfully. They are flourishing by means of cooperative systems of production and marketing and by dyeing, patterning and weaving textiles to suit the ephemeral tastes in colour and design of the markets at home and abroad.

Embroidered door hanging – a 'toran' – from Gujarat, India

Indepndence

THAILAND

MALAYSIA

Aceh   Malaya

Sabah

Sarawak

SULAWESI

BORNEO
Kaliman Tan

SUMATRA

MOLUCCAS

Palembang

JAVA   BALI   FLORES

LOMBOK

TIMOR

SUMBA   ROTI

Indonesia

The modern state of Indonesia is a collection of islands that meander over three and a half thousand miles of ocean and sea from South-East Asia to close by Australia. Bisected by the equator, these tropical islands have, from ancient times, acted as a sponge that has absorbed, developed and been enriched by the overflow of peoples, commodities and religions from mainland Asia. Like the Indian subcontinent, the Indonesian archipelago is alive with the interactions of hundreds of ethnic groups that have developed rich craft cultures over the centuries and of these, cotton weaving is central to a way of life that is a constantly developing blend of ritual and commerce. For over three hundred years from the fifteenth century onwards, international trade with the region was dominated by the export of luxury commodities such as spices, rare and scented woods and dyestuffs, especially indigo. Textiles from mainland Asia were used by the Portuguese and Arab coastal traders as goods for barter, so bringing to the islands weaving designs and influences from afar, and from the Indian subcontinent in particular. Of the indigenous textile production there are few records of large-scale export until this century when in the thirties and again in the sixties the international fashion demand for the batik sarong as exotic attire reached a peak. Of the loom-decorated textiles, it is the ikat work that delighted the Dutch settlers and such cloths were exported to Holland over a hundred years ago, to make striking bedspreads, curtains and loose furnishing cloth. Certainly, these ikat textiles and textiles woven on simple backstrap looms demonstrate the continuation and development of a weaving tradition that has ancient and complex roots.

Hinduism and Buddhism spread to the region from mainland Asia from about AD 100 and centred on the western islands of Java and Sumatra; to the north-east, the less populated islands of Sulawesi, Borneo and the Moluccas were inhabited by river valley and jungle tribes who, until the arrival of the Christian missionaries in recent times, mixed animist and ancient Asian beliefs that perfectly matched these hunter-gatherers' lifestyle of shifting cultivation. The current religion of Indonesia – Islam – was brought by the Arab and Muslim Indian traders to the region in the fifteenth century, and the pervasive message of the Koran soon spread throughout the western islands, evicting the believers of the local Hindu faith to the isle of Bali, an enclave of the original Indian religion to this day. From the fifteenth to the seventeenth

centuries, Portuguese and Dutch mercantile adventuring dominated the region and after the near-collapse of the dominant Dutch East India Company in the eighteenth century, the Netherlands' government inherited an empire that was to last until after the Second World War.

Textiles have been made on simple back-tension or backstrap looms throughout many of the islands since ancient times. Even today these most primitive looms are used to weave warp-ikat cloth for sacred rituals and, aside from their use as objects of exchange and wealth, it is their multivarious ceremonial significance that predominates. The preparation of the yarn, the dyestuffs and the weaving of the cloth is a woman's occupation, and this is a role that is in harmony with the male duties of housebuilding, loom making, metal working and erstwhile head hunting or other fractious habits. The textiles are seen symbolically as female and the finest are central elements in the ritual observance of the rites of passage – birth, circumcision, first haircutting, marriage and death. There are strict codes for the manufacture of these ceremonial textiles, from the types of dyestuffs and colours to the patterning and quality of work. Preserved within families, the specialized pieces of clothing, temple banners and hangings are unique to each tribal group, ranging from double ikat work from Bali, to weft-patterned textiles from Flores and including, even now, old patola cloth from Gujarat that has become sacred by use.

Textiles as costume provide a crossover point between ritual associations, the display of prestige and wealth, and everyday garb. There are records from the fourteenth century that indicate the presence of an established system of proprietary rights for the use of types and patterns of textiles and their value as gifts, a system maintained and protected until recently by the matriarchal members of the upper classes. Fine cloths were worn by men in association with personal weaponry such as the 'keris', and on Sumba impressive exhibitions of wealth would be colourfully achieved by temporarily dressing the extended retinue in ikat cloth from the royal storehouse. Fine ikats and other textiles would be amassed by the elite to wrap and bury the corpse in a final show of earthly prestige and religious ritual. The scanty traditional costume is in harmony with the tropical climate of the region by being flexible in use, light in weight yet filled with designs and colours that can display at a glance the status of the wearer, their stage in life and their com-

The production of Sea-Dayak cloth in Sarawak, c.1900. (Above) Cutting the lemba leaves, the fibres of which are used to tie the cotton threads before dyeing; (opposite, above) preparing to spin the thread that will be used to make an ikat cotton sarong as is worn by the weaver; and (opposite, below) cotton weaving on a backstrap loom

munity of origin. The backstrap looms are worked to produce rectangular cloths, which are draped or wrapped over the body in a variety of ways that show the patterns on the textiles to good effect. Smaller cloths are used as breast wrappers, belts and head wrappers, the larger cloths as sarongs and shoulder mantles. Although Western-style clothing has all but replaced traditional garb in the cities, villagers and rural peoples continue to sport hand-loomed textiles for comfort, and for identity and prestige.

The two most decorative forms of design and colour embellishment of textiles in Indonesia are ikat weaving and supplementary weft techniques. The shimmering colours and patterns of ikat cloth are achieved by resist binding groups of warps or wefts, or both, before the weaving process, and the blurred effect is caused and controlled by the seepage of dye into the resisted areas. By altering the position of the bound and protected areas for subsequent colour immersions – often by following a crude template or diagram – compositions may be dyed and woven which vary from the finest figurative detail to simple yet effective blurred associations of colour. The working of intricate designs onto plain cloth by the weft-patterning process reached a pinnacle of achievement in nineteenth-century Sumatra. The variety of textiles from this large island matches the ethnic mix of the population of Indian, Chinese, Javanese, Arabic, Portuguese and Dutch origin. South Sumatra is famous for two types of surface-decorated textiles, the women's sarongs known as 'tapis' and the so-called 'ship cloths'. Heavily embroidered, the tapis were prestigious items of ceremonial dress, and the rich natural dye tones of reds, blues and yellow-browns are contrasted by the wealth of banded stitchwork, highlighted with precious metal threads. Plain or warp-ikatted areas separate the decorated panels.

These tapis are certainly the most sumptuous textiles of the islands. The skills that were used to make the tapis and the ship cloths have been lost for nearly a century, and if the tapis are treasured for the rich indulgence of their embroidery, then the compositions of the ship cloths are valued for their strong imagery. The banner-shaped 'palepai' and 'tatibin' and the square 'tampan' panels are weft decorated with sombre images of boats, or a single boat, with arching bow and stern, filled with people, houses, animals, shrines and banners, and the cloths would be hung for the passage of life ceremonies.

Java is particularly well known throughout the world for its magnificent batik-decorated cloth and to the east the ikat tradition continues in eastern Bali with the exquisite double-ikatted cloth, known as 'geringsing', from the village of Tenganan Pageringsingan. Inspired in composition, it is thought, by the import of Indian patola cloths over the past four hundred years, these natural tan cotton cloths are resist dyed to create fine figurative motifs that link in geometric harmony when seen from a distance. Colours are deep tones of earthen red, purple and black, and these valuable cloths are traded for different ritual uses throughout the island. Weft-ikat work and plangi is common in Bali, and when worn at one of the ceaseless round of celebrations and ceremonies, they add to the rich tapestry of life on the island.

Following the chain of islands stretching to the east, the coastal district of eastern Sumba is famous for the men's mantle cloths. Ikat patterned and known as 'hinggi', the cloths are made in pairs, one to be worn over the hips and the second over the shoulder. As the island is famous for the breeding and export of horses it seems only natural that some of the most engaging ikat compositions depict cavorting stallions in a series of heraldic pairs. Sumban ikat patterns are often large and visually engaging, coloured with strong blue and red dyes, and the finest work of the past displays complex horizontal bands of small and large motifs. The ancient practice of exhibiting the severed heads of the enemy on staves finds expression nowadays in textile design, with ikat patterns of skull trees. Other subjects include lively interpretations of deer, fish, shrimps and well-endowed male figures.

The volcano-pimpled island of Flores is known for its regional textile production. To the west the Manggarai women weave indigo-dyed plain sarongs that are decorated with supplementary weft work in a rainbow of colours. An area of banded motifs creates a centre to the tubular sarong, with other stellar motifs scattered within the plain field of the cloth. Elsewhere, warp-ikat work predominates, and the Lio peoples weave patola-like compositions of light-coloured tiny human figures, insects and dogs on deep blue, brown or black grounds. Again to the east, the Atoni people of the island of Timor are known for their unusually brightly coloured hip cloth made up of warp bands. Plain strips of blue, yellow and red cloth alternate with warp ikat and supplementary decorative techniques. Northwards within the palm of the distorted fingers of the Sulawesi island group, the Toradja people's most decorative weaves are the striking warp-ikat funeral shrouds filled with interlinking images of hooks and arrows that are a reflection of their animist past. A jungle and swamp lifestyle has fostered the selective development of the tribes of Borneo as well. Now three nations, this large, relatively low-lying island is a mass of tropical rainforest that is inhabited by jungle peoples collectively known as the Iban. Away from the coastal enclaves of Chinese, Javanese and Malays, the Iban peoples pursue a lifestyle of shifting cultivation centred on their longhouse settlements. Their most famous textiles are the 'pua', warp-ikatted blankets and hangings reserved for ceremonial use. Woven in the shade and cover of a longhouse gallery the ikats are decorated, often on an attractive brick-red ground, with electric geometric patterning that almost overwhelms the senses. Only from a distance may one observe that these designs link to form interlocking chains of animal and human figures.

(Opposite) Where it all begins . . . llamas – and weavers – in South America

Indonesia

(Right) Tapis (woman's sarong), Sumatra, Lampong region. Warp ikat and embroidery of cotton and silk. This tubular skirt would have been worn as an item of prestige and wealth on ceremonial occasions.

(Left) Pua (blanket), Sarawak. Cotton warp ikat. A ritual textile of the Iban people, famous for their headhunting of the past, and their longhouse lifestyle.

(Below) Tampan (known as a 'ship cloth'), Sumatra, Lampong region. Cotton with supplementary wefts. Hung at passage of life ceremonies, this cloth is richly decorated with the beasts of the ocean which surround the vessel carrying four characters and their retinue on a sea voyage.

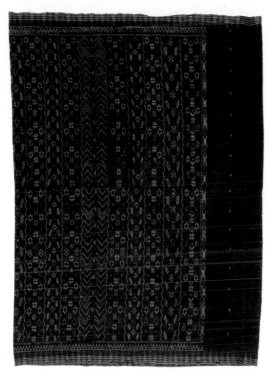

Hanging, made by the Toradja people, Celebes. Three panels of cotton, centre panel ikat. Made as funeral shrouds in the Rongkong valley but used elsewhere as clothing or hung at major feasts.

Sarong (woman's dress), made by the Manggarai people, Western Flores. Tapestry-woven of cotton with supplementary wefts. This sarong is worn knotted over the breast, and the dovetailing weave at the selvedge (the 'tumpal') indicates that it is the work of the highest quality.

Hinggi (man's mantle), Sumba. Cotton warp ikat. Made in identical pairs, one hinggi is wrapped around the hips and the other over the shoulder. The banded patterning and deep colouration of this refined example distinguish it as the exclusive garb of nobility.

The Indian subcontinent

(Right) *Abocchani* (wedding shawl), Sind, Pakistan. Embroidered with silken flowers on a cotton ground, this old dowry textile represents wealth and prestige for a Muslim family.

(Below) *Shamiana* (ceiling hanging, awning, or canopy), made by the Oswal Jain people, West Rajasthan, north-west India. Cotton appliqué. The lively colouring offers a decorative escape from their dry and dusty land, while the size of the hanging provides cool shade from the blazing sun.

Dhurrie, Bikaner, Rajasthan, north-west India. Cotton, single and double interlocking tapestry weave. This large dhurrie, made at the turn of the century, was probably commissioned for palace use at Bikaner.

(Right) Quilt cover, Kathiawar, Gujarat, north-west India. Quilted, silk-embroidered and appliquéd cotton. Made by the women of the Bhopa caste of itinerant performers and shaman characters, as a baby's or child's blanket.

(Above) Bullock cover, made by the Patel caste, Kathiawar, Gujarat, north-west India. Cotton appliqué and embroidery. A pair of bullocks would pull a cart at weddings and festivals, and both animals and the vehicle would be gloriously caparisoned with the very best textiles. Since one half of this cover would hang almost unseen between the animals, the embroidered work is more elaborate to the outside.

(Below) Chakla (wall hanging), made by the Mahajan people, Gujarat, north-west India. Cotton with floss silk embroidery. Chaklas are hung on the wall for weddings and special occasions.

Dhurrie, north-west India. Cotton, single interlock weave. This is a fine example of a modern dhurrie with a composition known as an 'eye dazzler'.

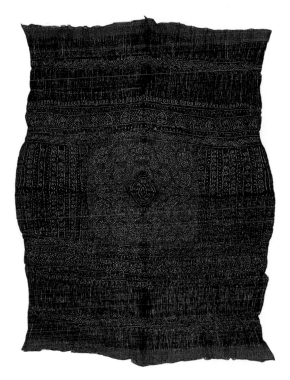

Shawl, from Mandvi, Kutch, Gujarat, north-west India. Tie-dyed cotton. Commercially made for Muslim women by tie-and-dye specialists. The degree of intricacy of the work would indicate the wealth of the owner.

61

Asia Minor to Central Asia

Pardah (wall hanging), Bokhara, Central Asia. Warp ikat of silk and cotton weft. Made of four panels stitched together at the selvedge in a way that further enlivens the shimmering ikat effect; used as a hanging at festivities and as a curtain.

(Above) Horse cover, made by the Uzbek Lakai people, north Afghanistan/Turkestan. Cotton with appliqué and silk embroidery. To a Turkoman, a horse is a prestigious and useful item of wealth, for work and play, and this pride in ownership is evident in the love and care that has been lavished on the making of this stunning horse cover.

(Below) Susani (embroidered hanging), made by the Uzbek people, Central Asia. Silk embroidery on cotton. The decorative inspiration of the susanis came to Central Asia from Persia.

(Below) Kilim, made by the Tartari people, north Afghanistan. Double interlocked wool. The Tartari, whose work, with its 'eight-legged spider' motif, is always distinctive, are also famous for their fine double interlocking weaving.

(Below) Kilim, Maimana, north-west Afghanistan. Slitwoven of wool. Very fine stepping slitweave, which creates colourful lozenges and diamonds with a multiple border, is a characteristic of kilims from around the town of Maimana.

Ghujeri (stripwoven kilim), made by the Uzbek nomads, north Afghanistan. Warp-faced patterned, wool. Woven in strips on tiny ground looms. The Uzbeki make rugs or saddle cloths and covers to almost any size by sewing many strips together.

(Left) Soffrai (eating cloth), made by the Rukshani Balouch people, west Afghanistan. Slitweave, weft-faced patterned and brocaded, of sheep's wool and goat hair. A classic eating cloth with an undecorated central field and simply coloured with madder and indigo.

Asia Minor to Central Asia

(Right) Kilim, Zarand, north Persia. Cotton warps and woollen wefts, slitweave. Always long and narrow, these kilims are finely decorated with floral motifs which, viewed from a distance, form three or more diamond-shaped medallions.

Kilim, made by the Qashqai nomads, south-west Persia. Slitwoven wool. For centuries the Qashqai have been brilliant and prolific masters of kilim weaving. Brightly patterned and warm in colour, they are bordered by a multiple 'tree' pattern.

(Top left) Modern kilim, made by Kurdish weavers, Senna, north-west Persia. Cotton and wool slitweave. Old (bottom left) and new kilims from Persian Kurdistan may be compared here. Both are inspired by a weaving commission – one for Persian court and noble use, the other for export to the West.

(Below) Kilim, Shirvan, Caucasus. Slitweave and brocade, wool. Shirvan kilims are borderless and patterned by stripes of small designs and bands of medallions.

Kilim, Kuba, Caucasus. Slitweave, wool. Large abstract medallion patterns and strong colouration are hallmarks of Caucasian kilims that have been entitled 'Kuba' by Western dealers and collectors.

65

Asia Minor to Central Asia

(Left) Kilim, Thrace. Slitweave with curved wefts, wool. The 'tree of life' composition is found in kilims from this region of European Turkey. A floral border with animal and leaf motifs is most common, and red and blue colours predominate.

(Below) Kilim, made by Kurdish weavers, Malatya. Slitweave of cotton and wool. These intricate kilims are often made in two pieces with three large medallions unevenly divided by the central axis of the rug. This is an unusually small example of a single, central composition.

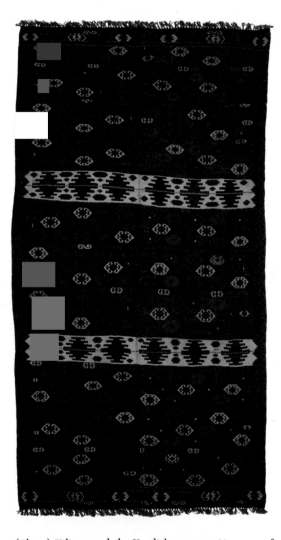

(Above) Kilim, made by Kurdish weavers, Van area of eastern Anatolia. Slitwoven wool. Often made in two pieces, these kilims resemble those woven by other Kurdish groups in the Caucasus and north Persia.

(Left) Kilim, known as a 'Karabagh' or 'Bessarabian' kilim, made by Kurdish weavers, eastern Anatolia. Slitwoven cotton and wool. Highly decorative, these kilims are instantly recognizable by their realistic floral compositions of roses and carnations.

(Below) Kilim, Konya. Slitwoven wool with outlining. Made in the hinterland of Konya in central Anatolia, these large kilims are woven in two pieces with a white or cream ground and a series of medallions running down the centre.

(Left) Kilim, Sivas. Slitwoven with outlining work, all wool. More often than not, these kilims are intended for prayer. This example contains a very subtle representation of the prayer arch – the mihrab.

(Right) Kilim, Erzurum. Wool, slitwoven. Often a fine ochre and green colour, Erzurum prayer kilims have distinctive floral and leaf borders.

(Above) Curtain, Ottoman Empire. Silk embroidery on cotton. Woven and decorated by embroiderers in service to the munificent Ottoman court, such historic floral textiles have inspired designers, weavers and artists the world over.

Africa

(*Above*) Tunic decoration, made by Coptic weavers, Egypt. *Slitweave with curved wefts, wool. Large numbers of fragments of Coptic tapestries have been exhumed in Egypt and all testify to a brilliant weaving tradition of floral and figurative compositions.*

(*Above*) Hanbel, made by the Berber people, Middle Atlas, Morocco. *Weft-faced patterned weave of wool. Laid over rush mats and beneath tufted carpets, or used as blankets, these are the North African equivalents of the Asian kilims.*

(*Right*) 'Kente' cloth, made by the Ashanti people, Ghana. *Silk stripwoven with supplementary weft-float patterns. A colourful example of a stripwoven chief's mantle made of imported silk.*

Flatweave, from Tunisia or Algeria. *Interlocking weave, wool. A colourful example of a rug from lands bordering the Sahara desert.*

(Left) Raphia textile, made by the Kuba people, Zaire. Raphia cut-pile embroidery. The many variations of traditional designs represented here are reminiscent of a sampler.

(Below) Skirt length, made by the Kuba people, Zaire. Raphia cloth with appliqué and embroidery. Many panelled lengths of raphia cloth are made as skirts, wrapped around in layers to show the embroidered and appliqué patterning.

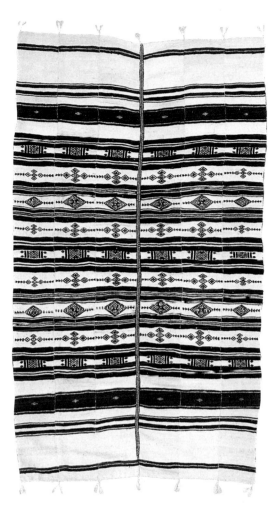

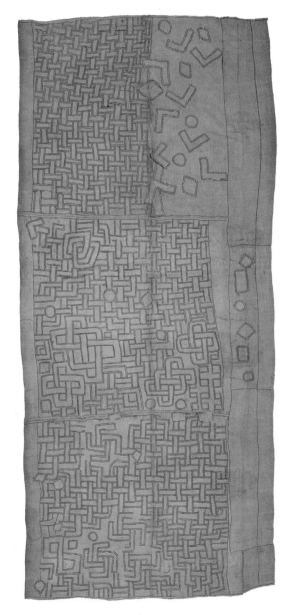

(Left) Blanket, made by the Fulani people, Niger bend, Mali. Stripwoven wool with weft-faced patterning. Used by the transhumant Fulani shepherds, these woollen textiles are essential as insulating blankets against the cold of the desert nights.

(Below) Robe, made by the Hausa people, Nigeria. Stripwoven cotton with silk embroidery. Decorated by male embroiderers, this fine gown is indigo dyed and silk decorated with the traditional 'two knives' pattern.

The Americas

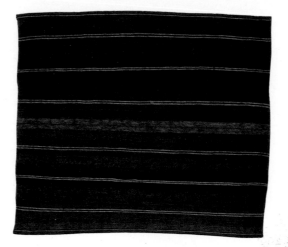

(Right) Iscayo (woman's mantle), made by the Aymara Indians, southern altiplano Bolivia. Alpaca hair, warp-faced weave. A garment of ancient origin and worn by chieftains' wives during official functions, such a fine cloth is a revered part of a 'q'epi' group of ceremonial textiles.

(Below) Guatemalan Indian skirt, Colotenango (Dept. of Huehuetenango), Guatemala. Cotton, hip-strap loomed in two pieces with cotton brocade. This type of skirt wrap is of pre-Columbian origin.

(Above) Llacota (mantle), made by the Aymara Indians, southern altiplano, Bolivia. Warp-faced weave, alpaca hair. Originally worn by men as an everyday shoulder cloth, the llacotas became ceremonial attire after the abolition of the mantle by the Spanish from the 1780s; later to be replaced by the poncho.

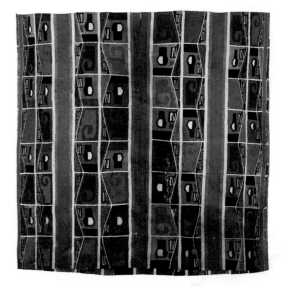

(Right) Tunic, Peru, Huari. (AD 600–800). Slit tapestry weave, alpaca. Decorated with feline and abstract motifs, this tunic is a fine example of weaving from a culture that represented their animal gods by abstract forms.

(Right) Serape, north Mexico. Interlocking tapestry weave of wool. A traditional wearing blanket, the serape is often made with a central motif of silk thread.

(Left) Poncho, South Coast, Peru, Nazca-Huari period (AD 700–1000). Cotton plainweave ground with applied feathers. Animal and stellar motifs compete for attention on this colourful poncho, most probably the garb of priests or royalty.

(Above) Mola (blouse decoration), made by the Kuna Indians, San Blas Islands, Panama. Cotton 'reverse appliqué'. These highly colourful textiles are made in pairs and sewn to the front and back of a blouse.

(Right) Flatwoven rug, Mexico. Tapestry woven, wool. This is a fine and robust modern copy of a nineteenth-century Navajo serape, which is ideal as a decorative floor rug.

The Americas

Chief blanket, made by the Navajo Indians, New Mexico. Single interlock weave, wool. This blanket is categorized as 'transitional Second Phase', denoting a period in the evolution of the Navajo blanket when triangular forms began to break out from the striped areas.

(Right) Flatweave, made by the Navajo Indians, New Mexico. Slitweave, wool. A good example of an early twentieth-century Navajo textile made as a floor rug with an 'eye-dazzler' composition.

(Below) Pictorial blanket, made by the Navajo Indians, New Mexico. Single interlock weave, all wool. The Navajo enjoyed copying the American flag, as it is so reminiscent of their own early striped weaves.

Chapter Two **Function**

Function

Of all the arts and crafts of the tribal and pre-industrial world, the production of hand-loomed textiles afforded the greatest opportunity for civilizing man to combine decoration with utility, both fundamentals in a primitive way of life. The most extreme examples of this expression are fast becoming historic, for the bright parrot and macaw feather ponchos of pre-Columbian Peru and the gold-threaded Sumatran sarongs of the nineteenth century share a common obsolescence: both represent aspects of elitist and decorative craft cultures that are now likely to be communicated in monetary terms, or by Western-orientated consumer wealth. Likewise, yet at the opposite extreme of wealth and status, the village and tented encampment domestic weaving of simply decorated storage and transportation bags has now, perhaps within less than a generation, been succeeded by the import and use of cheap and robust synthetic sacks. Such acculturation to the religious, social, and commercial habits of the 'civilized' world has permeated all but the most remote of tribes and is a process of mankind's development that may be charted in the use and decoration of hand-woven textiles over the last five hundred years.

The interlacing of threads of animal hair, wool or vegetable fibres to form cloth is one of the most important and liberating aspects of primitive technology. Successful habitation of the northern and southern hemispheres was reliant on effective insulation of the body from the extremes of the temperate and continental climes. From the hunting and trapping of animals for foodstuffs and the use of skins and fur for clothing followed man's realization of the potential of local domesticated animals and cultivated plants to provide raw materials for weaving. There are records and evidence for the prehistoric use of yarn spun from the indigenous cotton plant of the Indian subcontinent, Indonesia and South America, and of sheep's wool in the steppes of Central Asia.

Weaving techniques have developed, from the finger-plaiting of yarn to tapestry work on a loom, at different rates and with differing consequences for the production of multivarious types of textiles all over the world. Whereas the weaving of woollen blankets by the North American tribes is a phenomenon of no more than the past four hundred years, tapestry weaves from Peru may be dated beyond 400 BC. Aside from the obvious use of cloth as personal insulation and for the maintenance of a new-found modesty, in all societies in one form or another, a textile may instantly communicate, by pattern and colour, shape and size, the status, power, wealth and beliefs of the owner. This labelling of the bearer would have developed to include the dwellings of tribe or culture, whether tent, mud house, shrine or place of congregation and worship.

Subject to the survival and further intercultural development of weaving techniques and the successful establishment of trading networks of any scale, textiles became a manmade commodity for barter and commercial exchange. World trade in luxury textiles is certainly not a recent phenomenon. The Greeks knew of the fine muslins of India three hundred or more years before the birth of Christ, when the Chinese were already trading raw silk for such exotic cotton cloth. The development of inter-tribal and intercultural trading links continued at a relatively modest level of activity, such as by the trans-Asian Silk Route. These trails carried to the West some of the luxurious cloths from Cathay, Central Asia and the Levant that were seminal in maintaining a link between East and West, for these goods were part of the cultural inspiration of colour and pattern to a Europe in limbo during the Middle Ages. Such overland routes thrived until the fifteenth century when the coastal seafaring of the Portuguese extended European interests around the Horn of Africa to Asia, with its spices, silks and exotic raw materials.

Persian horse cover

Donkey bag from the Caucasus

Across the Atlantic the Spaniards colonized Central and South American territories with astonishing rapidity. At the expense of the local people these new empires and the adjacent territories became the overseas warring-grounds for the nations of Europe. At stake was the exportable mineral and agrarian wealth and a massive land area so ripe for colonization by the entrepreneurs, the malefactors and religious minorities of the Old World, a world that was fast bursting at the seams with a population explosion and with political ferment. The Dutch, English, French, Spanish and Portuguese and their colonial offspring disturbed the way of life of the tribespeople irrevocably, and at various rates and at various times they introduced social, religious and commercial influences, the ramifications of which are all-pervasive to this day. For the craft of weaving this destabilizing influence was associated with the power of international trade. Textiles that had functioned as garments of rank and prestige in Indonesia became the objects of many ephemeral decorative trends, as seen in nineteenth-century Holland and twentieth-century California. The ancient skills have been tapped since early trading days, as the South American Indians discovered when set to work in the obrajes, the erstwhile weaving work-shops of the Spanish colonials. Direct abuse by coercion has mingled for over four hundred years with the insidious influences of trade. Textiles that were developing as objects for traditional use within pre-industrial cultures have often become mere trading commodities. As such, the desire to satisfy a new and wealthy Western marketplace has, quite naturally, resulted in the production of textiles for monet-ary reward rather than for the slow pace of a local and traditional market.

Certainly almost no tribal group has escaped from the influences of Western-orientated trade and the colonization of the world by adventur-ous tourists. To the dismay of the traditionalists, chemical dyes and yarn were welcomed by tribal weavers because of their low cost and ease of use, and the shape, patterning and colouring of textiles and embroideries became

and, for the most part, remain conditioned by market demand. Cultures such as the Turkic nomads of Central Asia who lived in a fragile harmony of hardship and subsistence with their environment, and who wove essential textiles for family use, have been forcibly settled; their lifestyle was a bane to the territorially protective governments of the region. Invariably the de-mand for tribal textiles for a nomadic existence have ceased, so that their bags, animal trappings and tent decorations have now become items of historical interest.

Counterbalancing this inevitable destruction or dilution of the lifestyle of these weavers are two recent trends. The first is an attempt by some tribespeople to revert to a way of life governed by old tribal traditions and the second, the concern of the Western merchant and consum-er about the disintegration of the quality and authenticity of ethnic weaves. These factors are jointly responsible for the reintroduction, at different rates in different societies, of natural raw materials, traditional weaving techniques and the copying, where possible, of pre-acculturation textile compositions.

Such attempts to persuade tribal weaving communities that what is needed is a balance between financial profit and a maintenance of traditional values will certainly not call forth the production of the kind that was the hallmark of a pre-industrial and naive tribal past. Indeed, many textiles in Western collections are all that remains of lost techniques, forgotten cere-monies and mysterious symbology from as little as seventy-five years ago. There is hope, howev-er, that in some communities – in certain selected villages of Turkey, Thailand and India, for example – the new Western and locally inspired examination of and appreciation for the textiles of the past will set in motion a new and much needed recycling of design work and a raising of standards within weaving produc-tion.

The function of tribal textiles may be ex-amined in a historical context with reference to the nature of their practical uses and by an analysis of their qualities and purpose of de-coration.

Utility and trade

The range of uses for traditional tribal textiles is as varied as the lifestyles of their owners, whose dwellings range, in Western terms of sophistication, from the nomad's tent to the

palace of a maharaja, but it is the nomad who has retained the most sensible and traditional balance of utility and decoration. Nothing is superfluous in the spartan way of life of the

Double-headed bird design from Guatemala

Kuna Indian mola, depicting the mystical hero Ibeorgun

nomad for, from pasture to pasture, from area of water rights to well, all the paraphernalia of existence must be carried by camel or donkey.

The weaving of textiles by the nomads is a domestic affair and conforms rigorously to traditional values and uses. Bags, sacks, camel headdresses, horse and camel saddle covers and tent bands for ropes are made on the one hand for transportation and on the other, to afford some comfort at camp, with woven goat hair tents, tent bands as decorations, tent bags suspended as storage facilities, flatweaves on the floor as covers and blankets, and as curtains, and embroideries and patchwork as brightly coloured hangings. At celebrations, large rugs would be laid outside in the shade to welcome guests. The sizes and uses of textiles have evolved over the centuries as the nomadic lifestyle slowly developed, punctuated by inter-tribal feuding and trade and religious wars between local empires.

Most kilims of Asia and the North African hanbels of the nomads are rectangular and no more than three to five feet wide. Governed by the narrow width of a transportable loom, larger flatwoven rugs are made by weaving one or more strips to be joined at the selvedge. Small Balouch runners, known as 'soffrai' in Persian, are used as supplementary floor covers to edge larger rugs, and square kilims are used as cloths on which to lay the family meal. Balouch 'rukorsi' kilims, about three feet square, are laid over felts and a stove of charcoal embers, as a ceremonial cover. Larger rugs, such as the Berber hanbels, are used as floor rugs often over straw mats with knotted carpets laid underneath. In the winter the density of the flatweave means that the cloth affords much insulation when used as a blanket. Of great practical significance are the range of bags and bands made by the nomads. Tent bands that are sometimes over thirty feet in length and no more than four to nine inches wide provide lashing rope for tents and animal packs as well as tent trappings. Double bags known as 'heybe' in Turkish and 'hurgin' in Persian serve as donkey, camel and personal shoulder panniers. Small bags are used for food storage, such as bottle-shaped salt bags, for personal posses-sions and to protect the family Koran. Larger bags and frame covers include the rectangular 'juvals' and 'jaloors' of the Turkmen and the maffrash bedding bags of the Caucasus.

In contrast to the nomads, tribespeople set-tled within and associated with village, town or city life have considerable opportunities for the organized production of textiles and their use

as trading commodities. In Ghana, fine and traditionally patterned stripwoven cloth is to this day woven to commission on drag looms by the men; indeed, the clients were expected to provide the yarn. And in Bali, ikats that are not fine enough to be used as ceremonial gifts or hangings are sold to tourists without hesitation. The Kurdish village peoples of eastern Anatolia and north-west Persia have a long-established reputation for weaving fine kilims to order, and their ability to work to non-traditional com-positions is a boon for merchants and interior designers alike. Whole villages in Mexico, Guatemala, Ecuador and Peru have specialized in the craft of weaving as a viable economic activity, supplying tourists, cooperatives and commissioned export orders alike. The fine ikat robes of the gentry of nineteenth century Samarkand were made in urban workshops, wherein a highly organized network of special-ists contributed their skills of spinning, pattern creating, dyeing, warping, weaving, and the finishing of cloth. Away from the workshops of town and city, but still directly influenced by their decorative fashions, any village tribal weaving activity was very much more likely to be an integral part of daily life, balanced within a world of semi-subsistence farming or labour for landowners. With settled peoples, preoccu-pied not with the need to seek new pastures but with the desire to survive within the hinterland of the group of permanent dwell-ings, the production of textiles tends to reflect the stages of their cultural development.

The use of textiles within communities of fixed abode was determined by clothing needs, and by the decorative requirements for their animals and specific areas of the house, shrine or temple. Handloomed, embroidered, appli-quéd and quilted textiles remained objects of utility within the family, for insulation and as covering materials. Inevitably, wealth, rank and power was expressed by sporting finer cloths, and such elitism was a well-protected social more; in Indonesia, the right to use certain textile designs and colours was zealously guarded, and in the oasis cities of Central Asia similar dress codes were maintained by the rigorously enforced edicts of the ruling Khans. This extension of the textile's function, from an object of simple utility to such decorative trappings of wealth and authority, or as a ceremonial and religious accessory, may be examined by a journey through the tribal weaving communities of the world, appraising the religious and cultural basis for their textile traditions.

Decoration and symbolism

From the austere geometric patterning of Incan cloth to the lively figurative expression of the village embroideries of India, the beliefs and religions of peoples and tribal groups have influenced and controlled textile decoration for centuries.

Amongst the cultures of the ancient world that possessed no written language, the pre-Columbian peoples of Peru, Ecuador and Bolivia are known to have used the symbolism within their textiles as a form of communication. The priests and rulers of the Chancay, Huari, Nazca and Incan cultures used painted ceramics, carved stone reliefs and woven textiles to foster an acceptance and maintenance of religious principles of the day throughout their empires. Textiles were decorated with representations of gods and god-like creatures. Common motifs of surviving textiles vary from the representational – the two-headed snakes, birds of prey, fertility symbols and feline creatures – to the mysteriously abstract forms of colour and pattern association. Pre-Columbian textile patterning seems, from a contemporary Western point of view, to mirror some of the contradictions that have existed in European art since the late nineteenth century. Indeed, such parallels between cultures so very different hint at the complex genetic codes common to all mankind that control the more obscure processes of the brain. This is perhaps an explanation for the fact that the creative minds of many cultures – usually civilizations that have passed a certain point in their development, and may be coming to their end – will see and interpret in a similar way images that symbolize their existence.

These images decorate venerated objects such as textiles, ceramics, paintings and carvings, and will often assume forms, frequently of a geometric type, that are extraordinarily similar in different cultures and will be partly understood by the viewer as motifs or symbols. In ancient Peru, despite the overlapping of influences, one may chart a development of pre-Columbian textile designs from representational and realistic religious forms to the severe abstract compositions of the Incas that would not have offended the sensibilities of their living god. Within that Incan Empire, a refined system of rank placed textiles above food and ceramics and third in place below humans and cameloids. Such reverence for their weavings extended throughout life and into death in many of these pre-Christian cultures, whose death cults have fortunately resulted in the burial and preservation of thousands of textiles so that,

even now, we may enjoy the decorative qualities of their richest and finest wares.

For the Indians of Central and South America, the Christian faith of their European conquerors was absorbed and modified to suit a way of life that was intimate with survival within their mountain and jungle environment and influenced by the obvious as well as the more mysterious effects of the sun, moon and stars. In Bolivia, despite the efforts of the Church, memories of pagan rituals survive through the inheritance of the ceremonial textiles of the q'epi collection. Worn by the elected few at rituals such as weddings and saints' days, these eighteenth- and nineteenth-century blankets and capes are handled and stored with reverence. The mix of old and new beliefs is also evident in the dressing of models of saints in pre-colonial-style garb during feasts and processions and in the combinations of Christian and animistic motifs in their weavings. The calendar belts, the 'chumpis' of the Peruvian Indians, and many more of their traditional textiles, are packed with lively combinations of images – llamas, snakes, ducks and stars – which relate stories and traditions from both recent and ancient times. Guatemalan Indian textiles also betray such influences, mixing Mayan motifs of the sun, moon, double-headed birds and deer with the folk designs of the present.

More recent traditions, such as the weaving of the North American Indians and the appliqué of the Panamanian Kuna Indians, develop today in an uneasy relationship between supply and demand. For the Navajo a blanket was a functional trading commodity and the patterning of the textile was directly related to its mode of wear, so that a composition made sense when draped across the shoulders, worn as a poncho over the head, or used as a horse and tent blanket. This tribal use and local influencing of patterns were lost from the late nineteenth century onwards. The Kuna Indians, conversely, have adopted and developed a reverse appliqué technique for blouse panel production, most probably from contact with Europeans, using such colourful work as a powerful medium of tribal identity in the face of social and political acculturation. Mixing pagan and Christian symbolism, the molas depict local events, fashionable political messages and consumer ephemera with a beguiling freshness. Such work extends from pure decoration to simple messages of self-expression, and images of a symbolic nature, with a secret meaning that is probably linked with protection from errant evil spirits.

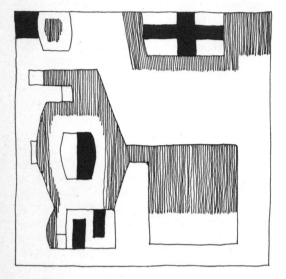

Puma motif from an ancient textile of the Huari period

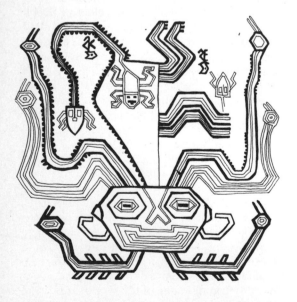

A cat being transformed into a god figure with snakes, from the Paracas culture

Pre-Islamic motif of ram's horns from a Central Asian embroidery

*Gujarat embroidery motifs: **a** peacock; **b** parrot; **c** tortoise; **d** ghee carrier*

In sub-Saharan Africa the decoration of textiles with motifs – when not governed by imported Muslim or Christian dogma – is associated with other art-and-craft decorative and ceremonial forms such as are found on ceramic pots and wood carvings. The textile motifs of the Kuba peoples of Zaire comprise geometric forms representing the physical phenomena of their habitat. Duplicating motifs on wood carvings, house decorations and on the body by scarification, the Kuba weave and decorate raphia cloth with complex geometric associations of designs with names such as 'the finger', 'the crocodile's back' and 'smoke'. Their fascination for expression through abstract and geometric designs was made evident with the first visit of a motor cycle to one of their villages. Rather than being bewildered by this apparition from an alien machine age, they focused their interest on the wonderful geometric imprint the rubber tyres left on the earth. The design compositions and shapes and sizes of the Kuba cloths differentiate their use; some types are for men, others for women, some are worn as ceremonial skirts, others for everyday use, but all have some social meaning, establishing the status of the wearer at a glance.

The Muslim weavers of North and West Africa, Anatolia, the Levant, Persia, Central Asia, Afghanistan, Pakistan, parts of India and Indonesia have inherited a happy melding of decorative arts and symbology that relates a pagan past with a statement of the Faith. Theoretically, Islam is a disciplined religion, enforcing a lifestyle wherein all words and deeds are seen to be derived from God. Islamic arts have tended to develop, therefore, as a composite and well-balanced blend of form, decoration and function, and the concept of art as art simply has no relevance in such a world. This dynamic creativity is seen through Western eyes to be a refined form of ornamental art. The endless unfolding of geometric, abstract and semi-natural forms that so amuses the eye may be contrasted so dramatically with the confinement of a Western art form, such as a self-contained image or set of images within a framed canvas. The Muslim development of the repeated geometric motif is not a direct reaction to a law forbidding representation of natural forms, but rather a response to the need to avoid idolatry. The animate tends, therefore, to be reinterpreted almost to the abstract, although amongst the tribespeople of varied origin within the Islamic world there is certainly an indistinct line between those images that are acceptable, and those that are not.

The motifs, designs, patterns and compositions found within the textiles of these tribes provide a key to their pre-Islamic origins. Balancing with these pre-Islamic factors are the restrictions imposed by the types of weaving since adopted and developed, and the variety of raw materials available. Contrasts range from the finest silk ikat work of Bokhara to the undyed and undecorated camel bags of the Balouch nomads. The simplest flatwoven techniques such as slitweave and simple interlocking weave will afford the repetition of stepped designs and patterns of blocks of colour, and from this stage developments include warp-and weft-faced patterning for rows of small and intricate designs, to the more flexible techniques that create a raised decorative surface such as 'zilli', 'cicim', 'soumak', brocade and embroidered work. Patterning by resist-dyeing techniques such as ikat and tie-and-dye work may be developed, as seen with the Hindu work of India and Bali, to incorporate naturalistic images, but resist dyeing and weaving truly suits the Muslim delight in the abstract association of form and colour.

The flatweaves of North Africa, Asia Minor, Central Asia and Persia display a fine combination of tribal motifs that have developed within the design restrictions and freedoms of Islam. The abundance of floral motifs, either realistically represented as in Kurdish Senna work, or stylized as rows of 'guls' in Turkic weavings, reflects an appreciation for the ephemeral beauty of a flower in the short spring of an often dry and dusty climate. Variations in the types of guls used on kilims and bags differentiate with clarity the nomadic Turkmen clans of Central Asia, and such was the importance of these identification symbols that conquering tribes imposed the adoption of their type of gul on the weavings of the vanquished. A common motif on flatweaves is the eye, intended to counter the effects of the evil onlooker, as well as ram's horns (a throwback to pre-Islamic fertility symbols), pairs of birds and a hands-on-hips design. A hand motif may be interpreted as that of 'Fatima' or the 'five pillars of Islam' and the 'tree of life' pattern and composition can be seen, at its most elemental, to be a model for the axis of the world.

Prayer rugs are symbolic in patterning, shape and function, providing a clean surface for the fivefold daily prostration. The orientation of the mat and the focus of the composition is indicated by the mihrab, and although commonly found for single use, multi-mihrab kilims and dhurries are found for family and mosque

Pair of birds kilim motif

Two dragons design on a Sumban ikat

Animals and figures on a Timor ikat

devotions. It is an unfortunate phenomenon that the motifs of Islamic weavings have been so misinterpreted over the centuries, for it is so easy to associate a crenellated line of colour on a kilim as a ladder and a simple cross with a squat base as a small tree of life. For the weavers themselves, the stylized repetition of motifs is part of a tradition perpetuated orally and visually over the centuries, causing a loss of understanding for the use and original meaning of a particular design, and when asked, a weaver will often respond, like a character from *Alice in Wonderland*, that that is always how it has been done. A clear understanding, and a categorization of these textiles (in itself, a peculiarly Western habit) are made difficult by the sheer volume of tribal weaving through the ages. Unlike the determinable origin of a good deal of Western artforms, the weaver of a particular textile can never be ascertained, only its region, and era of production to within twenty to forty years.

More exclusive weavings and embroideries – such as the commercially produced susanis and ikats of Central Asia, the fine textiles of the Ottoman and Safavid Empires and the jail dhurries of north-west India – have a history of production and commissioned design influences that may be charted with some success. The silk and cotton ikats depict stylized floral motifs, the susanis a high style of floridity in itself and the dhurries a range of influences from Persian carpets to marble chequerboard floors. Ottoman and Safavid embroideries and flatweaves invariably portray exquisite meanderings of vine leaves, carnations, roses and tulips – that have spawned endless ideas for reinterpretation by Western designers.

For the peoples of the Indian subcontinent, Hinduism currently predominates over the tenets of Buddhism and Islam. Indian clothing and household textiles are coloured, woven and embroidered with the vitality of the Hindu religion, which comes as a refreshing expression of clearly defined figurative forms after the more geometric aestheticism of Islamic design work. Figures for Hindu epics such as the Mahabharata cavort on embroidered textiles from north-west India, mixing with folkloric images of birds and other wildlife. Many Hindu houses will be decorated with an image of Ganesha, the elephant-headed god, son of Shiva, who removes obstacles and brings good luck. House deities are cloaked with embroidered covers, piles of quilts are hidden by appliquéd and embroidered hangings known as 'dharaniyo', temple ceilings are canopied with light and colourfully appliquéd cottons,

doorway lintels decorated with 'torans' complete with a fringe of symbolic leaves, and walls and areas to either side of a door made cheerful with square 'chaklas'. Textile decoration and symbology not only represent the vitality of the religion but are also clear expressions of status within an ancient class system. The style of the decoration of the home, of personal and animal garments and trappings and the types of materials used immediately establish the position of the owner within the caste system of the Indian subcontinent. Fine and antique double ikat patola cloth would be a ceremonial nicety for high caste Gujarati families, whereas merchants and moneylenders such as the Bansali would decorate their homes with cotton and raw silk embroideries, and itinerant snake charmers would wrap up against the cold with a simple quilted cotton cloth.

Although Islam is the state religion of Indonesia, such a relatively recent influence on the lifestyle of the people has become yet another facet on their jewel of a culture that shines with the energy of a mix of pagan, Hindu, Buddhist, Muslim and Christian beliefs – a mix that creates an all-pervasive atmosphere of ritual and ceremony. In these tropical islands, the use of textiles can range from shoulder wraps and sarongs, decorated with precious metal threads and fine ikat design work that is the zealously protected preserve of the elite, to cloth that enjoys a status of veneration by virtue of decades of ceremonial use.

Hand-woven textiles are an integral part of traditional Indonesian culture. They are woven by women and are symbolically female objects associated with fertility, fecundity and productivity. At crucial stages in life, textiles perform a vital and unifying symbolic role. The famous double ikat of Bali would remain uncut until used in the first haircutting ceremony, and other continuously warped textiles would symbolize the continuity of life and be evident at birth rites. To the east of Sumatra, the less heavily populated islands of Sulawesi and what was known as Borneo contain tribespeople of the river valley jungle who use textiles as funeral shrouds and ceremonial hangings. Filled with interlinking symbols of hooks, arrows and fierce zoomorphic creatures, these textiles represent tangible expressions of uncharted religious beliefs of peoples in tune with a simple yet severe jungle lifestyle that is in danger of being lost forever, buried by two of the many strange influences of the developed world – missionary zeal and the greedy extraction of mineral wealth and timber.

Chapter Three   **Raw materials and techniques**

Raw materials

For most of the tribespeople of the world, access to raw materials for the processes of weaving dictated, until about one hundred years ago, the nature of their textile production. Factors such as the climate and climax vegetation of an area, its mineral wealth and the pace at which hairy wild animals were domesticated dominated the development of weaving cultures. Trading influences of the ancient world, such as the trans-Asian silk and cotton routes between China and India, and the peripatetic nature of Greek and Phoenician traders, certainly spread the legendary sources and availability of luxury dyestuffs, yarns and finished textiles.

As with the use of raw materials, the tools and the mechanics of weaving seem either to have developed spontaneously and independently, as with the backstrap loom of South America, or to have been a transfer from their native cultures by overland or island-hopping routes, whereby the backstrap loom is thought to have been introduced into Indonesia, having spread from mainland Asia. Indigenous developments in the use of raw materials and weaving techniques took place at a comparatively slow rate, especially within traditional tribal communities averse to new ideas. Interspersed with these evolutionary periods were the revolutionary moments of great change, when new technologies and religions were thrust upon tribes people.

One such crucial interaction of cultures began with the early spread of the newly Islamicized Arab Empire from out of the Arabian desert. The ripples of cultural and political influence from this religious revolution continue to spread worldwide to this day. These effects, however, pale in comparison to the establishment of European-dominated international sea trading routes between the Orient, the New World and the Old. Sheep and horses were taken to South America, Indian cottons to Europe, Indonesian indigo to Holland and, more recently, inexpensive manmade dyestuffs and yarn were exported from the Western world to all but the most remote weaving peoples.

Since ancient times textiles have been woven of yarn that is of either animal or vegetable origin. Hairy or fur-covered mammals such as sheep, goats, camels (Bactrian and dromedary), horses, buffalos, dogs, rats, bats, humans, rabbits, mice and the cameloid family of llama, alpaca, vicuna and guanaco have been shorn, trimmed, plucked and killed so that enough animal fibres can be collected together to spin and ply into yarn. Bird feathers have been used as surface decoration and the insect family is represented by the cultivated and wild silkworms who busily secrete filaments of silk within their cocoons. From one cultivated cocoon the unravelled fine silk strand may exceed a kilometre in length. More obscure sources of filaments include spider silk and the byssus, pinna or sea silk threads that certain marine molluscs secrete to attach themselves to the sea bed. Plants yield a possible abundance of fibrous material for weaving purposes. Fibres from the seeds of trees and shrubs are in common use, most notably cotton and kapok. Leaf fibres of sisal and yucca are hard-wearing, often associated with nut husk fibres such as coir for machine-made floor matting. Of great historical importance are bast (inner bark) fibres from the stems of plants; best known are flax (linen), raphia, jute, hemp and nettle, and tree bark may be shredded to a fibrous state. Bright and often valuable decoration for a textile is afforded by the use of precious metals such as gold, silver and lurex threads, and eye-catching and percussive accessories of coins, beads, shells, and buttons are not uncommon.

Wool and hair Sheep have been domesticated and bred for centuries as a primary source of foodstuffs and weaving fibres for nomadic pastoralists and modern intensive farmers alike.

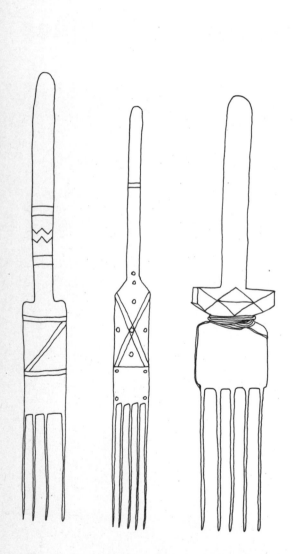

Kilim weaving combs

There are over one thousand breed types that inhabit temperate and continental climes, some suited to marsh and plain, others to rocky mountains and upland meadows. The nature and quality of their wool varies enormously between breeds, flocks of the same breed, between sheep within the flock and from one part of the fleece to another. The wool from around the shoulder is the finest, that from the hind quarters the coarsest. Myths and legends about fine fleece wool abound, from North Africa to the Caucasus and on to the High Pamirs of Central Asia; certainly, the average diameter of a fibre of sheep's wool may vary from twenty microns (thousandths of a millimetre) to over forty microns. A weaver looks for a wool staple which is neither too long nor too short, to ease spinning; of fine quality for weft work; and more coarse and stronger for warp use. Selecting by eye and feel, many tribal weavers are able to work to a two or three microns differential between fibres.

The elasticity of wool, its ease of use, its ability to take dye well and the good insulating properties of the woven textile have ensured that sheep have been introduced, distributed, reared and bred by man from Peru to Pakistan, from New England to Australia. Flocks of fat-tailed, fat-rumped, long-tailed, short- and long-legged sheep yield fleeces that vary in natural colour from white to black through grey, rust, sand and brown. Shearing of the sheep and lambs takes place once or twice a year, in late spring or early summer, and the fleece may weigh from three pounds to fifteen pounds. Preparation of the fleece may begin before shearing when the sheep are herded into a stream, river or lake in an attempt to clean the fleece. More often than not, however, it is the cut fleece that is washed of dirt and superfluous fats. Some tribes, such as the Qashqai of southern Persia, scour the wool in boiling water, Berber women often wash wool in the sea and Balouch and Navajo weavers use the carding of wool to remove debris, spinning and weaving the wool 'in the oil'. Most finished woollen textiles are washed to 'full' the cloth, whereby the weave is cleaned, softened and thickened for use. Wool fibres are prepared for spinning by carding or combing. In this way the fibres are aligned and spread evenly, curly wool separated from the straighter and longer hair, and the differing natural colours of fibres may be blended together. Tools for this process include fingers, a brush of thistles, wooden combs or wooden blocks with metal pins.

The goat is often praised as the cow of the poor, and throughout North Africa, the Middle East and Central Asia goat hair has been used since ancient times as a silky and robust adjunct to sheep's wool. Black and dark brown naturally coloured goat hair and wool tents are common in the Atlas Mountains, the Empty Quarter and Balouchistan, and the warps and selvedges of the bags and kilims of these nomads are frequently of goat hair. The most useful quadruped of the nomads, the camel, is an esteemed source of fine hair. Shorn from around the neck, throat and chin and plucked during the spring moult, camel hair has superior insulating properties to sheep's wool and is often used undyed to superb decorative effect on old Qashqai and Balouch kilims. Although complete camelines are rare, the ropes, cords, bands and belts of the nomads and semi-sedentary tribes are often twined with camel hair. For strength and sheen goat hair and camel hair is often plied with sheep's wool for the warp or the weft of a flatweave. Horse hair, too, has its uses, and is plucked and trimmed from the mane and tail for the reinforcement, binding and finishing of flatweaves.

Until the Spanish-borne arrival of sheep in the sixteenth century the Indians of the South American altiplano knew of no animal weaving fibres other than those of the domesticated and wild cameloids. The lustrous alpaca hair was treasured for fine textile weaving and hair from the timid, scarce and wild vicuna, the small relative of the alpaca, was woven into specialist textiles for tribal leaders. White alpaca were bred for their soft and shiny hair and the finest fibres selected from under the animal's chin; the lustre of the best alpaca cloth is legendary. The more robust llama hair and later, sheep's wool, were woven for more everyday cloth.

Silk Silk is an ideal fibre for weaving. It has length and elasticity, it is strong and even, fine to the touch and takes dye beautifully. The most refined of all cloth, silk has been woven for luxury garments and hangings for over two millennia. Sericulture originated in China, and the caravans on the Silk Route through Central Asia to the Middle East and Europe had spread the technology of silkworm farming through Persia by the third century and to England by the seventeenth century. Outside China, silk weaving reached various creative zeniths during the reigns of the opulent Byzantine, Ottoman, Safavid and Timurid Empires and in a direct line of creative descent from the latter come the silk ikats from the oasis cities of Central Asia.

Living on the leaves of certain trees, including some oaks in China, the tamarind tree in Nigeria and especially on the wild or cultivated mulberry, the larvae of the wild silkmoth pupate by spinning a cocoon of very long silk fibre and the gum sericin. After eight to ten days the chrysalid is ready to leave the cocoon and so discharges a solution that dissolves the sericin and damages the silk thread; the intern is finally released by eating its way out of the cocoon. The silk filaments are therefore short and must be carded and spun to use as yarn. Such thread is known as wild or spun silk. By killing the larvae in boiling water at the twilight of the cocoon stage the entire length of the silk thread may be preserved. The boiling water dissolves the outer layer of sericin, and the end of the thread is then found and wound off. The sericin-saturated filament may be degummed at this stage or after the weaving process.

Cotton Cotton is to the warmer climes what wool is to the colder zones and, until it was superseded by the machine-loom production from Europe and the USA, cotton was predominantly associated with the hand weavers, dyers and printers of India. Wild cotton is indigenous to the Indus valley, where techniques of mordant and resist dyeing are advanced: it is no wonder that the Indian subcontinent dominated the world trade in mass-produced cloth for over two thousand years, from at least 500 BC. Other centres of cotton weaving since ancient times include West Africa and central South America.

It is from the mass of fibres that covers the seeds of the cotton plant, bush or tree that cotton fibres may be teased and spun. The seeds are harvested from the plant and separated from this mass of fibres, the boll, by ginning. At its simplest, this may be done by rolling the bolls on a block with a rod to squeeze out the seeds. In Indonesia, a gin comprised of a wooden frame and twin rollers is found. The rollers are turned by hand to squeeze the seeds from the raw cotton. The cotton bolls are then disentangled by hand or, as in West Africa and elsewhere, with a bow, plucked against the cotton to hit and fluff the fibres into a loose mass.

Flax (linum usitatissimum) is a bast fibre best known as the raw material for fine European linens and many Coptic textiles were woven with flax warps and woollen wefts. Flax is a very useful agricultural commodity with an edible seed that, when processed, yields linseed oil – a famous moisturizer for carved willow. The finest flax thread is obtained from the green plant and the processing of the stalk fibres is long winded, involving retting, breaking, scutching, hackling and bleaching before being spun. Linen cloth is a delight to wear in a hot and moist climate.

Raphia The bast fibres of the raphia palm leaves are in common use as a weaving commodity in West and Central Africa. The raphia palm itself is a useful tree, yielding fish poison, palm wine and oil and is found wild in marsh and swamp areas. For the extraction of weaving fibre, young leaflets are harvested, the stems cut and stripped of the soft tissues whilst fresh. Dried slowly, the leaf membranes turn a pleasant yellow and may then be split into thinner fibres by hand or comb ready for weaving. Raphia staples are not spun or twisted together in sub-Saharan Africa, and so the size of the woven cloth is limited to the maximum available length of a palm leaflet, about three or four feet.

Spinning All natural fibres, with the exception of silk, occur in short staple form and must, therefore, be spun together to create a continuous yarn of a useful plying and weaving length. Threads may be twisted together by hand, with a spindle or on a spinning wheel. Hand spinning is a seemingly never ending yet soothingly rhythmical task and it is no wonder that the children of tribal weaving communities are encouraged to learn the craft from an early age. Spinning tools and machines are very simple, and can range from a stone weight to a hand-turned bicycle wheel. The drop spindle is in common use in South America, Africa and the Near East and is formed by weighting a metal or wooden rod with a disc or notched plate known as a whorl. Spindles with a whorl at the head or tail of the shaft are rolled the length of the thigh to spin the yarn, and this is a method used by the Navajo, the Kurds, the Kirghiz of Central Asia and the older members of the Balouch tribes. Simple spinning wheels have been in use in India for centuries but are a more recent introduction in South and Central America, Central Asia and Indonesia.

Drop spinning begins by drawing from a distaff or bundle of raw wool, hair or cotton a rove of fibres that is knotted onto the spindle. This is then given a slight twist and allowed to hang. By continuing to tease out and twist the rove, the weighted spindle will continue to wind the yarn as it spins unless it is allowed to touch the ground. With practice a strong, pliable and even thread may be spun in either a clockwise (a 'Z' twist) or anticlockwise (an 'S' twist) direction according to custom and superstition. Most right-handed people will spin with a clockwise twist. Two or more threads may be spun together on a larger spindle to create a strong yarn, and if the direction of the twist of the plied material is opposite to that of the single threads, the plied yarn is balanced and less likely to untwist or break. Threads of different type and colour may be plied together for effect and common combinations are camel or goat hair with sheep's wool, and cotton with wool. Whatever the constituents of the yarn, it is the sensitively manipulated action of hand spinning that gives a traditional tribal textile much of its supple character. Machine-spun thread feels dead by comparison.

Dyestuffs and dyeing From the brilliant red and blue silk ikats of Bokhara to the yellow and brown hues of Sumatran sarongs, the art of dyeing has always set the realistic yet mysterious possibilities of chemical processes against the creative imagination that so often craves to express a certain colour or relationship between colours. Until the Englishman W.H. Perkin synthesized the first chemical dyes from coal in the 1850s, the potential effect was limited by the technical expertise of the dyer and the availability of indigenous or imported raw materials. Local processes were developed to use naturally occurring substances.

The craft of dyeing in pre-industrial cultures has long been associated with the supernatural, ritual and great secrecy, and elevated social status. The ancient Persian, Indian and Phoenician cultures were famous throughout the known world for their scarlet, blue and purple dyed cloth respectively, obtained from the female kermes scale insect or the madder plant, the indigo plant and the purpura mollusc. The time and expense of extracting the purple dye from the latter sea shellfish partly explains why the colour is associated with nobility. Of the New World, the surviving textiles of the ancient Andean and the South American Pacific coastal cultures show a highly developed dyeing tradition, for the colours are fast and often brilliantly bright some two thousand years after the yarn left the dye bath.

Generally speaking, natural dyes work most successfully with animal fibres, whereas vegetable fibres will take only certain dyestuffs and then with lengthy processing. Natural dyes may be classified as either substantive or adjective. The only substantive dyes are obtained from certain lichens, the bark and heartwood of trees and the indigo plant. For a degree of permanency, adjective dyes need to be used with a mordant (from the Latin *mordere*, to bite) to take or 'bite' the fibres. Certain mordants will react with the fibres and weaken the textile – black fibres mordanted with iron pyrites, for example, will harden and disintegrate through time. Yarn may be mordanted before, during or after the dyeing process, but the best results are achieved if the fibres are mordanted before dyeing. The many different mordants that may be used produce different colours from the same dyes. Mordants include the metallic salts of alum, chrome, iron and tin, common salt, vinegar, caustic soda, slaked lime, urine and compounds or solutions of leaves, fruits and wood ash.

Certain dye processes, such as indigo dipping in West Africa, begat thriving town and village industries and the associated agricultural and mining activities. Traditional and professional dyers, often seen today in India and Nigeria, are instantly recognizable by their deeply stained hands, forearms and feet. Weavers in villages and amongst the nomadic peoples would sometimes have access to a complete range of natural dyestuffs – primarily the vegetation that grew wild in the animal pastures – and would possess the wherewithal to synthesize and fix colour on their weavings of woollen or fine animal hair fibres. The flowers, roots, bark, seed pods, fruit and leaves of herbs, other plants, trees and shrubs as well as insects and worms would be gathered and processed using personal and unwritten recipes. The secrets of these concoctions, often known nostalgically for their fine fixed colours that mellow gently over the years, more often than not have now been lost forever. Handed down through the generations by word of mouth, the use of natural dyestuffs has been superseded, for reasons of economy, by the use of synthetic dyes.

Synthetic dyes, especially the modern chrome dyes, are easy to use, the colours may be matched exactly, they are inexpensive and can offer a range of colours that most tribal weavers had previously only believed possible in their wildest dreams. What is so often lost, however, is that very lack of perfection that makes a naturally dyed and traditionally woven textile so pleasing. In the past, for reasons of economy or for ease of transport, only small batches of yarn would be dyed at any one time,

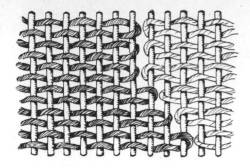

Slitweave

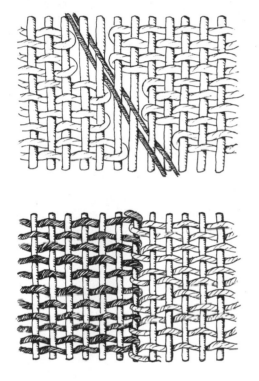

Outlining

Dovetailing

Double interlocking

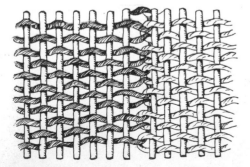

so that when yarns from different batches, dyed slightly or abruptly differing colours, were woven in the same area of pattern, an effect was created – known as 'abrash' in the rug trade – which may vary from a natural shimmer to an amusing and startling change of colour. Many modern facsimilies of old textiles now being woven for specialized export contain what may be tritely termed 'designer abrash', of synthetic colours. There are other problems of an aesthetic nature with manmade dyestuffs, for when a colour is fixed so well as not to run, it will not mellow, and colours that do mellow run when washed; it is no wonder that there has been a revival in the use of natural dyestuffs throughout the world.

Yarn or finished cloth must be immersed in a solution of a dyestuff, and so pots, pits and baths are used; there were reputedly over two thousand indigo dye pits in the West African Hausa city of Kano in the nineteenth century. Using the leaves of the indigo shrub, the unique dyeing process has long been associated with African, Indonesian and Indian cloth, and involves a sequence of repeated dipping and oxidizing to achieve a blue colour ranging from sky tones to new-moon black. A common source of red dyestuff is madder, a wild perennial native to Asia, with a colour range from terracotta, obtained by powdering young roots, through to purple, from older roots. Mordants must include a metallic salt and an alkali before the madder will bite the fibres. Mordanted with alum, madder yields a red and orange colouration, whereas iron fixes colours from violet to lemon-yellow.

Reds Madder, rose, rhubarb and apricot roots, kermes scale insect, cochineal worms, resin from the lac insect, poppy, cherry and pomegranate skins, bark of rhamnus, jujuba, camwood and barwood trees, straw, lichens, brazilwood, ivy and prickly pear fruit, tulip petals, guinea corn, safflower petals and henna, prepared yellow yarn boiled in a solution of the flowers of the hemp leaved hibiscus

Blues Indigo leaves, aubergine skin, and barberry fruit

Yellows Lemon and pomegranate rinds, fustic, weld, safflower petals and buds, saffron, turmeric, goldenrod, centaury roots, marigolds, dahlias and zinnias, onion skin, sage, daphne and black cherry leaves, flowers of larkspur and sophora, fresh stems of artemisia, kola nuts, leaves of brimstone, apricot, alder, willow, apple and wild pistachio trees and the heartwood of the jackfruit tree

Oranges Grass roots, saffron, henna, bark of plum trees, marigold leaves and combinations such as madder-dyed yarn dipped in solutions of poplar or willow leaves or pomegranate husks.

Greens Walnut and olive tree leaves, sweet violet, curled dock, sheep's sorrel and the dyeing of yellow yarn with indigo

White A solution of kaolin or the contrast of brilliant white cotton against wool or hair

Browns and black Natural wool, cotton and hair colour, tea, tobacco, charcoal, mud and volcanic mud, eucalyptus leaves, madder root, cochineal, leaves of wild pistachio trees or walnut bark with ferrous sulphate, acacia and locust bean tree bark

Looms It is much easier to interlace the warp and weft threads of a cloth tightly together if the warps are held in tension, and so a simple frame of wood – the loom – has been developed. The warps may be tensioned by bodyweight as with the backstrap loom, or by the drag on the warps of a ground weight. On a fixed ground loom the warps are stretched between warp beams that are pegged into the earth. Alternatively, a wooden frame set vertically or at an oblique angle may be built and the warps stretched by means of ropes and pulleys or wedges.

On all these looms the interlacing of the weft within the stretched warps may be speeded by using a device or devices to open and close the alternate warp elements separately. This opening between alternate warps is the shed. Shedding mechanisms range from a wooden batten, known as a shed stick or weaving sword used with a single heddle, to the rapid weaving achieved with double and many heddled apparatuses.

Although the shed stick will separate the warps into two groups, allowing the pick – the line of weft thread – to pass, for the return of the next pick the relative position of the warps must be reversed to create a countershed to continue a coherent interlacing process. By attaching with leashes each of these alternate warp threads to another stick – the heddle –

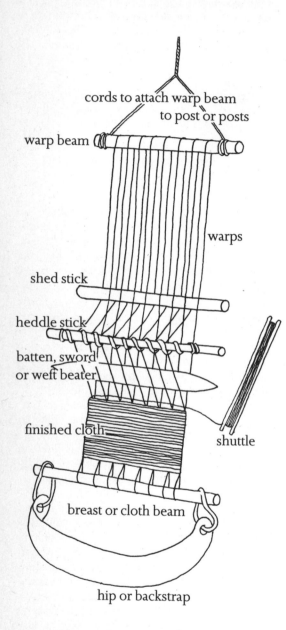

cords to attach warp beam
to post or posts

warp beam

warps

shed stick

heddle stick

batten, sword
or weft beater

finished cloth

shuttle

breast or cloth beam

hip or backstrap

Single heddle backstrap loom

and by constructing a tension and release suspension mechanism for the heddle, or by fixing the heddle and manipulating the shed stick, the shed and countershed may be rhythmically opened and closed for the passage of the pick. Double heddle looms leave the hands of the weaver free, for the alternate warps are connected to the separate heddles which are suspended on a pulley over the loom. Each heddle has a foot strap or is attached to a foot peddle, and the heddles are joined by a cord, so that by alternately depressing and releasing the pedals the shed and countershed are effected. With the hands free and the foot peddles operated efficiently, the pick may be thrown from side to side on a wooden carrier in a blur of coordinated movement. The pick of the weft may be carried from side to side by a stick, belt, shuttle or bobbin. The growing edge of the cloth, the fell, may be compacted to varying degrees of tightness with another flat batten, weft beater, weaving sword or reed, or with long- or short-toothed metal combs.

Backstrap or bodytension looms Single heddle backstrap looms are of ancient origin and use in Central and South America and Indonesia. Warp tension is maintained by securing the warp beam to a post, frame or set of pegs and by strapping the breast beam close to the body with a belt. Seated on the ground with the warps rising away at a slight angle, the weaver tensions the loom and beats down the weft by pushing against a ground beam with his legs, and by leaning back. Warp tension is released by slightly leaning forward for heddle and shed stick operation, allowing for the passage of the pick. Backstrap looms are often warped continuously, so that the finished cloth is pulled towards the weaver and under the breast beam. The length and width of cloth is thus dictated by the reach, strength and ability of the weaver. In South and Central America the two narrow halves of a poncho and the elaborately decorated belts are made on continuous warped backstrap looms, and in Indonesia the tubed sarongs are often made in this way. Discontinuous warped backtension looms are found in use in Indonesia, and for some tribes of the Congo region, short raphia warps are tensioned by the weaver's feet in warp beam stirrups, the breast beam is attached to a sturdy part of the hut and the weaver sits semi-suspended under his work.

Pegged ground looms Constructed with either a complete frame or merely two beams, these single heddle looms are often pegged out on the ground in the tent or in the shade of a tree and the warps tensioned by winding the beam-securing ropes or cord. Warps may be continuous, as on the tiny Andean Indian looms for making belts, or discontinuous; and the kilim-weaving nomads of North Africa, Asia Minor and Central Asia use a similar arrangement, often with a wooden tripod that holds the heddle in suspension. For the nomadic and semi-nomadic villager, the single heddle pegged ground loom strikes the perfect balance between portability and weaving efficiency. The loom is easily dismantled and rolled up for transport on a camel or donkey, and yet tightly woven and robust kilims and rugs and larger floor covers or tent panels may be made, by joining strips at the selvedges.

Vertical looms By stretching the warps vertically in front of the weaver on posts or on a wedged frame, an upright structure is created. Single heddle discontinuous warped vertical looms are in common use throughout Anatolian villages, North Africa and West Africa. The Navajo of the nineteenth century often used to set up a vertical loom between conveniently sited strong saplings to weave the wide chief blankets, and the discovery of wide cloth of pre-Columbian origin in Peru indicates that vertical looms were in use in ancient times. Vertical looms offer two possible advantages over ground looms: size of finished textile and speed of production. The structure may be large when securely fixed within the house to a wall and when fitted with a roller-beam mechanism, the finished textile may be rolled down and the work area of the weaver remains at a relatively constant height. Very large kilims are made in Maimana, north-west Afghanistan, on fixed roller-beam vertical looms.

Semi-mechanized looms The traditional double and treble heddle drag looms of West Africa, the pit treadle looms of the Indian subcontinent and the European treadle looms exported to the Americas are all examples of fixed looms made efficient by a limited degree of mechanization. Foot pedals operate the heddles and the weaver may work rapidly, on detailed patterning such as is found on the Ashanti stripweave in West Africa, or as in India, where the complex supplementary weft-patterned ikat cloth is woven on a wide loom, with the help of an assistant.

Techniques

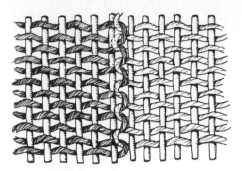

Double interlock reverse

Weft-faced patterning

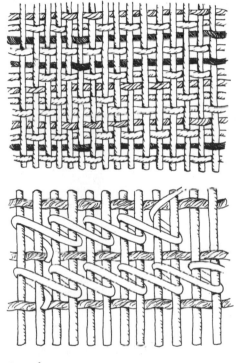

Soumak

Brocading

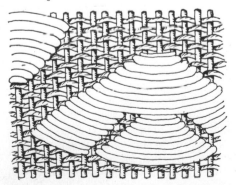

Balanced plainweave The simple interlacing of warp and weft elements of the same thickness, flexibility and tension on a loom is known as balanced plainweave. The colour of the warps and the wefts will show on the surface of the cloth and so this technique is ideal for surfaces where decoration is of no importance, as with kilim bag backs or plain grounds for decoration. The exceptions to this rule are the intricately pre-dyed double ikat textiles of India and Bali. Examples of a surface decoration on a plain ground include the Kuba raphia cloth with a pile, embroidered or appliqué finish, and the Anatolian zilli and cicim work.

Weft-faced or tapestry weave The wefts are beaten down onto each other so tightly that the warps are hidden. The colour of the textile is therefore dictated by the dyeing of the weft yarn and the warps may be left undyed. Patterning may be achieved by weft stripes of colour, or in the case of ikat work by the resist patterning on the wefts. Weft-faced ikat is found in India and in Indonesia. Most kilim and dhurrie weaving is weft-faced, and weft-faced plainweave and striped work is commonly found at the ends of kilims and on the backs of bags.

Warp-faced weave Here the warp is dominant over the weft and many of the striped cotton and silk weaves of West Africa are patterned in this manner. Most ikat work, often of patterned silk warps and hidden cotton wefts, is warp faced.

Slitweave This is a simple technique by which blocks of colour may be introduced into the weave. One coloured weft returns around the last warp of its own colour area and the adjacent, different coloured weft returns around the next warp, so leaving a vertical slit between the colour areas. Too long a slit would weaken the integrity of the weave and so most slitweave work uses small stepped patterns. Most kilims are woven in this way and should be reversible. The kilim slitweaver will work on a block of colour, so stepping diagonally up the textile rather than directly across many changes of weft colour. 'Lazy lines' occur when the weaver works on small sections of the same colour area. When returning to complete the colour area, the weaver often uses yarn of a slightly different colour or tone as well as slitweave, so successfully breaking up large areas of a single colour. The finest slit tapestry weaves are undoubtedly the ancient textiles of the pre-Columbian cultures of Peru and the figurative Coptic work.

Outlining or contour bands Slitweaving may be reinforced in a number of ways when the textile is on the loom. Contrasting colour bands may be woven between the blocks of colour, so outlining a design or pattern, or the weaver can wrap extra wefts of a contrasting shade around pairs of warp threads between different colour areas. These techniques are common on Anatolian kilims.

Dovetailing and single interlock work In dovetailing the weft threads from adjacent areas of different colours return around the same warp. No slit occurs, so the weave is stronger, but the relationship between the colours is slightly blurred. A link of 1:1 of each colour on the warp is known as dovetailing. Ancient Peruvian textiles use delicately executed interlock work as do the Navajo weavers, the kilim makers of North Africa, Persia, Afghanistan and the dhurrie makers of India.

Double interlock work Found occasionally in the flatwoven rugs of North Africa and Persia, this is a common technique in the kilims of Turkestan and the dhurries of India. The wefts of adjacent colours link once as they move in one direction and again in the next row in the other direction. This creates a very crisp outline between the colours, a very strong weave and a ridge on the reverse.

Weft-faced patterning Unlike the simpler techniques of slit and interlocking work where pattern changes are associated with blocks of colour, weft-faced patterning may be used to create rows of very fine designs. Extra coloured wefts only show on the surface of the textile when needed to form a design and for the rest of the time they float along the back of the weave. Fulani woollen blankets from West Africa and the kilims of the West Afghanistan Balouch peoples are finely woven and decorated with intricate weft-faced patterns. Associated with this technique is supplementary weft patterning, where a decorative thread is added to the basic weft of the ground weave. Such a decoration is not structural and may be applied with the help of special pattern heddles or with a small spool and needle. The historic ship cloths of Sumatra and other fine textiles from Indonesia and India are embellished with supplementary wefts.

Warp-faced patterning Warp-decorated and warp-dominated weaves such as the fine ceremonial capes and purses from Bolivia and Peru may be contrasted with the warp-faced patterned stripweaves of north-west Persia and north Afghanistan. The Persian stripweaves are made by the Shahsavan peoples and are known as 'jajim', and the Afghani Uzbek work as 'ghujeri'. As with the equivalent weft technique, where the patterning warp does not appear on the surface of the textile, it floats along the back. The associated, yet entirely decorative, supplementary warp work is found in India and Indonesia.

Soumak, zilli and cicim work Soumak is a fine weft-wrapping brocade technique for floor rugs that is thought to have originated in the Caucasus. Certainly the most intricate work is from that region and now soumak rugs are made in west Afganistan and Anatolia. Zilli and cicim work is found on central Anatolian kilims as a raised area of decoration. By wrapping warps with common ratios of wefts, the zilli technique creates a cording effect.

Embroidery Any type of accessory stitching that decorates or embellishes a fabric, whether serving any practical purpose or not, is known as embroidery. Such stitchwork, applied with a needle, is to the embroiderer what paint is to the artist. A separate volume could be compiled on stitching alone, and a good introduction may be found in Irene Emery's *The Primary Structure of Fabrics*. Throughout the tribal world, embroidery is practised, for the most part, on light cotton cloth for clothing or hanging use. Historic work includes the laid, couched, chain and buttonhole silk stitching of the magnificent susanis from the nineteenth-century oasis towns of Central Asia, the embroideries of the Uzbek Lakai nomads and the fine, golden-coloured and precious metal embroidery of the Sumatran tapis. The Ottoman Empire extended, by conquest and trading influence, the spread of the floral stitch designs and quality of techniques from North Africa to the Caucasus, and the courtly Safavid embroideries of Persia influenced and spawned copyists throughout Central Asia. Woven by the men, the raphia cloth of Zaire is still embroidered by the women. Their geometric designs

are outlined with overstitching or by inserting and trimming small bundles of raphia fibres under a ground thread, forming a tuft known as plush stitching.

By far the most prolific source of traditional yet mostly twentieth-century embroideries is the Indian subcontinent. From the tribes and castes of Rajasthan, Gujarat, the Punjab, Sind and the North-West Frontier provinces, embroideries have been sewn for millennia in a continuous and still developing tradition. Each region and each group within an area has developed a local style and tradition of use for embroideries. On clothing, and on house, temple and animal decorations, the embroidery captures the geometric representations of flowers and natural forms of the Muslim peoples, and of the lively figurative traditions of the Hindu followers. Parrots, cows, monkeys, bicycles, buses, networks of geometric forms – all and more are depicted on archways, doorway hangings, shawls, blouses and skirts. Darning, double running, closed herringbone, stem, cross, blanket, and satin stitches are just some of the many techniques, often combined together, and the bright colours and sheen of silk, cotton and metal threads are the decorative raw materials on a cotton ground.

Patchwork Defined as the cutting up of pieces of fabric, old and new, and the rejoining of the materials together to form a newly patterned cloth, patchwork is an ancient craft and as a tribal activity is associated with Central Asia and Sind. The Turkmen of north-east Persia in the border area with Afghanistan and Russia have a tradition of sophisticated pieced patchwork for horse and camel decoration. Patchwork combines with appliqué and quilting techniques on the 'rillis' from Sind that are used as general purpose covers.

Appliqué This technique involves the addition to the main cloth of a piece or pieces of accessory decorative fabric. On the raphia cloth from Zaire, skirt lengths are decorated and repaired with appliqué forms of arrows, circles and networks of moving geometric patterns. Animal trappings and festival wall hangings from Gujarat and Rajasthan are decorated with figurative and geometric appliqué work known as 'katab' as well as embroidery. On the other side of the world, the reverse appliqué molas, the blouse panels of the Panamanian Kuna Indians, are outstandingly decorative. Layers of coloured cut cloth made of cotton are sewn

together so that patterns are formed by the outlining of the ground material.

Quilting This is the sewing of two or more layers of fabric firmly together with lines of stitching. The rillis and 'derkee' coverlets of Sind and Gujarat combine quilting, appliqué and patchwork techniques in geometric forms to great effect. Bengali 'kanthas' combine quilting with highly decorative figurative stitching, and as hangings and covers are classic examples of the family folk art of the region.

Tie and dye Known internationally by the Malay-Indonesian term of plangi and in India as bandhana work, tie and dye is a simple process, found throughout the world. Selected portions of the textile are protected from the action of the dye by tying or shrouding with leaves, bast, string or rubber bands. Emerging from the dye bath and unravelled, the resisted areas appear as a negative pattern. The complexity and success of the composition may be enhanced by folding and by the detailed tying of small patterns that will open out as a mirror image after dyeing. West African tie-and-dye work often takes the form of white patterns on an indigo ground. Pre-Columbian Peruvian plangi work has been found dating from the late Nazca and Chancay periods and aside from such superlative historical examples, the finest tie-and-dye work comes from the Indian subcontinent and Indonesia.

Ikat A Malay word derived from 'mengikat', meaning to tie or bind, ikat is a dyeing technique wherein the warps or wefts, or both, are bound – resisted – and dyed before weaving. Meticulously planned, sometimes with the aid of a chart or wooden pattern guide, groups of threads are gathered together in bundles and those sections that are not to be dyed with each consecutive colour are bound with impermeable thread. These resisted areas experience dye seepage and the adept control of this effect creates a blurred or shimmering pattern. Silk and cotton warp-faced ikats were made into sumptuous coats for the elite of Turkestan in the last century or hung as decorative panels. Of Indian ikat, known as bandha, the double ikat patola work of Gujarat is a legendary and near historic production. Weft and double ikat is now being produced on a large scale in Orissa and Andhra Pradesh. Indonesia is famous for its ikat traditions and in the Americas, ikat work is found in Ecuador, Peru, Mexico, Guatemala and Bolivia.

Chapter Four **Decorative hangings**

Decorative hangings

There are numerous tribal precedents for the hanging of woven or embroidered textiles on the wall, and in addition to their decorative function, the design and placing of the cloth has symbolic significance. In Gujarat the embroidered hangings for the home adorn doorways, piles of quilts and shrines. On many Indonesian islands a fine local textile, often an ikat, or a venerated import such as an old patola, is hung in the temple or home as an integral part of one of the many ceremonial occasions of the year. In times past, the great Islamic patrons of the arts such as the ruling classes of the Ottoman and Berber dynasties commissioned the weaving of fine linen, silk, cotton and wool tapestries and embroideries to enrich the walls of their many palaces and, in the New World, the large size of some of the ancient textiles exhumed in Peru suggests that they were used as temple and palace hangings.

In the Western world, the positioning of tribal textiles on the wall is universally acceptable for decorative purposes and preservation of the weave. Most, save those whose age and fragility make them especially sensitive to the atmospheric conditions of light, temperature and humidity, may be displayed in a multitude of ways, from fine framing to hanging by clothes pegs. Indeed, the majority of textiles, except for kilims, dhurries, hanbels and some Mexican and American Indian work, were made to hang or wear and not for floor use, and so would not survive the rigours of daily tread.

Weaves as wall hangings may be regarded as pictures, even though they are often large and texturally alive; and as with a collection of paintings, the style of work is as varied as that of the different artists. With textiles, however, one may choose from the work of invariably unknown weavers, from an often strange land and from, at times, an era impossible to determine. It is no wonder that many enthusiasts recommend a method of selection based on a combination of parameters. These include size, colour and pattern of textiles, their style of arrangement, hanging and framing methods, and the possible amounts of wear and tear that they will receive, even on the wall. Yet all these sensible considerations may be delightfully cast aside by such unforseen factors as the strangely compulsive desire to purchase a certain weaving on first sight.

Size and shape

The greatest choice of available textiles will be from those of small to medium size, of rectangular shape – that is to say, up to six or seven feet by two, three or four feet. There is an abundance of everyday as well as ceremonial articles to be found from all the weaving communities, such as skirt lengths from Indonesia, shawls and doorway decorations from India, blankets and capes from the Americas; and the smaller kilims, hanbels and dhurries will make ideal hangings. Square textiles are less common, with the exception of the chaklas, molas, some of the eating cloths and ship cloths, and the cut-pile raphia and appliqué panels of the tribes of the Congo. Very long or narrow textiles include kilim runners, certain ship cloths, sashes, more complete lengths of raphia appliqué panels and tent bands. Unusual shapes can be provided by articles of clothing such as coats, tunics and blouses, woven capes and embroidered hats, and by textile fragments, bags, animal trappings and complete or composite archways.

The availability of larger weavings and embroideries is limited by comparison. The largest textiles to be found are the cotton appliqué work and dhurrie production from north-west India, the kilims of Anatolia and Afghanistan, and the West African stripwoven cloths. Weavings and textiles such as these are often made for ceremonial use and as a store of wealth. Whether one cares for the finished product or not, when witnessing the unfolding of a large textile it is humbling to remember the length of time and the technical difficulties involved in the weaving. Such constraints ensure that evenly made tapestry-woven textiles rarely exceed twenty feet in length or fifteen feet in width. Embroidered, appliqué and stripwoven work and patchwork may be formed to any size, which is determined as a rule by their traditional function and the strength of the materials – usually cotton and silk – that are used in their making.

Scale

The scale of the hanging textile in relation to the size of the wall is a decorative consideration of fundamental importance. A textile may be used to cover the entire wall area, large or small, and whatever the colour or patterning of the textile, it will be a dominant presence in the living area. To soften the impact of a large wall area, one very long textile may be hung, landscape, at eye level. Alternatively, a long textile may be hung well off-centre in a portrait style, dividing the area vertically, instead of horizontally. An ideal location for such a shape is in a deep stairwell, tower or turret. If a large expanse of wall must be covered, another solution is to break up the area with one large yet unusually shaped weaving, or perhaps with several textiles. These may be of the same shape – as with an arrangement of square Kuba cloths, for instance – or a random selection of shapes and sizes. The orientation of the hanging is important. In a long hallway a row of rectangular sarongs hung in a portrait format will alter one's impression of the ceiling height, whereas a series of narrow textiles, hung landscape, will lengthen the look of the room.

The hanging of weavings of the same pedigree – from the same tribe or region – would present interesting possibilities, especially if such textiles – Navajo rugs, perhaps – were chosen from different periods of production, thereby charting the stages of development in their weaving traditions. A collection of the range of ikat-patterned cloths from the islands of Indonesia would certainly cover a long and lofty wall, as would the variations in the traditional textiles, from clothing fragments to wedding kilims, of a nomadic tribe such as the Balouch. Another solution would be to group textiles with similar compositions or designs but from utterly dissimilar origins. The eye-dazzler compositions of the rugs of the Navajo of North America, the kilims of the Qashqai of southern Persia and the dhurries from the villages of north-west India, which arise in part from the technical constraints of their flatweaving, would create stunning juxtapositions on a wall.

Colour and pattern

The traditional use of natural dyes will provide colours, when fixed well, that may vary from sharp and bright to dark and subtle tones. Textiles with particularly lively colours

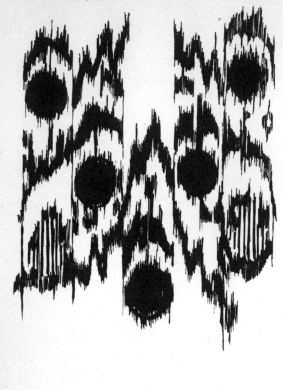

include many of the silk Ashanti stripwoven cloths, susanis and the ikats of Central Asia, India and Indonesia, the Anatolian, many Persian and some Afghan and Tunisian kilims, early Navajo textiles, the Kuna Indian molas, some Mexican weaves and the village embroideries, appliqués, tie-and-dye cloth and patchwork of India. The most rash yet often charming use of near fluorescent synthetic dyes may be sought out in Central and South American weaves and in the kilims of the early chemical dye years. Whatever the combinations of bright colours used – blues, reds, yellows, oranges, pinks and greens – they will form a dominant and characterful focus of attention in almost any room. By comparison, subtly coloured textiles will blend more easily, and may form background decoration. The rich brown and blue tones of Balouch kilims, the plain and simply striped indigo cloth of West Africa, pastel coloured kilims, Navajo rugs and dhurries, and many of the elegant old sarongs of Sumatra will hang with understated individuality on the wall.

As with the colours of tribal textiles, there are both strong- and weak-patterned weavings and embroideries to choose from. Strong-patterned textiles tend to dominate, especially when seen from a distance where the full effect of the composition may be appreciated. A Bokharan large medallion susani may be bracing to the eye from across a room, yet when viewed close to, the detail in the embroidery technique is marvellously subtle. It is often important, therefore, to place the intricate textiles that have a powerful composition, such as many embroideries, appliqués, patchworks and resist-dyed cloths, on a wall where they may be enjoyed from many viewpoints. This is particularly true for geometric work, such as is practised by Muslim weavers and embroiderers of kilims and appliquéd textiles.

Strong designs may include large figurative work featuring monsters, men, birds and fish – as seen on many Sumban ikat cloths, as well as in combinations of geometric forms and shapes such as the eye-dazzler, tree of life and the powerful mihrab composition of Muslim kilims and prayer cloths. Central Asian ikat is invariably stridently patterned, with shimmering forms that are a fine match to the blurring effects of the resist-dyeing technique. The molas of the Kuna have finely cut and stitched appliqué work that depicts forceful images of local events, spirit forms and even political slogans. The cut-pile raphia panels of the Congo are filled with powerful geometric designs.

Subtlety in textile patterning is often achieved by banding and the blending of bands of harmonious colours together, by using small and detailed motifs, often figurative, in proportion to the size of the textile, and by ensuring that there are no focal designs such as medallions. Examples of this include some of the Ewe and Uzbek stripweave work, many of the old Bolivian alpaca shawls and purses, most Balouch kilims, Coptic tapestries and the raphia appliqué of the Kuba. Such types and combinations of compositions are described as having 'movement' and are soothing to the eye, for there are often no jarring or strong motifs which some people may find unsettling.

Formal and informal styles

As with pictures, textiles hung on the wall may relate formally or informally with each other and their surroundings. A formal tone may be created by the loneliness of a framed and spotlighted textile on a large white wall, and indeed spotlighting and mounting, stretching or framing, especially behind glass or perspex, makes the textile the subjugated object of attention. Two textiles of near identical size and tribal origin, such as a pair of Sumban ikats, will hang with solemnity on either side of a fireplace in a drawing room and a defined wall-space will frame a textile – over the mantelpiece or in an alcove, for instance. Rows of frames the same size containing textile fragments will create an atmosphere akin to a gallery or museum, and a display of weavings from the same tribe on the same wall will establish a formal setting. Some rectangular or very long textiles may look formal or informal according to the way they are hung.

Informality is very easy to achieve with hanging textiles and many of the tribes themselves pin their textiles on the walls of their huts, tents and houses with a disarming lack of care for the niceties of order and visual effect; for many, it is enough that the cloth is present. Weaves with textural qualities, such as the mixed knotted and flatweave work of the Berber and Balouch peoples, and bags, garments and trappings that will not lie perfectly flat against the wall, will create an informal effect, often enhanced by a naive adornment of beads, shells or buttons. On a large plain wall, a mêlée of textiles of different shapes and sizes – especially of garments, framed or loosely hanging, which amusingly combine areas of colours and patterns – will seem like a completed collage. Bags, or other textiles of the same use yet diverse origins, will combine well together, and so will an arrangement of pictures, carved wooden panels, textiles and flat ceramics. Many textiles derive their patterning from ceramics and carved wood; thus, an Ottoman Iznik tile with floral designs will enhance the impact of an adjacent Ottoman embroidery, and a Kuba cut-pile raphia piece can relate directly to a panel of carved wood from the same tribe. This interaction of creative expression may be extended yet further by positioning ceramic ware, wooden carvings and pictures of modern Western origin adjacent to hanging textiles with similar designs or colour relationships, whether these have influenced the others' conception or not.

Informality also owes much to the arrangement of electric light and hanging style. Whereas the spotlight may create a gallery-like effect, a shaded wall light or lamp and shade can spill a diffuse light more naturally across a textile. By hanging a textile loose with a rod and sleeve or Velcro on a batten, the weave will be shown more naturally. There is, after all, no substitute for feeling the front and back of many textiles – providing, of course, the owner does not object. The rod or pole may be made more interesting with turned, carved or cast finials to the ends, and a swag of a complementary embroidered or woven ribbon across the face of the hanging to the sides completes the informal image.

Durability

Rugs and floor coverings are expected to be durable, and when hung on the wall should, if well looked after, last a very long time. There are, however, good and bad locations for textiles as wall hangings. Textiles will experience little wear and tear when hung above reach and as far away from humans and animals as possible, in little used or private rooms such as the bedroom or study. Narrow hallways or corridors, where passers by may brush repeatedly or catch against a hanging are not ideal. Rooms much in use or where there will be great fluctuations in atmosphere and light will be detrimental to the long life of a textile. Hanging a weave in a bathroom or kitchen is an unusual idea – indeed, kitchens may be delightfully decorated with eating cloths, spoon and coca bags – but this is not recommended for a prized possession because of the constant variations in heat, humidity and quality of air. A bathroom is often a condensation trap and the frequently damp conditions will rot the cloth. On whatever wall of the house the textile finds itself, the two totally undesirable places are over a radiator and in full sunlight – especially if the cloth is of wool or hair.

Lighting

It must be remembered that light is energy and consists of a broad spectrum of visible and invisible rays. Both will damage textiles, by fading and by breaking down the fibres; to guard against this, the ambient illumination should, theoretically, not exceed 50 lux. In the open air, the direct sunlight on a summer's day will measure over 100,000 lux and inside on a dull day, some 750 lux. Old, ancient or especially fine textiles, or those of great personal value, should be lit with care. Many ancient textiles are preserved by their owners in the darkness of a curtained room, chest or cupboard, to be viewed only on special occasions. Most of the textiles depicted here have been hung or positioned within certain sensible lighting parameters so that the weavings may be both enjoyed and preserved.

If textiles are, of necessity, fixed to a wall where strong natural light may fall across the hanging, windows may be screened with an ultra-violet filter coating or by the judicious placement of coated plexiglass. These spray-on filters have a limited lifespan and the glass will have to be recoated from time to time.

Fluorescent tubes emit ultra-violet radiation and ought to be screened by filters, but their cool running temperature is an advantage when lighting a cabinet or small room. Incandescent light bulbs and spotlights emit almost no ultra-violet rays but, unless of low voltage, much heat. Spotlights may be mounted on ceiling or wall tracks to flood or highlight the display so long as the heat of the bulb is not in proximity to the cloth. Movable lamps and floor stand or table spots are useful for highlighting and for creating a more informal atmosphere. Certainly the optimum solution is illumination by low voltage incandescent sources, on tracks, recessed in the wall, flush with the ceiling or as a self-contained unit. The drawback is high cost.

Hanging methods

Of primary consideration is the even support of the weave, and there is a variety of ways, both simple and complex, to ensure that a textile does not permanently sag, crease or tear with its own weight.

The nature of the structure and decoration of the wall should first be examined. The weakest surfaces to fix into are partition walls, constructed of little more than board and a skin of plaster, but by using the requisite expanding plugs or by finding the internal timber cross-members and uprights, all but the very heaviest of textiles may be hung securely. Brick, stone and building-block substrates, if in solid condition, will be relatively easy to fix into, and the heavier the textile, the longer the bolts or screws required and the more frequently the hanging apparatus will need to be fixed to the wall. Uneven walls present problems and the textile may need to be blocked flat on a scribed batten. Walls with damp are to be avoided.

Hanging without a framework All but the very lightest and smallest of textiles and fragments may be hung without a frame. Many fine and old textiles need to be lined before hanging so that the backing material is supportive and may itself be used to fix the textile to the wall. Textiles that have a tendency to curl may be weighted to drop straight with curtain weights. For advice on lining techniques and service, please consult the list of restorers and framers in Chapter Seven.

Carpet gripper Available in shops and warehouses that sell wall-to-wall carpets, carpet gripper is wooden beading, about one inch wide and one-quarter inch thick, covered on one face with the heads of many small diameter pins.

Normally used by the fitters to secure carpet invisibly to the edges of a room and available in various lengths, carpet gripper is ideal for hanging many textiles on the wall. Carpet gripper should be prepared about one-half inch shorter than the hanging edge of the textile so that it cannot be seen, and secured to the wall, pins pointing outwards from the wall and upwards to the ceiling, with drilled fixings of a suitable nature. The textile may be centred on the gripper rod and the weave gently but securely pressed onto the pins. Two people are really needed for this operation. The advantages of this hanging technique are many: the textile is supported evenly at at least one-quarter inch intervals and the hanging may be easily removed and replaced after dusting, mothproofing, cleaning or storage. Small adjustments to the level of the textile may be made with ease and this is often necessary as tribal weavings are rarely perfectly symmetrical. Carpet gripper is ideal for kilims, hanbels, dhurries, rugs and the blankets of the Americas.

Back view of sleeve hanging method

Tab method of hanging

Rod and sleeve A regularly shaped textile whose weave is not too loose or too fine and delicate may be hung by sewing a cotton sleeve or length of webbing to the back of the cloth with matching cotton thread, slightly below the required hanging edge and one-half inch shorter. By then sliding a length of metal or wooden pole inside this sleeve, the overhanging ends of the rod may be suspended from wall- or ceiling-mounted brackets. An alternative method is to leave a gap or gaps at the back of the sleeve for single or multiple, visible or invisible suspension of the rod with wire, cord and hooks. Garments such as coats and tunics are best hung by sliding a rod covered with acid-free paper through the sleeves and across the neck to support the textile with arms extended or akimbo. The tab-hanging method is a variation on the sleeve technique. Suitably coloured sleeved cotton tabs may be sewn at intervals to the hanging edge of the textile or backing, and a rod passed through the tabs and suspended by wire or hooks on the wall or ceiling. This method best serves the hanging of a plain cloth mount, the same colour as the tabs, onto which has been sewn a light and small textile.

Velcro Lightweight textiles may be held to the wall with Velcro. As with the carpet gripper technique, this is a flexible hanging method well suited to the repeated adjustment, removal and replacement of textiles. The more flexible strip of Velcro is sewn onto the hanging edge and the strip of 'hooks' stapled to an exactly sized flat wooden batten secured to the wall. The strips of Velcro may then be pressed together and the hanging position adjusted with ease. Many collectors hang large and light textiles using this Velcro technique onto battens suspended from the ceiling with pulleys and nylon yachting cord. In this way the battens or beams may be effortlessly hoisted and lowered to change the textile when desired.

Other techniques Curtain tape may be sewn to the back of the textile and hung with hooks and eyes onto a wall- or ceiling-mounted curtain rail. Textiles are sometimes stapled to a wooden batten that will then be suspended against the wall. This is obviously a technique best reserved for less important decorative textiles. Very light textiles may be held up by a series of small wire butterfly clips, individually suspended by nylon line or wire on hooks.

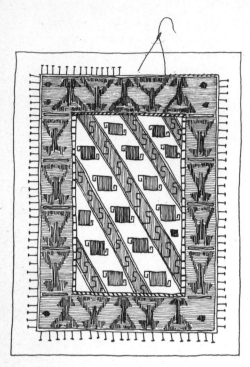

Front and back view of a framed textile on a wooden stretcher. Securing pins are being removed as the sewing progresses round the textile.

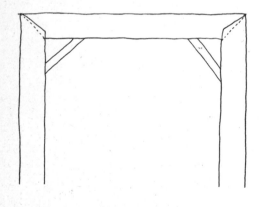

(Opposite) Quite often the simplest solutions for the problems of hanging a textile are the best. Six pushpins secure this Kuba skirt length from Zaire to the wooden panelled ceiling. Matisse, Klee and Picasso all found inspiration in the naive abstraction of African textiles such as this.

Hanging with a frame Many textiles may best be enjoyed and their construction understood only by handling, and many other weaves may be used as garments or bed and floor covers, and so will need to be easily detachable from the wall. Indeed, the enclosing and mounting of a textile on a frame of any kind immediately tends to divorce the onlooker from the nature of its original use and its structure. However, some textiles are enhanced by a frame and many must be framed in order to be seen and hung at all. Fragments, fragile embroideries and ancient tapestries are too delicate to handle and need support and protection from the environment. Some framing techniques are described here; for further advice please consult the professional framers listed in Chapter Seven or the textbooks listed in the bibliography.

Mounting without glazing This technique is the most popular of all framing methods, for the face of the textile is exposed to view and touch, and a border of backing cloth may be used to good decorative effect. A first consideration is the size and shape of the wooden stretcher in proportion to the textile. Many different-sized stretchers may be purchased from framing and craft shops. When the stretcher is larger than the textile, a frame of mounting cloth will be seen, or when nearly identical in size (and this is only possible when the textile is of very regular shape), only the textile will be seen, proud from the wall. Once the size of the stretcher and colour of the mounting cloth – of either silk, cotton or linen – has been chosen, the wooden frame should be sealed with polyurethane varnish or covered with acid-free paper to prevent staining caused by the wood sweating. The mounting cloth should be stretched over the frame and secured to the back by rustproof staples or brass tacks. The textile may then be positioned onto the mounting cloth with pins and sewn in place with cotton, silk or linen thread using a running blind hem stitch. The thread should catch between a crossing of both the warp and the weft threads on the face of the edge of the textile. Stitching should continue around the textile with a half-inch to one and a half-inch floats according to the size of the textile. The pins may be removed as the stitching advances and the finished frame hung on the wall with mirror plates, or invisibly with picture wire and hooks.

Glazed mounts At its simplest, two sheets of perspex may be bolted together and the sandwich, created by spacers, then contains a textile sewn to the backing perspex with thread through a series of pre-drilled holes. The textile must be small and very flat for this method to succeed.

A larger, bulkier textile may be mounted on a stretcher and a perspex sheet cut to the size of the frame. This protective sheet may then be secured over but off the surface of the textile with perspex dowel rods and screws or bolts. A textile on a stretcher may also be sealed behind perspex by ordering a sheet with sides that are greater in depth than the combined measurement of the stretcher frame, the mounting cloth and the thickness of the textile. This cover may then be positioned over the frame and secured away from the textile by screw fixings to the wooden stretcher. Traditional picture-framing techniques are good for small and fine textiles or fragments as long as the mount is cut deep enough to prevent the glass from touching the textile. All papers and mounting board should be acid free. Linen, silk or cotton covered mounts may be used in conjunction with a hidden or decorative sub-frame to separate the glass from the textile.

(Opposite) Lit largely by diffuse natural light, the centrepiece of a south Californian den is a Germanstown Navajo rug whose electric patterning, on close examination, is a masterpiece of colour movement in stripes. At the foot of the rug is an arrangement of walking sticks from New Guinea and a number of fine American Indian baskets.

Hung behind the table covered with ebony sculptures and other objects is a bark-cloth patchwork from the Congo.

This large colonial house in Philadelphia is home to a well-matched collection of modern Western and old ethnographic art. Few walls escape an exciting juxtaposition of colours and patterns of the arts and crafts of worlds Old and New. Here, in the dining room, the geometric designs of a Sulawesi ikat form a perfect decorative backdrop for an array of finely shaped ceramics and glass.

(Above) A lofty, long yet narrow hall is one of the few places where a full-length raphia skirt from the Congo may be seen to best effect. Mounted on a cloth-covered wooden frame, the many panels of this appliqué and embroidery work are illuminated by spotlights.

(Top left) This New York loft apartment is a splendid living space for the enjoyment of many types of textiles. The living room is dominated by a silk and cotton embroidered gown made by the Hausa craftsmen of Nigeria. Stripwoven and decorated with a traditional 'eight knives' pattern, such designs are first drawn on the cloth and then painstakingly embroidered, a process which takes many months.

(Left) This angular and powerfully formed sculpture is more than matched by the character of the sacred cloth from Sumatra.

(Right) Two striking silk embroidered hangings from Central Asia on the wall in the music room of a Philadelphia home provide a rich and inspiring patterning and colour for the pianist to enjoy, as well as improving the sound qualities of the room.

(Below) A Manhattan apartment, sparsely furnished yet richly decorated with textiles. The subtly ikatted silk cloth from Central Asia is sumptuously embroidered and coloured with floral trellises; when mounted on a cloth-covered frame, it forms the focal point of the room.

(Bottom right) In this hallway, textiles, pottery, baskets and a Sepik river ancestral figure have been effectively lit and formally positioned to give an impression of a museum or gallery. Here the finest combination of embroidery and ikat work on a south Sumatran woman's cloth is strongly contrasted with the simple, dark and celestial patterning of the Moki Navajo wearing cloth.

(Left) *Acting as two points of heat and colour in a brilliant kitchen are a pair of Kuna Indian molas from the San Blas Islands off Panama; these reverse appliqué blouse fronts have been sandwiched between sheets of perspex and hung to striking effect without frames or clips.*

(Below) *An unusual south Persian tribal bag – most probably for storing salt – brings character with texture, shape and colour to a corner of this kitchen.*

(Left) *If carefully and expertly mounted and covered with plexiglass for safety, there is no reason why even the most valuable textiles cannot be used almost anywhere in the house. Here a thousand-year-old Huari feather and cotton poncho adds a colourful focus to the adobe kitchen. Care should be taken, however, to determine ambient light, humidity and temperature levels; too much variation will damage so ancient a textile.*

(Opposite) *Many disparate shapes of wood, stone and iron combine with appliqué and cut-pile raphia cloths from Zaire to frame a doorway.*

(Left) The double ikat patola cloths from Gujarat have been revered throughout eastern Asia for centuries, inspiring imitations. In this study, a framed fragment hangs over a day bed.

(Opposite) A child's bedroom is a perfect home for the village embroideries, appliqués and quilts of India, which are comfortable and warm to play on and easy to hang. The multitude of animal, floral and mechanical images provides a delightful and stimulating environment for children of all ages.

(Left) In the bedroom of this house in Philadelphia, striped flatweaves from Morocco and Afghanistan cover the wall, floor and part of the bed – rich textures that highlight the mix of collectables which ranges from the finest bleached linen to a triad of Venetian carnival masks.

The memories of trying to keep warm in the depths of a Kabul winter under this patchwork and embroidered quilt are enough to spur on the unwilling exerciser. Callisthenics on the Caucasian Shirvan kilim are made safe and comfortable with rubberized underlay.

(Left) The sumptuous dark purple of a north Sumatran silk shoulder cloth, here draped over a wooden rail, was derived from cochineal. Silk from China has been dyed and woven with supplementary weft threads of gold by Aceh people and such fine cloth would have been a valued ceremonial gift between families.

(Above) On an inner hallway wall, safe from the fading effects of the sun, are hung these Central Asian bedding decorations of the Uzbek Lakai nomads. Such fine stitching rests well in a simple yet effective frame of stretcher, cloth and perspex sheet.

(Opposite) A still-life arrangement of china and textiles decorates a chest of drawers in a bedroom, setting up simple yet evocative associations between East and West.

(Above) This is part of the living room of an early twentieth-century Santa Monican bungalow that overlooks the ocean; a landmark of the area, this glorious example of craftsmen's architecture is an unusual backdrop for a fine collection of North American Indian textiles. Drawing the eye away from the sturdy beams, table and the old-style furniture from New Mexico are the simple designs and colours of the late classic Navajo serape on the wall and the more modern Navajo rug fragments made up as sofa cushions.

(Left) In this large Santa Fé house, tribal textiles blend with modern furniture to good effect. In the hallway, a gypsy kilim from Afghanistan on the brick floor and the Caucasian maffrash bag piece on the wall vie for attention with the more familiar design of the Navajo Indian 'Stars and Stripes' blanket over the door.

(Left) A magnificently arranged library is the setting for two fine Indonesian cloths, whose decorative and technical merits and quirks may be appreciated equally from near and afar.

(Below) In the entrance hall of this Santa Monican bungalow, the imposing brick fireplace forms a central core of warmth during the chill Los Angeles evenings; American Indian weavings and baskets provide shape, pattern and colour, thus creating a characterful first impression.

(Above) These Navajo blankets have been placed away from the harmful southern Californian sun. The rugs have been positioned as low as possible and are illuminated by a strong wash of light from above, detracting from the high ceiling. Californian and Arizonan Indian baskets and New Mexican Pueblo pottery bowls complete an American Indian theme.

(Left) Dominated by a nineteenth-century English copy of a French four-poster bed, this opulent bedroom is decorated with textiles from the Silk Route, nineteenth-century Russian tin mirrors and an eighteenth-century North African embroidery from Algeria – then part of the Ottoman Empire. The colour and composition of the old English quilt on the bed provides an admirable contrast to the deep colours and geometric patterns of the Muslim wall hangings.

The embroidered mirror work of an ox cover, a woman's blouse and small purses will gleam and glow by bedside candlelight. All are linked, by region of origin, with the colourful north-west Indian appliqué ceiling hanging that adorns the bed.

Flanked by an American folk sculpture of the last century, the framed Central Asian silk embroidery swirls with delightful floral motifs that radiate from the centre. In a room such as this, with ceilings of average height, textiles may be successfully hung in a landscape style, here providing a backdrop to a fine collection of Asian ceramics. Nestling amongst them is a pre-Columbian smiling head from Mexico.

(Left) Imaginatively combined in a medley of colour, shape and texture are animal trappings, a salt bag and prayer mat, kilims, a soumak and embroideries. These textiles were collected in the Caucasus, Afghanistan, Pakistan, Persia and India.

(Opposite) This is the London studio home of a collector of fine and unusual Islamic art. Family heirlooms mingle with recently acquired textiles – often layer upon layer – celebrating the owner's pleasure in colour and pattern; here, a large Thracian kilim looks down on a Nepalese bronze door, Japanese porcelain and Persian and Turkoman carpets and cushions.

A modern Mexican Indian copy of a Navajo chief blanket lies by an adobe fire in a house outside Santa Fé. This is truly a Mexican corner, with a chest, table, indigo-dyed poncho, sombrero and floral tray, all from south of the border. The unsightly view is covered by a cotton Guatemalan shawl.

(Below) In Bolivia the sacred and ceremonial textiles are preserved for generations, wrapped as bundles known as 'q'epi'. Here, in New York, a collection of Bolivian Indian textiles is stored in a chest, under a man's mantle. Rolled on acid-free cardboard tubes, each is ready to be hung by a sewn strip of Velcro. In this way a collection may be moved from store to wall with ease.

This very early example of a Bolivian Indian woman's mantle has been attached to the wooden bar with Velcro. It is bathed harmoniously and harmlessly in the last rays of the sun's light, reflected from the windows of an adjacent building. Although this apartment is above a busy street in Manhattan, peace and harmony reign in the simply furnished living room.

(Left) Decorating a cupboard door is a panel of cut-pile raphia skirt length, made by the Kuba peoples of Zaire. Despite the rigidly geometric patterns, the gentle colouring – or lack of colour – in Kuba cloths ensures that a room will not be dominated by their presence.

(Below) Kilims look splendid on varnished floorboards, and this north Persian example is no exception. Some fine textiles, on the other hand, and especially embroideries, are enhanced by formal framing; the gold and red stitching of this North-West Frontier cushion cover is well matched by a gilt frame.

(Above) While poring over a computer print-out, an executive's tired eyes may be intermittently soothed by turning to gaze upon the Navajo blanket that hangs quietly behind the desk.

(Right) Quiet concentration on one's work in an office or study can be assisted by the pleasure of contemplating a favourite textile. This Sumatran tampan is finely decorated with supplementary wefts, and mounted for protection on a perspex framed panel.

(Far right) Tucked away in the depths of the corporate headquarters, a small office is delightfully dominated by a modern Anatolian kilim of fine quality that has been designed to blend some traditional patterns with acceptably decorative colours.

(Opposite) From floor to wall, this is a room inspired by the arts of Africa. The fine, stripwoven kente cloth is hung by a pulley and wooden beam system, and fills the room with ordered colour and pattern. The arrangement of wooden floor blocks is derived from Kuba textile designs, and a rare split cane floor mat from the same tribe is framed and rests on the fireplace surrounded by masks and loom pulleys from West Africa. The chair was a present to a departing English governor of Kenya and has been carved in the style of the palace designed by Charles Rennie Mackintosh.

Objects collected on travels from all over the world are on display throughout this apartment. Here a narrow-necked salt bag and accompanying Persian tribal bag faces vie for attention amidst the trappings and carvings from Asia.

Hanging on the curved wall of the central stairwell in this modern house is a cheerful marriage canopy from north-west India. The mirror work and stellar or floral patterning gives the room a focus of attention, to which the hanging cradle from Gujarat is an unusual accessory.

Chapter Five **Unusually decorative**

Matisse, in his South of France apartment, surrounded by paintings and tribal textiles: over the sofa, a Senna kilim; on the wall, a cut-pile raphia panel from the Belgian Congo. Many of the artists of the late nineteenth and early twentieth centuries, such as Picasso and Braque, as well as Matisse, found inspiration in tribal art. Below: Henri Matisse, Pianist and Chequer Players, 1924

Unusually decorative

The most traditional use, in a Western sense, for a handloomed textile of the tribal world is as a floor rug. Before the nineteenth century, it had become accepted that the finest floor coverings were imported Turkey or Persian carpets, and for many expatriates and colonials exposed to the utilitarian tribal and village wares, the kilims, hanbels and dhurries were robust mats for the dogs to sleep on. Today, in a world of rapidly changing design styles, tribal textiles of all origins are beginning to be seen for what they are – useful, original and highly decorative.

Judging by the rate at which ethnographic textiles are being absorbed into fashionable Western interiors, not only will an unusual trend of the recent past – such as hanging a textile on the wall – become normal, but also, by demand, the availability of so many more unfamilar styles of textiles of diverse origin will increase. The ethical implications of a world trade in ethnographic art aside, an increased appreciation for the technical and creative expertise of these weavers and embroiderers might play a role in awakening general awareness of the highly developed processes of the 'natural' creativity of semi-tribal cultures.

Unusual yet traditional

Westerners often associate the 'unusual' use of textiles with the legacies and traditions, or vestiges of traditions, of a transhumant way of life. The great fairs, festivities and wedding celebrations of West Africa, Central and Southern Asia are, and always were, a time for the gathering of tribes, clans and families, when gaily caparisoned animals and tented cities temporarily made colourful a dusty and often drab and desiccated environment. Through this uncomfortable, hard and fragile landscape the nomads and semi-nomads passed, carrying their world from place to place in bags and panniers; and when temporarily settled in tented encampments, they would adorn their living quarters with symbolic, decorative and useful textiles. Some of the most highly organized and famous nomads were the Turkoman tribal groups of Central Asia.

Generations of wanderers on the great steppes, deserts and mountains of the region developed the use of the circular nomadic tent – the yurt. Formed with interlocking and bent green willow staves, the inner structure of the yurt is light and strong. Covered with heavy felts, the interior is warm and dry in winter and comparatively cool in the torrid heat of the summer, especially when the side panels of the yurt are rolled back. Cooling breezes may then enter the shade afforded by the yurt. At the setting of camp the men will invariably rest and relax as three or four womenfolk set up the tent. Carried in its dismembered state by a trio of camels, with a lifetime of practice the yurt may be erected in less than half an hour. The diameter of the yurt and the number of yurts in a family camp is proportionate to the wealth of the owner, and this is reflected on the inside, too, by the lavish nature of the unusual textile decorations.

In this windowless interior where the smoking central fire is vented by a narrow opening at the apex of the tent, the appliqué, patchwork and flatwoven trappings add colour and comfort to the cosy scene. Aside from the tent bands used to lash the structure together, wider bands with decorative brocade run the circumference of the interior of the yurt. The dome is hung with bright printed Russian cloth and the rear walls decorated with 'kurachis' – the patchwork panels of silk ikat, red cotton and embroidery that also caparison the flanks of the bride's camel in a wedding procession. On the latticework sides of the yurt hang flatwoven bags such as the juvals, as well as bags for utensils, clothing, tent components and cooking apparatus. The earth floor is cushioned and made clean and warm with felts and flatweaves, and the other colourful textile accessories which make up the bedding are stored during the day on top of the wooden chests – such coffers are likely to be the only pieces of 'furniture'.

The scene is complete when the yurt is filled with the extended family group, each jostling for a good position near the fire in the winter and aware of the traditional codes of conduct that govern the seating of family and guests in the smoky confines of the tent. The owner of the yurt takes his place to the right of the wooden door or felt cover, and to the left, his wife; the guest immediately faces the door. Bathed by the glow of the central fire the atmosphere in a yurt is made colourful not only by the hangings, bedding and bands, but also by the rich texture and patterning of the clothing. Silk and cotton coats, often padded and ikat decorated, brightly coloured turbans and women's dresses of a patchwork of multicoloured Russian printed floral cotton – all contribute to a lively mix of colours and textures.

Personal effects are carried in small bags, and purses are in common use, whether embroidered with rayon and gilt thread or plainwoven of undyed sheep's wool and goat hair for durability. Tent bands are woven on very narrow and highly transportable ground looms by many of the nomads of Asia and North Africa. Often warp-faced patterned, these strips are sometimes cut into equal lengths and sewn together at the selvedge to make a rug or animal cover of almost any size. Rolls of narrow tent bands are used as rope, to tie the tent together and to lash bags to donkeys and draught animals. Wider bands of the Turkoman of Central Asia, decorated with brocade, are strung around the yurt as a decorative frieze. In India and Pakistan the horses, camels, oxen and cows are frequently caparisoned with embroideries and appliquéd cloths for village festivities and the animals then match the gaily dressed men, women and children.

The shapes and decoration of flatwoven bags have developed through the ages according to their usefulness. Jaloors and juvals are the rectangular kilim sacks of the Turkic tribes of Central Asia which, when filled, are strapped to the sides of an animal or hung around the yurt for storage. The double bags, the hurgin of the kilim world, are used as personal panniers or to throw over a donkey's back. The five-panelled maffrash covers of the Caucasus and north Persia are fitted over wooden frames or boxes, or when filled with bedding, lashed together with straps. Their use is vividly described in Harper's Magazine, November 1893, by Edwin Lord Weeks, when travelling 'From Tabreez to Ispahan': 'As the Persians know how to travel in their own country, we have adopted their fashion of carrying valises and small trunks, and have invested in two pairs of long woven sacks, in which these articles are packed. Each sack is called a "ma-fresh" and two of them are a load for a horse, one placed on each side of the saddle, with the weight carefully adjusted. These receptacles are six feet in length by eighteen inches in depth and width, shaped like long narrow boxes, with stout leather handles at each end, and a multitude of straps and buckles. In each of these sacks all the small packages and valises are placed, waterproof bags with bedding, our own camp bedsteads, stools, tables and carpets are laid on top and after being tightly strapped on, they are lifted into place by the combined efforts of all the men, and corded onto the bulky pack saddles of the horses.'

In Peru the archaeological excavations and the less controlled plundering of the grave sites of the pre-Columbian cultures have yielded a bewildering assortment of fine textiles of obscure use and unusual nature. In one Chancay culture grave, more than a dozen bales of strong cotton fabric were found; they are patterned by warp striping and two feet wide by over fifteen yards in length. The reasons why such a stock of cloth was entombed will never be known; their subsequent use, however, is most unusual. After samples were secured for the museum, the cloth was given to the site workers who then sold the textiles as covers for deck chairs, hammocks and garden furniture – an extraordinary final use for thousand-year-old weavings.

The last and most notorious of the South American Indian empires was that of the Incas and, by means of the show of fine and unusual clothing, personal status within their highly developed class system was communicated. The lower classes made do with undecorated, plain and functional garb whereas the Inca and his various wives were adorned with the finest cloth, often decorated with tropical birds' feathers. One may imagine the conquering Spaniards speechless with wonder, albeit temporarily, at the sight of the Incan ruler clad in a shimmering robe of brilliant reds, blues and yellows – the plumage of the Amazonian macaws, smaller parrots, and such exotic birds as the toucans. These composite cotton and feather textiles were great achievements of technique and imagination in the use of resources and their senstive use of plumage colour, together with the manipulation of the subtle variations in feather tones and shading, are extraordinary. Capes have been found with designs of animal and supernatural forms, created by the unusual juxtaposition of many different birds' feathers.

What became of the many fine cloths and clothing of the Incas is not clear. There are reports that any item worn once by the Inca was ceremonially burnt on an auspicious day of the year, whereas a near contemporary Spanish writer, Garcilasco de la Vega, maintains: 'There were plentiful supplies of new clothing both for daily use and for the bed; for the Inca never wore his clothes twice, but gave them to his relations. All his bedclothes were woven of vicuna wool, which is so fine that Philip II had it brought to Europe for his bed, together with other Peruvian products.'

For the peoples of the villages of Indonesia, Central and South America and Central and West Africa, a ceremonial occasion usually of religious significance has always been a time when the finest and most traditional textiles would be disinterred and displayed. Men's and women's mantles of alpaca would be taken from the q'epi and worn on a particular saint's day in the villages of the Bolivian altiplano. Many of the patterns and colours of these cloths, as well as their use in the religious ceremonies, relate to a pre-colonial and pagan past that stubbornly refuses to be buried by acculturation. In West and Central Africa, displays of rank, wealth and symbolism are

Embroidered tent decoration of the Uzbek Lakai people, Central Asia

combined in the fine silk or raphia textiles worn as skirts or body cloths, and in Indonesia specific textiles are worn and hung at the many ceremonial gatherings of families, clans and villages.

Certain Indonesian textiles enjoy an ancient and widespread function as objects that clearly define an area of particular religious significance. On the island of Roti, nine large textiles would be hung to close off the bridal room , so imitating a 'room in the sky', and a corpse is embowered by a cloth known as the 'broad cloth of heaven'. In South Sumatra the major ceremonies were accompanied by the hanging of the palepai – the ship cloth – within an inner room, so creating an area of ritual significance. The Iban of Borneo use their strikingly decorated pua cloths to enclose the dead, to act as a sacred enclosure and to decorate a room within the longhouse where a person could await a 'spirit helper' in the 'dream room'. Such spiritual reverence for textiles and their subsequent 'unusual' use is extended by custom to include enclosing the resting places of royalty or leaders of a society. The regal trappings of the beds-of-state of Java and Sumatra echo by their rich adornment the decorative treatment of medieval European carriages, palanquins, beds and biers. Opulence and prosperity are a common denominator for such textile display within these two cultures. Yet, as ever, the Indonesian use of textiles has deeper meaning, conveying powers of fertility and well-being by their ceremonial use.

Unusually decorative

Upholstery Of all handloomed weaves and sewn embroideries, the strongest furnishing textiles are the flatwoven kilims and dhurries. These and other textiles may be adapted for use in one piece, as with a bag, or – and this is a very delicate subject amongst textile collectors, scholars and dealers – the textile may be cut and fitted to specification. There are many bags, from purse to pannier, that may be filled with a prepared feather pad and used on the sofa as a comfortable and visually interesting cushion. The larger bags, such as the jaloors and juvals, will, when stuffed, make ideal floor cushions and seats, and the hurgin panniers may be filled and sat against, or a frame made to form a free standing legless chair. Conveniently, the appliqués and embroideries are often originally square, and a panel with a cotton, linen or silk back will be an ideal cushion cover. The molas, chaklas and North-West Frontier blouse panels and sleeve pieces may be adapted in this way for cushion use. Any lengths of cloth will either have to envelop the cushion pad or be cut. Here the possible choices are limitless, for very many shawls, mantles, skirt and flatwoven rug lengths are suitably decorative. Most dealers and decorators, thankfully, will only use textiles that are damaged, will not lie flat or are so new as to have no sentimental or historical value.

One of the most striking and unusual uses for a tribal textile is as fitted upholstery. A chair designed for Western decorative tastes, whether a reproduction Louis-Quatorze seat, a sofa, or an antique or modern high-backed chair, will be transformed by a fitted cover of ethnic origin. An old susani on an English antique wing chair, a near matching collection of Sumban ikats on a set of dining-room chairs, a sofa covered in a colourful kilim, and ottomans, foot stools and stools decorated with Navajo rug, kilim or dhurrie-fitted upholstery – there is a wealth of possibilities. The maffrash box covers and bedding bags are ideal for unusual furnishing use, for they are, of course, originally made as fitted upholstery, and so, without cutting, they can cover a purpose-built ottoman or chest.

(Opposite) The wife of a prince of the Congo, dressed in an appliqué raphia skirt with matching body scarification

Unusually casual A good many people will use a pliable, light and colourful textile to throw over and hide a mess of clutter in a corner of a room: a useful but decorative aid on the appearance of that surprise visitor.

Rather than cut and fit a kilim or dhurrie, a sofa may be loosely enveloped with a large flatweave or with a selection of different textiles. In this way the seat and back may be covered by weaves of various origins that display matching or related designs and colours. A kilim from Anatolia and a Mexican eye-dazzler serape would be a fine choice. For some, the decoration of the home extends beyond prepared furnishings to the swagging and draping of chairs, tables, beams or stands with interesting examples of ethnic textiles. A long table, when not in use, may, in a somewhat liturgical manner, be decorated with a central band of cloth such as a narrow Indonesian breast cover or a nomad's tent band. A table may be completely covered by a textile, provided that the latter is inexpensive and suitably ornate, washable and able to stand up to daily use. When not in use, a fine table or sideboard may be protected and decorated by a textile that is instantly removable, to avoid spills and misuse. The beams of houses with open and lofty ceilings may be draped, in heraldic manner, with open or folded textiles that might serve to trace the development of the textile design traditions of a village or tribe; a good collection, which may be found with relative ease, would show the various examples and ages of Kurdish floral weaves of north-west Persia. In the bedroom or bathroom a screen may be draped with different textiles for contrasting decorative effects, and a bed covered completely by a colourful embroidery or appliqué such as a susani or an Indian cotton hanging. The bedroom is also just one ideal venue for draping or fitting a robe or garment of tribal origin over an old tailor's dummy – although waking up in the night to see a Hausa robe or a Berber shepherd's cape on a figure in the room may prove too much for some. Tent bands, sashes or woven ribbons that often end up in a drawer or cupboard for want of use may be rolled, draped or hung over a wall-mounted crossbar.

In the knowledge that the sun will fade, eventually, all textile colours, one may use light kilims, shawls, dhurries, mantles and sarongs as window covers. Curtains and blinds of over-zealously bright colours might well improve with a decorative sun-fading treatment. The style and nature of their use will be made complete by using tend bands, woven ribbons or sashes as tie backs.

(Opposite) Under the New Mexican sky, the sundeck of this modern adobe country house is set ready for breakfast; here the untreated willow furniture is made colourful and comfortable with a mix of tribal textiles. Modern Indonesian ikat placemats, Persian printed cloth cushions, an Indian appliqué wrap and a Caucasian maffrash bag face – all mix together in diverse yet decorative harmony.

In this Californian ranch-style house, textiles from the great tribes of Persia and America co-exist with ease. Hanging in the eaves are three Navajo Indian rugs that look down upon a Qashqai (South Persian) kilim that has been draped over the back of the sofa. A Moroccan donkey bag and a number of Navajo rug cushions lie on an adjacent seat, completing a living space decorated with flatwoven textiles from the Northern Hemisphere.

(Opposite) A New England barn, now a spacious sitting room, provides an unusual setting for this exciting collection of early Navajo blankets. The blankets, which chart the birth and development of an ephemeral but great North American weaving tradition, have been draped over the tie beams – as if ready to be worn again.

After years of careful collecting, the owner of this adobe house was able to use a number of Indonesian Sumban ikat cloths as dining chair covers, to dramatic effect. The complicated resist-dyeing and weaving technique gives dazzling patterns in blues and reds. The excellence of the weave ensures that the covers will be tough enough to withstand daily use.

(Left) Oblivious to the Crimean War scenes behind, Georgie, the family pet, waits in the main hall beside two kilim-covered chairs, the patterns of which are so similar to the Persian ceramic tile decoration on the table.

The flowing floral designwork on the Ottoman glazed tiles is echoed by vases of flowers and textiles. Contrasting with such splendour is the simple cotton and linen appliqué tunic of a Sudanese dervish, worn by the Mahdi's troops against Gordon of Khartoum. The French tapestry nestles amidst the exotica.

(Opposite) Inspired by a sixteenth-century Ottoman velvet, gold stencilling richly embellishes the hallway, and the delightful floral palmette motifs are repeated in a Central Asian form on a nineteenth-century Bokharan robe of honour.

(Above) The fringed square textile over the sofa is a chakla, a wall decoration for the dowry of a Hindu farming family of north-west India. The footstools are covered with a kilim from Van, east Turkey, and the easy chair is splendidly cushioned with Tashkent embroidered covers. Most of the textiles made into the sofa cushions were originally clothing; there are mola blouse fronts from Panama, Gujarati skirt pieces and a Guatemalan blanket fragment.

(Left) The early morning light strides into the living room of this adobe house, lighting the rich, vegetable-dyed flatwoven textiles. From the bright Persian Garmsar kilim in the distance, to the Mexican and New Mexican blanket and poncho and the Persian Kurdish cushion, all these tribal textiles beautifully complement the antique American furniture.

(Left) The mixtures of vegetable and synthetic dyes in the flatwoven cushion covers, from origins as distant as Afghanistan and New Mexico, are a delightful foil to the dazzling colours of a south Californian garden in the spring.

(Right) In the corner of this sitting room, which opens onto the garden by way of full-length windows, is a quiet reading area. Surrounded by books, a peaceful and comfortable seat is made colourful by a Navajo fragment that complements the Navajo rug-covered ottoman.

(Right) From the long, light living and dining room through to the master bedroom, tribal textiles add colour and texture to the wall, table and chair. Wrapped around the Mexican terracotta urn is an Indonesian Sumban ikat cloth, on the wall a tantalizing glimpse of a twentieth-century Navajo rug and over a chair another American Indian flatweave.

(Right) Nothing could be more startling and original than an English Chippendale wing chair covered by fragments from a cotton and silk susani from Samarkand. In contrast to this vivid yet delicate floral embroidery is American folk art of the 1920s – a Tennessee crazy quilt hangs moodily over the country kitchen cabinet.

135

This galley kitchen has been made a pleasure to work in by the stencilling of Mughal floral patterns, originally seen on a sixteenth-century tent, over the high walls. The illusion of space, light and warmth is complete.

(Opposite) In this potter's home there are few corners of a room left bare. Paintings and collections of pots, books and textiles vie for space. Over the sofa seat a Mexican serape cloth contrasts energetically with a Kurdish kilim from eastern Anatolia.

Over the kitchen refectory table of this old cottage is an eastern Anatolian kilim. The floral patterning of this flatweave is in harmony with the shapes and curves of the fruit, vegetables, pots, plates and plants that bestrew the room.

(Left) In a Los Angeles home, two reproduction Louis-Quatorze chairs have been unusually covered by robust pieces of an *Afghani* kilim.

(Below) A mix of photographs, paintings, drawings, and textiles – framed and unframed – transforms a corridor wall. Each tells a story, from the picture of a weaver spinning, to the woollen cape of the Middle *Atlas* that evokes memories of haggling in a Moroccan bazaar.

In this New York apartment, a seasoned traveller of *Afghanistan* has effectively framed behind glass the textile clothing fragments, purses and ephemera collected from many journeys. Much as with fine paintings or drawings, delicate textiles may be framed set on a deep acid-free mount, or a sub-frame constructed to keep the glass from touching the weave.

(Right) A sofa has been decorated with a mix of an Anatolian kilim-covered seat and cushions of Syrian, Thracian and European origin. This mix of ages and cultures is subtly highlighted by the fragments of pre-Columbian and Thracian tapestries, whose designs complement the shape of the Afghan brass bird.

(Right) Mixing with congruity amidst the paintings, a framed fragment of Huari tapestry from ancient Peru hangs on the living room wall of a London apartment.

(Left) This spare bedroom, which is also host to an impressive library of books on textiles, offers an informal setting for a collection of hats and belts from *Central Asia;* casually yet effectively hung on a clothes hanger is a Moroccan Berber cape, strikingly decorated with an eye symbol that deflects the evil of the unsolicited glance.

(Opposite) The French gilt decoration in the window competes with the wrought-iron grille for the view beyond, and the rounded belly of a Mexican grain liquor pot nestles onto a Guatemalan carrying-cloth, forming a most unusual decorative stand.

(Above) In this Santa Monican living room, the tables and chairs are bedecked with puppets, dolls, textiles and statues, collected in the course of travels through North Africa, Mexico and Asia. The strikingly patterned kilim was made and found in Tunisia and hangs seemingly unsupported against a bare white wall – an effect that is simple to achieve with the use of a strip of carpet gripper.

(Left) On one of the first warm days of a mid-western spring, a collection of cowboy boots and jewelry has been brought outside to be cleaned and polished. Over the antique Russian rocking chair rests a waistcoat made up from a damaged sixty-year-old Navajo rug, and another flatwoven fragment, this time from *Afghanistan,* has been made into a small cushion.

Over the seat of the chair a Maimana kilim fragment is cushioned with a modern English appliqué that enlivens this room with the colours of summer flowers.

(Opposite) Tribal textiles have here been used as soft furnishings. Anatolian kilim fragments are sewn together to make cushion covers, a Peruvian poncho from the Amazon is draped texturally over the chest, and a Navajo blanket backs the white sofa.

(Below) At first this bedroom seems the exclusive preserve of the kilims, embroideries and carpets of the East. The eclectic spirit of the apartment is emphasized by a lonely embroidery from the New World: a child's blouse of Guatemala is almost swamped amidst the richness and patterning of the Islamic textiles.

Small kilim fragments have great potential; here, an Anatolian example has made a comfortable and colourful seat cover for a low bedroom stool.

(Right) An appliqué hanging from India is a perfect-sized bed cover.

144

(Right) The possible domination of this bedroom by the high bed and the eighteenth-century Venetian gesso headboard is lessened by the large patterns and strong colouring of the susani bed cover. Inspired by such floral colouring as is found in these gladioli, the framed textile depicts one of the Ottoman favourites, the tulip.

(Left) A brilliant idea for the use of a damaged kilim fragment – as a padded headboard cover. On the bed, a Bokharan silk ikat is a striking and luxurious counterpane.

(Above) A high-raftered bathroom in New England is a strikingly unusual setting for these North African weavings. A Moroccan Berber ceremonial wedding belt hangs over the mirror, in which one may see a portable screen covered by a Berber hanbel.

Lined with Bokharan silk ikat, this gold-embroidered velvet robe from Central Asia swags a fine marble fireplace with exotic colour and texture.

Laid over the back of a sofa is a Bolivian Indian woman's carrying-cloth that was originally woven for ceremonial use as an offering to pre-Columbian gods. In the fast-sinking sunlight of a late afternoon in fall, the naturally coloured alpaca cloth appears as a relic of a lost age.

At the foot of these farmhouse stairs, a pair of Iban ikat cloth-covered cushions rests on a simple seat.

(Opposite) Tribal and folk textiles are visually very effective when placed in a living environment of wood, plain furnishings and white walls; here, a Navajo Indian horse blanket thrown over the plain-covered chair offers subtle geometric patterns to counter the strength of form in the baskets and statues.

(Below) An inspired way to show a colourful mix of Guatemalan embroidered sashes. Wall-mounted wooden rails and picture lamps are useful for the display of light and unusual textiles such as tent-band lengths, sarongs and small animal trappings.

148

(*Above*) Beneath the samplers is a row of hats that vary in origin from England to Persia and from Yugoslavia to India.

(*Right*) On an antique English chest lie embroidered cones and cupolas, the evocative forms of old hats from Central Asia.

(*Below*) Embroideries, tapestries, carpets and hangings complement the photographs of nineteenth-century Persian Turkestan and the floral and colourful Persian tiles and Russian porcelain.

Chapter Six   Decorative floor covers

(Opposite) Overlooked by a majestic Florentine portal, this formal dining room is an ideal location for a fine kilim. Little used, yet visible from many other rooms, the Kurdish kilim and Indonesian ikat table decoration add a glow of colour and texture to a rich setting.

Decorative floor covers

Most tribes that weave textiles suitable for use on the floor live in semi-deserts or mountainous areas, and there is, therefore, a simple and essential reason for their weaving habit – namely, the need for insulating covers. The flatwoven rugs with the longest history and the greatest range of construction techniques and patterning are the kilims of Asia and the hanbels of North Africa. The floor covers of the Indian subcontinent, the cotton dhurries, have ancient roots and the oldest and finest examples a historical association with the arts and crafts of the Mughal Empire. Navajo floor rugs are the product of late nineteenth- and twentieth-century consumer demand, and of more recent commercial inspiration are the Mexican Navajo copies and the small floor rugs of the Andean Indians.

There are many factors that determine how a flatwoven rug may be used on the floor, from practical considerations which take into account the type of underlying floor surface and durability of the textile, to matters of a more aesthetic nature, such as the sizes, shapes, colours and patterns available.

Floor surfaces

Flatwoven rugs may be found in so many colours and patterns that selecting a textile to match the existing floor covering is relatively easy. The primary consideration should be safety, as a sliding or moving rug is a hazard to bipeds and quadrupeds of any age. Floors with a high shine are slippery and fitted carpets with a deep pile tend to become a cushioning layer on which the rug will float about. The answer to these problems for all but the deepest shag pile nylon carpets is underlay. The right underlay will increase comfort, safety and durability. To be hidden under the rug, the underlay should be cut, overall, about one inch smaller than the flatweave. Many underlays are available in rolls that are often four feet wide, and so single-sided tape will be needed to join the strips together to go underneath a large rug or wide runner. Cushioning underlay for bare wood, stone and tile floors will not only prevent movement but also prolong the life of the weave. The abrasive action of dust and grit underfoot irrevocably damages the fibres of the flatweave; an underlay will act as a cushioning pad between such particles and the floor. It also absorbs any rucks or small creases caused by minor imperfections in a rug. Most underlays will not need to be attached to the flatweave itself or to the floor, and unless guaranteed by the manufacturer not to leave a residue, and to be suitable for repeated lifting, the use of double-sided tape as a securing agent is to be avoided.

(Opposite) Major Sandeman stands among his Balouch chiefs, who proudly display their finery: swords, embroidered clothing and a fine weft-faced patterned kilim.

155

Tufted or piled carpet Flatweaves on broadloom carpets of tufted construction tend to 'walk' and may be corralled by the use of specialist underlay of either a 'string vest' or thin synthetic felt type

Looped pile carpet Often known as berber, this is an ideal and inexpensive base for flatweaves, which then do not require an underlay.

Sisal, coir and sea grass matting An underlay is usually not necessary, but for comfort underfoot, especially on the coarsest of vegetable weaves, a thin rubberized or felt underlay should be used.

Wood and tiled floors Highly polished examples of wood, glazed ceramic or terracotta floors are a skating-rink for flatweaves. Underlay must be used and solutions vary from ordinary felt to rubberized matting (the corrugated rubber surface rests on the floor) to more specialized webbing, synthetic felts, and a sponge-type lining designed in Germany especially for flatweaves, and there is another, similar type from America.

Stone floors Unless sealed and polished, stone flags and concrete floors are safe for flatweaves without underlay, but for warmth and comfort underfoot and to prolong the life of the textile, underlay of a sponge or thick felt type is recommended. Flatweaves will not survive well on stone floors with damp problems.

Size and shape

Traditional flatweaves, in particular dhurries and some Afghan kilims, can be over twenty feet long and of a maximum width of twelve to fifteen feet. Originally made for palaces, festivals and celebrations, these textiles may represent more than a year's work at the loom and will need a room of worthy dimensions to allow a true appreciation of such effort and skill.

There is no doubt that the problems presented by an awkward-sized floor or an expansive area in need of a large textile can be solved by the modern dhurrie. Inspired by market forces and aided by the commissioning traditions of the colonial and pre-colonial past, dealers and designers in the West and within the Indian subcontinent itself are able to take orders for the manufacture of bespoke dhurries. Theoretically, the length of a dhurrie is unlimited and will depend on the weaving facilities available, whereas a maximum width of about fifteen feet is possible. The Anatolian weavers are also making kilims to order, albeit of wool, or wool and cotton, and, governed by the smaller sizes of their looms, the maximum sizes are confined to about thirty feet by about eight feet.

Flatweaves of eight feet in length or less are in abundance, from the Americas to Asia, although very small textiles of old age are hard to come by and many were originally bag faces or parts of animal trappings. For technical reasons, square flatweaves and rugs of a traditional nature over six feet wide are a problem to find, except for the small square rukorsis and the similarly shaped soffrai of Persia and

Afghanistan. Part of the pleasure of collecting kilims and hanbels is their originality and, unless governed by commercial demand, most tribal flatweaves – especially of nomadic origin – are each unique, yet made for a specific and time-honoured use that is often not in league with the decorators of the Western world.

Most flatweaves are likely to be placed on the floor in the traditional and somewhat formal Western decorative manner, occupying a central position with the border or frame of the underlying floor covering around. This style of use is particularly successful when the floor is interesting, as with a stone-flagged or wooden-boarded surface, and when the design composition of the textile is enhanced by a floor border, such as a rug with a central medallion or with many varied borders of its own.

Rather than covering, or partly covering, a large floor area with one flatweave, a less formal solution would be to use more than one rug. In this way a room is broken up into many areas, and rooms that open onto each other may be linked by the size and patterning of different rugs or of one rug placed between the two rooms. The never-ending search for a particularly wide flatweave may be resolved with stunning simplicity, by placing two rugs, perhaps runners, of near identical length, side by side. The smaller rugs are also always flexible in use over time, for at a future date, after moving house or with a change of decoration, the flatweaves may be moved and used again with ease.

Colour and pattern

Certainly, a large flatwoven textile might tend to dominate a room by the sheer bulk of its presence, but a busily patterned and coloured rug of any size will also attract a good deal of attention. Subtly coloured rugs, available from all flatweaving regions, will blend; they are often old and naturally faded examples, or very new rugs woven with decoratively acceptable colours such as pastels, or bright rugs that have been sun faded. The brown tones of early twentieth-century Navajo work and the muted indigos and earth colours of traditional Balouch weavings are particularly enjoyable to live with. Bright-coloured rugs may have been dyed with natural or chemical dyes, or both; and some of the most electric colour combinations may be found in early Navajo eye-dazzler examples and the old kilims of the Qashqai. Indeed, most of the old kilims of Persia, Anatolia, the Caucasus and of the southern oases of Tunisia are sought after for their naturally bright and cheerful colours.

The decorative nature of the room itself will determine the colouring of textile suitable. A hot-coloured rug may draw attention to a gloomy part of a room or house and, conversely, a light and bright beach house with whitewashed walls will make all but the fiercest coloured textiles seem dull. Dark rugs on dark wood or stone floors may, to some, seem to disappear and to others, be a perfect match of tone and texture. Rugs from totally disparate origins and ages will blend in harmony on the floor of one room if they have mutual colour or tonal balance. Most older hanbels, kilims, dhurries and rugs of the Americas quite shimmer with colour – the result of abrash. In decorative terms, rugs with such tonal colour movement will be easier to live with.

The patterning of flatweaves can be figurative or abstract. Most rugs with patterns that have no focus, but instead stripes or bands of colour between rows of small motifs, will tend to blend more easily than those with a clearly defined pattern of a central medallion or medallions and border or borders. The red and cream hanbels of the Atlas Mountains, the Balouch dowry kilims, Persian and Afghan stripweaves and some Navajo textiles are all examples of banded decoration. Figurative designs are less common, save those birds and beasts that decorate modern Andean rugs, the tiny goat and camel motifs of kilims and the animals of the Tunisian desert flatweaves. Floral decorations abound, from the stylized guls of Central Asia, to the realistic such as the flowing floridity of the Senna kilims.

Flatweaves with a central and dominant pattern may need positioning in the centre of a room with a good border of floor to soothe the busyness of the composition. Without a doubt, the kilims, hanbels or rugs with any strength of pattern or colour will look best, in an aesthetic as opposed to an eclectic sense, when laid in a room without floral wallpaper, chintz curtains or upholstery. Plain yet interestingly coloured furnishings, painted walls and simple furniture seem to work so well with the naive and refreshing powerful simplicity of some flatweaves.

For those with very particular requirements, the modern Mexican, Anatolian and Indian weavings may be made to order. In Anatolia thousands of historic kilim and carpet designs have been recorded on the ubiquitous computer, and a complete design plan for any of these examples may be printed and handed to the weaver for reproduction. In Mexico, inexpensive and accurate copies of nineteenth-century Navajo blankets and rugs are now made that are highly suitable for floor use, and the dhurrie weavers of India and Pakistan are well known for their abilities as copyists.

Durability

The durability of a flatwoven textile used as a rug is subject to many factors. The type of yarn and weaving technique determines the structure and strength of the rug, and its longevity is subject to the wear already received, as well as the likely wear to be meted out. Many finely woven old textiles that may have been used on a mud or matting floor, or in layers, or trodden by bare feet or soft shoes, should be treated with respect and laid to rest in a quiet area of a room, and likewise with thin or worn out flatweaves. By contrast, some rugs, especially woollen kilims, are so tightly woven and tough that it is difficult to penetrate the weave with a needle. The double interlocked kilims of the Bakhtiari and the Tartari peoples, the weft-faced patterned Balouch kilims and some cotton dhurries are good examples of very hard-wearing floor rugs. Generally speaking, the textile is strongest when no pronounced slitweave work is evident. By comparing different flatweaves by feel and by holding a textile up to the light, one may gain an impression of the strength of the rug.

The placing of furniture on kilims will tend to disturb their decorative effect, especially when a central design or the subtle relationships between designs are hidden. It is unlikely that the resting furniture, unless very heavy, will damage the weave of a robust textile, but the repeated and clumsy movement of chairs, benches, beds and tables should be avoided. The greatest hazard is of chair legs getting caught in the slitweave. If in doubt, either lay the rug away from furniture or use plastic or wooden cups for the chair and table feet to distribute some of the weight. Partially covered rugs will wear unevenly and so should be lifted, shaken and turned as often as is convenient.

Possible positions for flatwoven rugs are here examined, room by room, and the house divided into areas of hard use and soft use. Finer and more precious textiles are obviously best suited to rooms with little foot traffic and the more robust, perhaps newer, yet still characterful rugs may be used throughout the home.

Soft use

Bedroom Often the most private and least used room in the house, the bedroom is an ideal location for the appreciation and preservation of flatwoven rugs. The bed often dominates, and this effect may be combated by the addition of an interestingly patterned or coloured flatweave. Kilims of similar use, patterning or shape, such as prayer mats and small runners, may be placed either side of a free-standing bed and will be a welcome soft texture to step onto with bare feet.

Study Flatweaves associated with journeys to faraway places are often too extraordinary for traditional Western decorative use and may therefore find refuge in the calm of a study, to be enjoyed in an atmosphere of quiet contemplation. A strongly patterned and coloured kilim that is part of the memory of a bustling bazaar may compete for attention with a plain indigo and madder-decorated Balouch meal cloth, a textile that so often sums up images of their nearly barren desert and scrub lands.

Hard use

Bathroom An unlikely room for a flatwoven rug unless considerable care is exercised in the choice of textile and the need for underlay recognized. Many old kilims will not experience colour run when gently washed and yet are probably too valuable for the damaging extremes of temperature and humidity. An inexpensive modern flatweave is a solution and the small dhurries of India or the kilims of Maimana in north-west Afghanistan are often colour-fast. Tile bathroom floors are a hazard at the best of times, and so, if a rug is placed on such a surface as a bath or shower mat, a non-slip rubberized underlay should be used, and the rug will need to be dried and aired frequently.

Kitchen This is so often the centre and most lived-in area of the home that any flatweave on the floor will have to be able to stand up to unremitting punishment. The kitchen floor usually has a surface that is easy to clean, such as sealed and polished wooden boards, cork, ceramic, vinyl or marble tiles; these are all very slippery surfaces and a flatweave will need a truly effective underlay to prevent accidents. A rug for the kitchen must lie flat, and if it is not washable, a steam or shampoo cleaning bill must be expected from time to time.

Playroom Children spend most of their time on the floor, and so any flatwoven textile will need to be tough yet comfortable. Underlay is essential on all but looped pile fitted carpets, and it would help if colours are fast to cope with the inevitable spills. A brightly coloured and patterned kilim can prove to be an amusing racetrack for toy-car drivers and at another moment a chequerboard for games.

Dining room A rug will receive much wear when placed under the table and, in any case, most of the pattern will be hidden; only the most tightly woven dhurries, or kilims without slitweave, should be considered. Underlay should be used if necessary and protective cups placed under the feet of the table. If possible the rug should be wide enough to accommodate the chairs when pushed back so that the edge of the textile is not repeatedly caught. Colours should be fast so that any inadvertent spills will not ruin the evening. A kilim or dhurrie placed right away from the dining area will form an alternative focus of attention in the room.

Living room This is a room where there are often areas of floor that are either abused or disused, and the floor covering should be chosen accordingly. The living room is often the entertaining room, and much money may be lavished on the decorations into which a flatweave must fit or be fitted around. To cover the central part of the floor area, or to become the focus of comfortable chairs, a rug is needed that balances quality with practicality – some of the Persian kilims of the Turkic tribes of the south are relatively tough and decorative, but are now becoming difficult to find, as are the Kuba and Shirvan weaves of the Caucasus. Wear is liable to be greatest by an open fire and near any doors. If the room is to be decorated with many small flatweaves, these are areas where the least valuable and toughest rugs should lie. Underlay should be used if necessary and any armchairs or sofas should rest on furniture cups.

Hallway A hallway leading in from the front door will create first impressions and receive much dirt. Flatweaves here must be strong, decorative and firmly set to rest on a slippery floor with underlay. Hallways lead from one area of a house to another and, if possible, a textile such as a runner may be used as a linking element, or more than one rug can visually define each area by their variations in colour and patterning.

The look of narrow hallways may be extended lengthways by a thin runner or series of runners, and compressed, or expanded widthways by a wider rug or rug with banded patterning and no distinct border. Large and lofty hallways may be decorated with a brightly coloured and highly patterned flatweave of large size, such as a Maimana kilim or dhurrie that will provide a strong focus of attention. Dark and narrow halls or passageways will need to be well lit by artificial light and, ideally, a series of low voltage recessed downlighters or surface fittings used. These will bring alive even the most sombre of runners. Hallways and corridors often meet with stairways and this may provide the rare opportunity for a flatweave to be seen from above, and from a distance. The character of a rug with many different scales of patterning that are often unappreciated at eye level may then be discovered and enjoyed from different vantage points.

(Opposite) A Parisian apartment is the refined setting for tribal textiles and carvings. Hanging from a chair from the kingdom of Swat, erstwhile home to the Akond, is a Seychellian coca de mer begging bowl from Persia, whence came the colourful Qashqai kilim.

(Opposite) In the office, study and library room of a house in Philadelphia, two desks stand on a south-west Anatolian kilim. Over a chair rests a contemporary alpaca sweater from Bolivia, decorated with colours and patterns directly inspired by pre-Columbian textiles of the Peruvian Huari culture.

In this home of a painter and experienced traveller of Persia, small Kurdish kilims decorate the floor and wall of the bedroom, providing a vivid contrast between the floral and banded decorative styles of weavers from the same region.

In this Parisian apartment textiles and textile fragments are a decorative focus of attention, either as a kilim in a traditional position – on the floor – or as upholstery.

The characteristic adobe construction of this house is strikingly evident in the dining room, as is the international flavour of the furniture and furnishings. Nineteenth-century Mexican altar retablos look down on seventeenth-century chairs, and the Welsh pine table sits on a Mexican reproduction of a Navajo rug.

(Left) In an English country cottage, small rooms need small rugs. Beside a Spanish writing table lie two simply decorated Balouch prayer kilims.

(Opposite) At an elevation of eight thousand feet, the winters in Santa Fé are bitterly cold and so this adobe fireplace becomes a focus of warmth and comfort. Under an elk antler mounted Mexican monastery granary door is a soft-coloured High Andes Indian blanket. Almost invisible amongst the eclectic mix of ornaments is a Bolivian wool carrying-cloth.

The honey-coloured tiles on a kitchen floor have been decoratively enhanced by an Iraqi embroidered flatweave. Full of animal and floral images, this is an exciting and cheerful rug for a bright and busy room.

Wound round a wooden rod, these tent bands from the Balouch tribespeople of west Afghanistan are displayed in a most unusual and effective way. Woven with silk, the bands would have been both decorative and functional. Similarly, under the table, the kilim – woven by south Persian Turkic tribespeople – has two virtues useful for both nomads and New York city dwellers, for it is tough and colourful.

(Right) Here, in a light-filled kitchen that looks onto the garden, the shine of the French terracotta floor tiles is contrasted by the subtle colours of a kilim from Anatolia decorated with cicim work. When laying a kilim on such a floor it is important to use a suitable non-slip underlay.

Deep in the English countryside, this cottage is happily festooned with all manner of textiles. Indian appliqués hang on the wall and fall from the chair, and robust kilims from *Afghanistan* and *North Africa* adorn sofa, chair and floor.

Bright with the bursting colours of flowers, an oil hangs adjacent to a Persian kilim from Senna, and the rug is itself packed with floral motifs. On the most heavily used part of the floor carpet, a tough Balouch kilim runner has been laid as a protective strip. The model is, quite naturally, a Persian vertical loom.

Inspired by its archaeologist-owner's many years of work in Persia, this country home has been imaginatively decorated with a mix of tribal horse trappings and rugs. The south Persian horse cover is hung without a frame to facilitate a close appreciation of the multivarious textures of the weave, and a wall-mounted picture lamp subtly lights up the rich and deep colours.

(Below) Hanging as a bedroom decoration is a ceremonial ship cloth from south Sumatra. Although the room is dominated by Indonesian textiles, a brightly coloured Anatolian kilim matches well as a useful floor cover.

(Left) The bathroom can be an ideal place in which to hang textiles that are neither too fragile nor too valuable to be worried by fluctuations in temperature and humidity. On the carpeted floor is a robust Maimana kilim, while on the back of the door, a silk chapan, also from Central Asia, hangs ready for use as a dressing gown. A mirrored, quilted and appliquéd cover from Gujarat is supported on the wall without needing a frame.

(Right) On either side of the bed are two Mexican Indian copies of Navajo rugs, while at its foot is an early twentieth-century Navajo flatweave. The bed cover and cushion are both modern appliqué work from Thailand.

(Right) In this Spanish house, a 'second home' for a New York ballet dancer, a newly woven and fine quality 'reproduction' Turkish kilim looks splendid amidst the traditional furniture of the bedroom.

171

(*Above*) Lying at the foot of this metal collage is a Navajo rug from the late nineteenth-century 'transitional' period.

This is the Philadelphia home of a designer and textile collector whose roving eye selects examples from many weaving cultures with a gifted spontaneity. Here, on a small landing, a still-life arrangement of textiles and another great passion, fine art books, aesthetically link an American Indian floor rug, a Central Asian silk ikat, a wall-mounted Bolivian ponchito and, in the distance, a pair of richly decorated Sumatran tapis.

On the end wall of the cabinet-filled hallway is hung a fine example of a Third Phase woman's chief blanket. This Navajo weaving, with its expansive composition, is a stirring focus of attention at eye level in this long corridor. By contrast, the more modern Navajo floor rugs, with their formal and balanced diamond patterning, are well suited to performing the task of decorative floor coverings — that is, of blending, rather than challenging. On such a polished wooden floor, these flatwoven woollen rugs have to lie on a suitable non-slip underlay.

(Below) Clustered around this front door is a magnificent selection of decorative tribal art. The Tunisian hanbel on the floor shares a common African origin with the Tuareg saddle. The soumak and knotted bag faces and donkey bags are so robust they may simply be pinned to the wall.

(Above) Being robust and relatively inexpensive, Mexican copies of Navajo rugs may be used on the floor with impunity. In this entrance hall, the Teotitlan rug lies on underlay over wooden boards. Over the Bar Harbor chair cushions are a mixture of Guatemalan carrying-cloths and a Mexican silk and wool serape piece; their unusual colours contrast with the chilli-red ristra which hangs on the veranda in a traditional New Mexican style.

(Above) A kilim of the Qashqai nomads is finally at rest under the dining-room table of a New England country home.

(Left) A quiet, almost monastic writing and reading area to a bedroom in a Spanish house, where the robust and lively patterning of an Afghan kilim lies half obscured under the desk.

174

(Left) In this Long Island converted farmhouse, the stained and varnished wood and open brickwork of the narrow hall create a fine setting for a Persian Kurdish kilim. Tough and decorative, this kilim will withstand wear on the floor for a long while if laid on underlay and shaken vigorously from time to time to dislodge dirt and grit.

(Below) The meeting of modern and tribal art in this formal dining room is a decorative success. Hard-wearing and original, the west Afghani kilim contrasts with the delicate nature of the tabletop Batak sacred cloth from Sumatra.

Chapter Seven Collector's guide to sources and services

(Opposite) In this hallway of an eclectically furnished New York City apartment, there is a mêlée of textiles, both useful and simply decorative, from Africa and Asia. In between the Thracian kilim fragment on the floor and the Indonesian Sumban ikat on the wall, the table and seat are made colourful and comfortable with Moroccan, Tunisian and Persian flatwoven cushions.

Collecting textiles

The whole atmosphere of textile collecting has developed, in at least the past twenty years, into a highly specialized and hierarchical world of suppliers and consumers. A complex series of relationships between the activities of dealers, museums, private and corporate buyers ensures that, as in the fine art world, the netting of the finest works at the highest prices is almost always achieved. The difference, however, between this world and that of the fine art circus is that, within reason, the individual may participate without unreasonable expenditure. For the price of a new family car fresh off the assembly-line, one may build a representative collection of exquisite Bolivian alpaca mantles of the nineteenth century. A holiday in the Falklands would pay for a framed series of cut-pile raphia panels from the Congo that would bring character to any setting. By buying a robust and decorative floor covering, such as an old Tartari kilim from Afghanistan, one might have to miss out on a new dishwasher that year. By comparison with other highly lauded and traditionally 'acceptable' art forms, the old, antique and ancient textiles of the ethnographic world are ridiculously under-valued.

There are four main reasons for collecting ethnographic textiles: to meet a specific requirement — a cheerful kilim of a particular size for a dull room, perhaps; to make an investment; to add to an existing collection; and last, and least predictable, to satisfy those needs which spring from falling in love with a textile or type of textile and imagining where it may go, until, by an insidious process, one becomes unable to stop collecting and hoarding a wealth of beautiful weavings or embroideries.

For investment purposes there is no doubt that the older and finer the textile and the rarer its origin, the more valuable it may become. Not all old textiles are wonderful, for not all weavers of the past were great masters or mistresses of the loom or needle. Weaving cultures tend to pass through phases and cycles of creative development. Only when enough examples are gathered together from each era may one attempt to determine by comparison which is the finest — in academic or personal terms. If contemplating an investment in a new textile that may be the collectable of the future, then it is worth examining the fine 'facsimile' or reproduction textiles of Anatolia and Persia. Naturally dyed and woven with the patterns of their past, before Western interference, these flatweaves might well age as beautifully as their inspirational ancestors. Rooted in a more recent tradition of American Indian weaving, the fine Navajo copies from Mexico are also well worth considering.

When thinking of a textile for a particular floor or wall use, it is best to examine the quantifiable parameters of likely wear and tear, lighting, and safety if it is to be used underfoot. Armed with these provisos and with accurate measurements, suitable textiles may be sought whose prices and qualities of strength and finish should be compared. There is no way of avoiding, unfortunately, the arduous fact-finding missions to many reputable dealers. For those smitten by the textile collecting bug, you have my sympathy as a fellow sufferer. Any advice might best be expressed as 'always buy what you like, but know just what you are buying'.

Buying There is no substitute for a journey to a foreign land and a foreign culture in an attempt to appreciate their traditions. The stories and memories of the people and their often colourful and aromatic markets and bazaars are an integral part of the textile that one may buy and bring home. Unless very lucky, however, one is unlikely these days to find a textile of great rarity. Even in some lost village, such textiles will either have been destroyed by use or, if of ceremonial value will not be, or should not be, for sale. Most major cities in countries with a weaving tradition have a network of local merchants who gather interesting textiles for export, or for sale in a Western-style gallery, fine hotel or airport shop. This news should not be too depressing, however, for what can be found is an abundance of old and new textiles at reasonable prices. Do consider the possible extra costs in tax when the goods, if declared, are exported and imported. If sent independently, there will be handling and shipping charges.

Buying from a retailer or dealer in the developed world should be a rewarding experience for both parties. Ancient and antique fine textiles may be sought from highly specialized dealers, so that one may have to travel the Western world itself for a particular acquisition. These dealers are accustomed to sending high quality photographs to seriously interested parties and will give a money-back guarantee, after expenses, if a textile is purchased unseen and deemed to be unsuitable. Suppliers of antique textiles are to be found, usually in the towns and cities, throughout the West; some specialize, many have a general stock. More recently, commercially made ethnographic textiles of a useful and decorative nature are now found for sale quite cheaply in locations as varied as enlightened department stores, shops selling decorative and ethnic arts and crafts in general, and small warehouses. Whatever the source, be sure to enquire whether a trial-by-approval system is possible, as a textile in a gallery might look quite different when taken to a home environment. The cultivation of a friendship or relationship of mutual respect with a gallery owner is a wise course of action, especially when advice is needed for the building of a collection of textiles.

Buying a textile at auction can be a fun-filled experience, for there are many provincial auction houses who will sell ethnographic textiles in a general sale, or who will not have the specialist knowledge to recognize the value of an obscure weaving – often described as 'Oriental' or 'African'. Auction sales of fine collections of textiles will be well attended by dealers and collectors and one will probably have to pay a more representative market value for a textile.

Selling The best way to sell a textile is through an established auction house or, if accepted, on commission through a specialist textile dealer. Some idea of the possible value of equivalent examples might be gleaned from the pages of *Hali* magazine or from the lists of prices realized, and the catalogues of recent auctions.

Valuation A collection of textiles should be valued for insurance purposes on a regular basis. If a textile is of family origin, perhaps a legacy of a relation in the colonial or Foreign Service, and has a history as yet unknown, it is best to find out what part of the world it must have come from and, after consulting the list of specialists in this book or in *Hali*, have the textile examined and valued by the relevant specialist. A complete valuation certificate should include a colour photograph of the textile, its dimensions, source, age and value. There will be a charge for this service, usually fixed at a percentage of the valuation.

Care, repair and cleaning

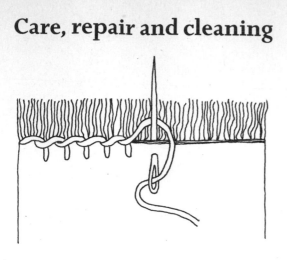

Blanket stitch oversewing to prevent unravelling of the weft – a common affliction in flatweaves

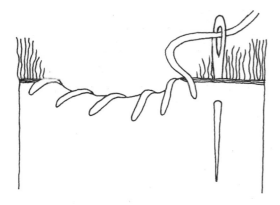

Oversewing of damage to prevent further cause for concern until professional restoration may take place

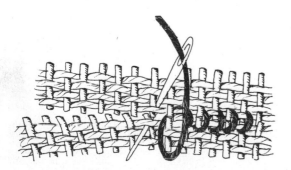

Oversewing a hole or cut in a textile – obviously complementary coloured thread of wool, silk or cotton should be used

Care Textiles will need to be cared for from the moment of acquisition, whether stored in a chest or in use on a hallway floor. A collection of textiles ought to be catalogued and this may take the form of a coded cotton tape attached to each weaving. A system may be created in a variety of ways, perhaps based on dates of purchase, or tribe of origin, or estimated year or period of weaving, or simply in sequence around the house or within a chest. These codes should cross reference with a log book that contains price, date and place of purchase, value, dimensions and notes on origin and weaving or embroidery technique information. If possible, photographic records of each textile should be made.

Textiles may be stored, rolled onto acid-free paper-wrapped cardboard tubes, in a chest, cupboard or room where extremes of temperature and humidity can be avoided. The destructive effects of daylight and electric light have been discussed in Chapter Four. Needless to say, these storage areas should be dark. Damage by insects, especially moth, may be avoided by proofing the textiles with suitable insect repellent and by examination for possible infestation at least twice a year, especially at the end of winter. Muslin bags containing solid insect repellent should be placed above but not touching the textiles. Anyone who has experienced the shock discovery of a favourite textile or textiles festooned with clothes-moth larvae will appreciate the need for preventative measures of a zealous nature. Moths like peace and quiet and a woollen textile hanging freely against a wall is a comfortable egg-laying surface. Moth proofing by spraying should be a biannual activity and moth balls should be hung in muslin bags by the structure on which the textile is hung. The nesting of mice or other small quadrupeds within a textile collection may be avoided by keeping a cat or by laying down trails of suitable poison.

Repair The techniques involved in the restoration and conservation of textiles are highly complex. It is recommended that professional advice be sought for all but the simplest of repairs to a weave and there is a selection of specialists listed at the end of this chapter. More recently made textiles that are not of great value, such as some flatweave rugs, or those that have received minor damage, should be repaired or temporarily made good with simple stitching. As long as the minor blemish of a darn is not a visual disturbance to a textile, then a cut, tear or small hole in the weave may be sewn over with needle and suitably coloured cotton or woollen thread. A common cause for concern is the unravelling of the wefts at the fringe of a textile and this may be held in check by oversewing, or with a blanket stitch. Any damage to the edge of the textile, whether at the fringe or along the selvedge, should be temporarily oversewn with suitable yarn of a matching colour. This will at least prevent the damage from spreading if the textile remains in use.

Cleaning All textiles in use will require cleaning from time to time. The frequency of this operation will depend on the nature of their use. Flatwoven textiles on the floor will need to be hoovered carefully or shaken or beaten over a line at frequent intervals to prevent the accumulation of fibre-grinding dirt and grit. The floor underneath a rug will need to be cleaned as well. Textiles draped over sofas, chairs, tables or beds will be easy to remove and shake clean from time to time. Free-hanging textiles on the wall should be taken down and the dust shaken off once or twice a year, and this will be an opportune moment to check for the dreaded moth's presence.

Many restorers and conservationists are adamant that the wet or specialist dry-cleaning of textiles should be left to the professionals. If in doubt it is better to have a grubby textile than a textile ruined by colour run; colour fastness may be ascertained by rubbing gently each and every different colour area of a textile with a slightly damp white cotton cloth. If any of the colours appear on the white cloth the textile will have to be professionally cleaned. If the colours seem to be fast then proceed to wash with caution. Cold water, very mild detergent such as good quality, colourless washing up liquid and repeated rinsing in clean water will remove most dirt. Stubborn stains may be teased with a soft nailbrush and oil or grease worked on with small quantities of hand cleanser such as motor mechanics use. Textiles should be dried flat, away from excessive heat and all sunlight; many flatweaves will need to be stretched slightly and pinned to prevent wrinkling.

The accidental spillage of liquids or foodstuffs onto a textile should be treated rapidly and with common sense. The spilt matter should be dabbed or shaken off the weave and if necessary the floor underneath covered with newspaper to absorb the residual damp and possible colour run. Large-scale saturation will necessitate the cleaning and drying of the complete textile.

Further reading

Magazines   The *Oriental Rug Review* and *Hali* , especially, are the two main periodicals covering many textile subjects. Both are available throughout the world by subscription, and *Hali* publishes a German-language supplement.

Hali Publications Ltd, Kingsgate House, Kingsgate Place, London NW6 4TA, UK Tel: 0171 328 9341

Oriental Rug Review, Beech Hill Road, Meredith, NH 03253, USA Tel: 603 279 5574

Books and catalogues   *African Art* Frank Willett, 1971

African Textiles J.Picton and J.Mack, 1979

Ancient Peruvian Textiles Ferdinand Anton, 1987

Animal Regalia Moira Broadbent, 1985

The Arts of Islam Hayward Gallery, 1976

Arts & Crafts of Rajasthan A. Nath and F. Wacziarg, 1987

Arts & Crafts of Turkestan Johannes Kalter, 1984

Aymara Weavings L.Adelson and A.Tracht, 1983

Caravans to Tartary Roland and Sabina Michaud, 1985

The Care and Preservation of Textiles K.Finch and G.Putnam, 1985

Carpet Magic Jon Thompson, 1983

Consideration for the Care of Textiles and Costumes Harold F.Mailand, 1980

Court and Village Merrily Peebles, 1981

Courtyard, Bazaar, Temple: Traditions of Textile Expression in India K.F.Hacker and K.J.Turnbull, 1982

The Craft of the Weaver A.Sutton, P.Collingwood and G. St. Aubyn Hubbard, 1982

Double–Woven Treasures from Old Peru A.Cahlender with S.Baizerman, 1985

Dowries from Kutch Vickie Elson, 1979

The Dyer's Art: Ikat, batik, plangi Jack Lenor Larsen with A.Buhler, B. and G.Solyom, 1976

Flat Woven Rugs of the World Valerie S. Justin, 1980

Flat Woven Textiles Cathryn Cootner, 1981

Folk Art of the Americas General Editor: August Panyella, 1981

From the Bosporus to Samarkand: Flat Woven Rugs A.N.Landreau and W.R.Pickering, 1969

From the Far West: Carpets and Textiles of Morocco P.L.Fiske, W.R.Pickering and R.S.Yohe (eds.), 1980

Golden Sprays and Scarlet Flowers: Traditional Indian Textiles Marie-Louise Nabholz-Kartaschoff, 1986

A History of Textile Art Agnes Geijer, 1982

Ikats from South East Asia Jonathan Hope, 1977

Ikats: Woven Silks from Central Asia The Rau Collection, 1988

Indian Costumes from Guatemala Krystyna Deuss, 1981

Indonesian Textile Techniques Michael Hitchcock, 1985

Kilim, Cicim, Zili, Sumak Belkis Balpinar Acar, 1982

Kilims Yanni Petsopoulos, 1980

Latin American Brocades: Explorations in Supplementary Weft Techniques S.Baizerman and K.Searle, 1980

Living with Kilims A.Hull and N.Barnard, 1988

Master Dyers to the World Mattiebelle Gittinger, 1982

Mola Art Capt. Kit.S.Kapp, 1972

Native Arts of North America Christian F.Feest, 1980

Nigeria's Traditional Crafts Alison Hodge, 1982

Nuristan L.Edleberg and S.Jones, 1979

Otavalo Lynn Meisch, 1987

Patchwork Pamela Clabburn, 1983

Patterned Threads: Ikat Traditions and Inspirations Lotus Stack, 1987

Patterns of Life: West African Strip–Weaving Traditions Peggy Stolz Gilfoy, 1987

Pueblo Indian Textiles Kate Peck Kent, 1983

The Primary Structure of Fabrics Irene Emery, 1980

The Qashqai of Iran Lois Beck, 1986

Shoowa Design: African Textiles from the Kingdom of Kuba Georges Meurant, 1986

Spanish American Blanketry Harry P. Mera, 1987

Splendid Symbols: Textiles and Tradition in Indonesia Mattiebelle Gittinger, 1979

The Techniques of Rug Weaving Peter Collingwood, 1976

Textile and Weaving Structures Peter Collingwood, 1987

Textiles in Archaeology John Peter Wild, 1988

Textiles of Baluchistan M.G. Konieczny, 1979

Textiles of Indonesia Indonesian Arts Society, 1976

Textiles of the Kuna Indians of Panama Herta Puls, 1988

Threads of Life: A private collection of textiles from Indonesia and Sarawak Dr Monni Adams, 1981

Threads of Tradition: Textiles of Indonesia and Sarawak Joseph Fischer, 1979

Traditional Textiles of Tunisia Irmtraud Reswick, 1985

Tribal Rugs Jenny Housego, 1978

Tribes Peter Marsh, 1988

Tulips, Arabesques and Turbans: Decorative Arts from the Ottoman Empire Y.Petsopoulos (ed.), 1982

Turkish Flat Weaves W. T. Ziemba, A.Akatay and S.L. Schwartz, 1979

The Unappreciated Dhurrie Steven Cohen; D.Black and C.Loveless (eds.), 1982

Walk in Beauty: The Navajo and their Blankets M.H.Kahlenberg and A. Berlant, 1977

The Weavers of Ancient Peru Mo Fini, 1985

Weaving Arts of the North American Indian Frederick J. Dockstader, 1977

West African Narrow Strip Weaving V. and A. Lamb, 1975

Woven Air: The Muslin & Kantha Tradition of Bangladesh Whitechapel Art Gallery, 1988

International textile collections

There are many museums and galleries worldwide with famous, rare and important ethnic textiles among their other collections. Those listed here are likely to have some of their textiles on show to the public, but particular examples or collections may have to be seen by appointment.

Australia

Australian Museum,
6-8 College Street, Sydney, New South Wales 2000

Australian National Gallery,
Canberra, ACT 2601

University Museum,
James Cook University, Townsville, Queensland 4811

Austria

Museum of Applied Art,
Stubenring 5, A-1010 Vienna

Ethnological Museum,
Ringstrassentrakt, Neue Burg, A-1014 Vienna

Canada

National Museum of Man,
Victoria & Metcalfe Streets, Ottawa, Ontario K1A 0M8

Textile Museum,
585 Bloor Street West, Toronto, Ontario M6G 1K5

France

Fondation Dapper,
50 Avenue Victor Hugo, Paris 75116

Germany

Islamische Museum,
Staatliche Museen zu Berlin, 102 Bodenstrasse 1/3, Berlin

Kestner-Museum,
Trammplatz 3, Hanover

Museum für Islamische Kunst,
Staatliche Museen Preussischer Kulturbesitz, Stauffenbergstrasse 41, Berlin 30

Museum of Ethnography,
Schaumainkai 29, 6000 Frankfurt, Hessen

Rautenstrauch-Joest-Museum
Ubierring 45, 5000 Cologne, Nordrhein-Westfalen

Hungary

Museum of Ethnography,
Konyves Kalman Korut 40, Budapest VIII

India

Calico Museum,
Ahmedabad, Gujarat

Indonesia

Municipal Museum,
Palembang, Sumatra

Provincial Museum,
Mataram, Lombok, Nusa Tenggara Barat

Textile Museum, Jakarta

Netherlands

Ethnographical Museum,
Agathaplein 4, 2611 HR, Delft

Museum of Geography & Ethnography,
Willemskade 25, 3016 DM, Rotterdam

Museum of the Tropics,
Linnaeusstraat 2, 1092 AD, Amsterdam

National Museum of Ethnography,
Steenstraat 1, 2300 AE, Leiden

Poland

Asia and Pacific Museum,
ul Nalczowska 40, Warsaw

Turkey

Bursa Turkish & Islamic Art Museum,
Bursa

Mevlana Museum,
Konya

Topkapi Sarayi Muzesi,
Istanbul

United Kingdom

Fitzwilliam Museum,
Trumpington Street, Cambridge CB2 1RB

Horniman Museum & Library,
London Road, Forest Hill, London SE23 3PQ

Museum of Mankind,
Burlington Gardens, London W1

Petrie Museum of Egyptian Archaeology,
University College London, Gower Street, London WC1E 6BT

Pitt Rivers Museum,
South Parks Road, Oxford, Oxfordshire OX1 3PP

Royal Scottish Museum,
Chambers Street, Edinburgh EH1 1JF

Victoria & Albert Museum,
Cromwell Road, London SW7

Whitworth Art Gallery,
University of Manchester, Oxford Road, Manchester M15 6ER

United States of America

American Museum of Natural History,
79th Street and Central Park West, New York, NY 10024

Boston Museum of Fine Arts,
Boston, MA 02115

William Hayes Fogg Art Museum,
Harvard University, Cambridge, MA 02138

Metropolitan Museum of Art,
Fifth Avenue, New York, NY 10028

Peabody Museum of Archaeology and Ethnology,
11 Divinity Avenue, Cambridge, MA 02138

Smithsonian Institution,
1000 Jefferson Drive SW, Washington D.C. 20560

Textile Museum,
2320 S Street NW, Washington D.C. 20008

University Museum,
University of Philadelphia, 33rd & Spruce, Philadelphia, PA 19104

M. H. de Young Memorial Museum,
Golden Gate Park, San Francisco, CA 94118

International auction houses

Many auction houses will value and sell textiles, often in biannual or more frequent specialist auctions, and many have branches in other countries and in provincial towns.

France

Ader Picard Tajan
12 Rue Favart, Paris 75002
Tel: 42 61 80 07

Germany

Ketterer
Brienner Strasse 25, D – 8000 Munich 2
Tel: 089 591181

Rippon Boswell
Friedrichstrasse 45, D – 6200 Wiesbaden
Tel: 06121 372062

Switzerland

Galerie Koller
Ramistrasse 8, 8024 Zurich
Tel: 01 475040

Ineichen
C.F. Meyerstrasse 14, 8002 Zurich
Tel: 01 2013017

United Kingdom

Christie's
8 King St., St. James's, London SW1Y 6QT
Tel: 0171 839 9060

Phillips
7 Blenheim St., London W1Y OAS
Tel: 0171 629 6602

Sotheby's
34/35 New Bond St., London W1A 2AA
Tel: 0171 493 8080

United States of America

Butterfield and Butterfield
220 San Bruno Avenue, San Francisco CA 94103
Tel: 415 861 7500

Christie's East
219 East 67th St, New York, NY 10021
Tel: 212 606 0400

Grogan & Company
890 Commonwealth Avenue, Boston MA 02215
Tel: 617 266 4200

Phillips
406 East 79th St, New York, NY 10021
Tel: 212 570 4830

Robert W. Skinner
Route 117, Boston, MA 01451
Tel: 617 779 5528

Sotheby's
1334 York Avenue, New York, NY 10021
Tel: 212 606 7000

Dealers, importers and services

In this section, the names and addresses of textile dealers from all over the world are listed, together with the services they offer (e.g. cleaning and repairing) and the kinds of textiles stocked. Obviously it is not possible to list everybody, but we have tried to give details of well-established houses and traders, as well as some more unusual and specialist galleries and businesses. It is advisable to call before you visit a dealer or showroom – some are only available by appointment, and it is always worth checking opening times.

Key to services and types of textiles stocked:

Imp.	Importer	N Am.	North America
Ret.	Retailer	S Am.	South America
W.	Wholesaler	N Af.	North Africa
Manu	Manufacturer	Africa	Africa
Rep.	Repairs	Anat.	Anatolia
A.	Antique	Cauc.	Caucasus
O.	Old	Pers.	Persia
N.	New	Afgh.	Afghanistan
		India	Indian subcontinent
		Indon.	Indonesia
		World	World

Australia

Nazar Rug Galleries Pty Ltd,
583 Military Road, Mosman,
New South Wales 2088
Tel: 02 9692659/ 02 3311505
Imp. Ret. W. Rep.; A.O.N.; Anat. Cauc. Pers. Afgh.
A well-established business which does expert repairs and valuations.

Austria

Herbert Bieler
Erlaufstrasse 25/8, A – 2344 Ma. Enzerdorf
Tel: 0223 623 9562
Imp. Ret.; A.O.; Anat.
Two exhibitions per year of primarily old and antique kilims, and domestic weavings.

Hannes Boesch,
Hans Sachs Gasse 7, A – 8010 Graz,
Tel: 0316 78730
Ret. Rep.; A.O.; Anat. Cauc. Pers. Afgh.

Galerie Safor,
Naglergasse 29, A – 1010 Vienna
Tel: 01 533 3289
Ret. W.; A.O.; Anat. Cauc. Pers.
Dealing with outstanding and antique carpets and kilims.

Galerie Sailer,
Wiener Philharmonikergasse 3, A – 5020 Salzburg
Tel: 662 846483
Imp. Ret. Rep.; A; World
Only antique kilims, Oriental tapestries, North American Indian textiles.

Beate von Hartem,
Burggasse 24/12, A – 1070 Vienna
Tel: 01 933 0493
Expert repairs.

Belgium

Coppens Tribal Art,
Grote Peperstraat 69, 2700 Sint-Niklaas (Antwerp)
Tel: 03 776 99 39
Imp. Ret. W.; A.; Indon. Africa
Fifteen years' experience importing and specializing
in Borneo and Sumatran textiles.

Geert Keppens
Ruilare 54, B – 9130 Zeveneken, Lokeren
Tel: 091 559 617
Imp. Ret. W. Rep.; A.O.; Anat. Cauc. Pers. Afgh.
Travels frequently to Middle East and Central Asia
collecting unique kilims, carpets and ethnographica.

Etienne Roland,
Noville Les Bois, B – 5068 Fernelmont
Tel: 328 183 4005
Imp. W.; A.O.; Anat. Cauc. Pers.
A selection for collectors, antique dealers, decorators
and interior designers.

Herman Vermeulen,
Kraanlei 3, B - 9000 Gent
Tel: 091 24 38 34
Imp. Ret. W. Rep.; A.O.; Anat. Cauc. Pers.
More than twelve years travelling experience in
Anatolia.

Canada

Country Furniture,
3097 Granville, Vancouver V6H 3J9
Tel: 604 738 6411
Ret.; O.N.
Accessories and trifles for the selective shopper.

Frida Crafts
39, Front St East, Toronto, Ontario M5E 1B3
Tel: 416 366 3169
Ret.; O.N.
Handicrafts from Africa, Latin America and Asia,
including new kilims.

Sharanel Inc.,
763 Woodbine Ave, Toronto, Ontario M4E 2J4
Tel: 416 694 1399
Imp. Ret. W.; O.N.; Afgh.
Travels to Central Asia to buy, sells to trade and retail.

Vernacular,
1130 Yonge St, Toronto, Ontario M4W 2L8
Tel: 416 961 6490
Ret.; O.N.
Specializing in kilims, masks, tribal arts and textiles.

Woven Gardens,
1451 Sherbrooke St West, Montreal H3G 2W4
Tel: 514 937 6273
Ret,; O.N.
Wide selection of floor coverings, kilims, ethnic and
antique artefacts.

France

Apamée,
3 Rue Maître Albert, 75005 Paris
Tel: 46 34 04 40
Imp. Ret.; A.; Anat. Cauc. Pers. Afgh.
Antique kilims and carpets.

L'art Turkmene,
26 Rue Auguste Comte, Lyons 69002
Tel: 78 38 21 54
Imp. Ret. W. Rep.; A.O.; Anat. Pers. Afgh.

Haga,
22 Rue de Grenelle, 75007 Paris
Tel: 42 22 82 40
Ret.; A.; World
Textiles of the Orient and Europe a speciality.

Galerie AK Kurt,
72 Rue du Cherche-Midi, 75006 Paris
Tel: 42 22 10 49
Imp. Ret.; O.N.; Anat. Pers.
The owners visit Turkey each year to buy kilims,
carpets and textiles.

Galerie Kartir,
11 Rue Bonaparte, 75006 Paris
Tel: 43 26 90 28
Imp. Ret. W.; A.O.; Pers.
Art and textiles of the Middle East.

Galerie Triff,
35 Rue Jacob, 75006 Paris
Tel: 42 60 22 60
Ret.; O.A.N.; Anat. Cauc. Pers.

Gerard Hadjer,
22 Rue Drouot, 75009 Paris
Tel: 48 24 96 67
Imp. Ret. W. Rep.; O.A.N.; Anat. Cauc. Pers.
Dealer in arts and textiles.

Germany

Galerie Antiker Kunst,
Oberstrasse 110, 2000 Hamburg 13,
Tel: 040 45 50 60
Ret.; A.
Fine dealer in ancient art including Coptic textiles.
By appointment.

Peter Hoffmeister,
Rosenauer Strasse 20,
D – 96487 Dörfles-Esbach,
Tel: 09561 54343
Rep.

Koken,
Esslingerstrasse 14, 7000 Stuttgart
Tel: 0711 233416
Imp. Ret.; A.O.N.; Anat. Pers. Afgh.
Handwoven home furnishings from Anatolia through
to the East.

Ilona-Marie L. Lemberg-Richtermeier,
Atelier und Werkstatte, Schulterblatt 1,2000
Hamburg 6
Tel: 040 439 15 26
Rep.; A.; S Am.
Restoration and conservation of Coptic and pre-
Colombian textiles. Maxim is 'Sew, not glue'.

Galerie Mashallah,
Schellingstrasse 52, 8000 Munich 40
Tel: 089 272 3623
Imp. Ret.; A.O.N.; Anat. Pers. Afgh.
The same company as Koken.

Galerie Neiriz,
Kurfürstendamm 75, 1000 Berlin 15
Tel: 030 882 3232
Imp. Ret. W. Rep.; A.; Anat. Cauc. Pers.
A private kilim collector who sells antique pieces in
four exhibitions each year.

Galerie Ostler,
Ludwigstrasse 11, D – 8000 Munich 22
Tel: 089 285 669
Ret. W.; A.; Anat. Pers.
Their focus is weaving as art.

Alfred Walter,
Cremon 35, Hamburg 11
Tel: 040 2802306
Handwashing, restoration and conservation.

Holland

D.W. Kinebanian,
Heiligeweg 35, Amsterdam
Tel: 020 267019
Ret. W.; A.O.; Anat. Cauc. Pers. Afgh.
Traditional family business specializing in antique and
old kilims and carpets.

Saskia Wessel,
Overtoom 19, Amsterdam
Imp. Ret.; A.O.N. Afgh.
A collector and retailer of ethnographica from Asia.

Italy

The Carpet Studio,
Via Monalda 15/R, 50123 Florence
Tel: 055 211423
Ret.; A.; all but mostly Anat.
Primarily specialists in antique carpets and textiles,
but does have small selection of kilims.

Luciano Coen,
65 Via Margutta, 00187 Rome
Tel: 06 678 3235/679 0321
Ret.; A.; Anat. Cauc. Pers.
Stocks a few and very selected antique kilims. His
Swiss wife speaks fluent English and German.

Eskenazi,
15 Via Montenapoleone, 20121 Milan.
Tel: 02 700020
Ret.; A.O.; Anat. Cauc. Pers.
Dealer and exhibition organizer in rugs, kilims and
textiles from Asia.

Ghalibaf,
40 Corso Vittorio Emanuele, Turin
and 19 Via Cavour, Alessandria
Tel: 011 539303/531146
Imp. Ret. Rep.; A.O.; Anat. Cauc. Pers.
A large choice of antique and prestigious carpets and
kilims.

Kilim Arte & Antichita,
Via Fama 15, 37121 Verona
Ret.; A.O.
Kilims and textiles.

The Kilim Gallery,
Via di Panico 8, 00186 Rome
Tel: 06 68 68 963
Imp. Ret.; A.O.N.; Anat. Cauc. Pers.
Kilim specialist.

Il Mercante D'Oriente,
Corso S Anastasia 34, 37121 Verona
Tel: 045 594 152
Ret. Rep.; A.O.N.; Anat. Cauc. Pers.
Buys and sells tribal and village textiles.

Daniele Sevi,
6 Via Fiori Chiari, 20121 Milan
Tel: 02 87 61 69
Ret.; A.O.; Anat. Cauc. Pers.
Carpets, rugs, and kilims; also European carpets.

Dario Valcarenghi,
6 Via F. Corridoni, Milan
Tel: 02 54 83 811
Imp. Ret.; A.O.; Anat.
A large collection of antique and old kilims.

Portugal

De Natura,
162a Rua da Rosa, 1200 Lisbon
Tel: 1 366081
Imp. Ret.; A.O.N.; Anat. Cauc. Pers. Afgh.
A gallery selling fine oriental art and kilims.

Spain

Puerto Galera,
Dr. Roux, 30, Torre, Barcelona 17
Tel: 3 205 05 12

Sweden

J. P. Willborg AB,
Sibyllegatan 41, 114 42 Stockholm
Tel: 08 7830265/7830365
Imp. Ret. W. Rep.; A.; Anat. Cauc. Pers.
Antique textile gallery.

Switzerland

Alt Amerika, Arts Primitifs
Neumarkt 21, 8001 Zurich
Tel: 01 251 9118
Ret.; A.O.; S Am. Africa
African and old Peruvian textiles and objects.

Djahan Orientteppiche,
Freilagerstrasse 47, Zollfreilager, CH 8043 Zurich
Tel: 01 491 9797
Imp. W.; A.O.N.; Anat. Cauc. Pers.
A well-established firm renowned for their great collection of kilims.

Galerie Kistler Dekor KI AG,
Bernstrasse 11, 3250 Lyss
Tel: 032 81 44 33
Imp. Ret. W.; A.O.; Anat. Cauc. Pers. Afgh.
Nomadic art gallery.

Graf & Raaflaub AG/Ltd,
Rheingasse 31/33, 4005 Basel
Tel: 061 25 33 40
Imp. Ret. Rep.; A.; Anat. Cauc. Pers.

Nomadenschätze,
Weyrmuhle, 5630 Muri/AG

Tel: 057 44 42 18
and at Kirchgasse 36, 8001 Zurich
Tel: 01 252 5500
Imp. Ret.; A.O.; Anat. Pers. Afgh.
Tribal flatweaves, rugs, textiles and jewelry.

Ali Shirazi
Zollfreilager Block 1, Kabin 337, Postfach 159,
CH 8043 Zurich
Tel: 01 493 1108
Imp. W.; A.O.; Pers. Afgh.
A collection of unusual nomadic pieces.

Teppich Stettler AG,
Amthausgasse 1, 3011 Bern
Tel: 031 21 03 33
Imp. Ret. Rep.; O.N.; Anat. Cauc. Pers. Afgh.
An enterprise specializing in nomadic and cottage rugs, kilims and bags.

United Kingdom

Aaron Gallery,
34 Bruton Street, London W1X 7DD
Tel: 0171 499 9434/5
Imp. Ret. W.; A.O.N.
Islamic and ancient art.

Meg Andrews Antique Costumes & Textiles,
28 Cowper Rd, Harpenden,
Herts AL5 5NG
Tel: 01582 460 107
Ret.; A.; World
Decorative embroidered, woven and printed hangings.

J. L. Arditi,
88 Bargates, Christchurch, Dorset BH23 1QP
Tel: 01202 485414
Ret. Rep.; A.O.N.; Anat. Cauc. Pers.
Old Oriental rugs, runners and kilims bought and sold, cleaning and restoration service.

Nathan Azizollahoff,
Oriental Carpet Centre
Top Floor, Bldg. A
105 Eade Road
London N4 1TJ
Tel: 0181 802 0077
Imp. W.; A.O.N.; Anat. Cauc. Pers. Afgh.
Traders in antique kilims, and direct importers of new kilims from Persia, Afghanistan and Turkey.

Sara Bamford,
The Workhouse,
Presteigne Industrial Estate,
Powys, LD8 2UF
Tel: 01544 267849
Ret. Rep.; A.O.; Anat. Cauc. Pers. Afgh.
Restorers, cleaners and repairers with an interesting collection of rugs and kilims.

Benardout & Benardout,
7 Thurloe Place, London SW7 2RX
Tel: 0171 584 7658
Ret. W.; A.O.; Anat. Cauc.
Antique and semi-antique Oriental carpets and rugs, European textiles.

David Black Oriental Carpets,
96 Portland Road, London W11 4LN
Tel: 0171 727 2566
Ret. Rep.; A.N.; Anat. Cauc. Pers.
Long-established collector and dealer of antique kilims and dhurries. Author and publisher of many books on kilims and textiles.

Chandni Chowk,
1 Harlequins, Paul Street, Exeter, Devon EX4 3TT
Tel: 01392 410201
Imp. Ret. W.; A.O.N.; Anat. Pers. Afgh. India. Indon.
A comprehensive gallery of old tribal art.

Coats Oriental Carpets,
4 Kensington Church Walk, London W8 4NB
Tel: 0171 937 0983
Ret. Rep.; A.; Anat. Cauc. Pers. Afgh.
A small specialist shop dealing in the more rare and esoteric examples of village and tribal weaving.

de Quorum Lifestyle,
11 Colville Terrace, London W11 2BE
Imp. W.; N.; India
Twice yearly collections of decorative Indian hangings and rugs; made-to-order service available.

Fantasia Designs,
20A Conduit Mews, London W2 3RE
Tel: 0171 402 6278/370 0917
Imp. W.; O.N.; India
Importer of old and new Indian decorative textiles.

Christopher Farr Handmade Rugs,
115 Regents Park Road, Primrose Hill,
London NW1 8UR
Tel: 0171 916 7690
Ret.; A.N.; Anat. India. Africa
Decorative and useful, antique and new rugs and textiles a speciality.

John Gillow Oriental Textiles,
50 Gwydir Street, Cambridge CB1 2LL
Tel: 01223 313 803
Imp. Ret.; A.O.N.; India. Indon.
Peripatetic for six months a year in South and South-East Asia, collecting textiles, especially embroideries.

Graham & Green,
4 Elgin Crescent, London W11 2JA
Tel: 0171 727 4594
Ret.; A.O.N.; World
An eclectic selection of beautiful objects from all over the world.

Joss Graham Oriental Textiles,
10 Eccleston St., London SW1W 9LT
Tel: 0171 730 4370
Imp. Ret.; A.O.; World
Specialist in Indian, Central Asian, Middle Eastern and African textiles.

David Hartwright Ltd,
Unit 15c, Farm Lane Trading Centre, 101 Farm Lane,
London SW6 1QJ
Tel: 0171 381 3276
Rep.; A.O.N.; World
Cleans and restores all types of textiles.

J. P. J. Homer Oriental Rugs,
'Stoneleigh', Parabola Road, Cheltenham, Glos
GL50 3BD
Tel: 01242 234243
Ret. Rep.; A.O.; Pers.
Sale and repair of antique rugs, saddlebags, runners
and occasionally kilims.

Jonathan Hope,
20 Roland Gardens, London SW7 3PH
Tel: 0171 373 3704
Imp. Ret.; A.O.; Indon.
A well-known specialist in Indonesian and other
textiles. Open by appointment.

Paul Hughes,
3A Pembridge Square, London W2 4EW
Tel: 0171 243 8598
Imp. Ret. W. Manu. Rep.; A.O.N.; S Am. Africa, Indon.
Specalizes in ancient textiles as well as more contemporary West African and Congo weavings. Open by
appointment.

Tessa Hughes,
Denmark Lodge, Crescent Grove, London SW4 7AG
Tel: 0171 627 2145
A.; India
Private dealer open by appointment.

Alastair Hull,
The Old Mill, Haddenham, Ely, Cambs CB6 3TA
Tel: 01353 740577
Imp. Ret. W.; O.N.; Pers. Afgh. Indon.
Travels frequently to Afghanistan buying kilims to
sell from his home and from exhibitions and tribal
art galleries.

Kathryn Jordan,
19 Bailbrook Lane, Swainswick, Bath BA1 7AH
Tel: 01225 331858
Rep.; A.O.N.; World
Restoration, conservation, cleaning, estimates and
advice.

Alexander Juran & Co.,
74 Bond Street, London W1Y 9DD
Tel: 0171 629 2550/493 4484
Ret. Rep.; A.O.
Long-established and reliable Oriental carpet dealers.

The Kilim & Nomadic Rug Gallery,
5 Shepherds Walk, London NW3 5UE
Tel: 0171 435 8972
Ret. Rep.; A.O.; Anat. Pers.
A dealer who travels extensively around Anatolia
seeking old and unusual kilims.

The Kilim Warehouse
28A Pickets St., London SW12 8QB
Tel: 0181 675 3122
Imp. Ret. W. Rep.; A.O.N.; Anat. Cauc. Pers, Afgh.
A well-known importer of Anatolian kilims, with an
interesting gallery in an unusual location.

Alison Kingsbury
No 1 Lodge, Great Hampden, Great Missenden,
Bucks, HP16 9RD
Tel: 01494 488571
Repairs carried out personally by experienced trained
weaver.

Christopher Legge Oriental Carpets,
25 Oakthorpe Road, Summertown, Oxford,
Oxon OX2 7BD
Tel: 01865 57572
Imp. Ret. W. Rep.; A.O.N.; Anat. Pers. Afgh.
Buyers and sellers of all types of Oriental rugs, also
offering valuation and cleaning services.

Liberty plc,
210/220 Regent Street, London W1R 6AH
Tel: 0171 734 1234
Ret.; A.O.N.; S Am. Anat. Pers. Afgh. India. Indon.
A well-known store.

Martin & Frost,
130 McDonald Road,
Edinburgh EH7 4NN
Tel: 0131 557 8787
Ret. Rep.; O.N.; Anat. Afgh.
Quality house-furnishers with a specialized Oriental
rug and carpet department with knowledgeable staff.

Moroccan Rugs and Weavings,
5A Calabria Road, London N5 1JB
Tel: 0171 226 7908
Imp.; A.O.N.; N Af.
Viewing by appointment. 5-day exhibitions twice a
year.

M & M Oriental Gallery Ltd,
Block D, 4th Floor, 53–79 Highgate Road,
London NW5 1TL
Tel: 0171 267 5973
Imp. W.; A.N.; Cauc. Pers. Afgh.
Traders in antique kilims, and direct importers of
new kilims from Persia and Afghanistan.

The Odiham Gallery,
78 High St., Odiham, Hants RG25 1LN
Tel: 01256 703415
Imp. Ret. Rep.; A.O.N.; Anat. Cauc. Pers. Afgh.
Specialist in rugs and kilims for interiors; an empha-
sis on colour and design as opposed to rarity.

Orientis,
Digby Road, Sherborne, Dorset DT9 3NL
Tel: 01935 816 479/813 274
Ret. Rep.; A.O.N.; Anat. Pers. Afgh.
Oriental textiles and costumes.

Indar Pasricha Fine Arts,
22 Connaught Street, London W2 2AF
Tel: 0171 724 9541
Ret.; A.; Anat. Pers. India
Islamic fine arts.

Rau,
36 Islington Green, London N1 8DU
Tel: 0171 359 5337
Imp. Ret.; A.O.; Pers. Afgh.
A long-established collector and traveller.

The Read Molteno Gallery
Nomads House, High Street,
Stockbridge, Hants SO20 6HE
Tel: 01264 810888
Ret.; O.N.; Anat. Pers. Afgh. India. Indon.
An exciting tribal and folk art gallery.

Rufus Reade,
21 St. Leonards Lane, Edinburgh EH8 9SH
Tel: 0131 662 1612
Imp. Ret.; O.N.; Anat.
An Anatolian kilim exhibitor.

Gordon Reece Gallery,
Finkle St., Knaresborough, Yorks HG5 8AA
Tel: 01423 866219/866502
Ret. Rep.; O.N.; Anat. Cauc. Pers. Afgh.
An ethnic gallery with eight different exhibitions
each year, and a large permanent kilim stock.

Clive Rogers Oriental Rugs,
22 Brunswick Road, Hove, Brighton, Sussex BN3 1DG
Tel: 01273 738257
Imp. Ret. W. Rep.; A.O.N.; Anat. Cauc. Pers. Afgh.
Carpet and kilim dealer, importing new, natural-dyed
Anatolian rugs. International commission agent,
valuations and restorations.

Philippa Scott,
30 Elgin Crescent, London W11 2JR
Tel: 0171 229 8029
Ret.; A.; N Af. Anat. Pers. India
Collector and writer who deals and consults privately.
Open by appointment.

David Seyfried,
759 Fulham Road, London SW6 5UU
Tel: 0171 823 3848
Kilim-covered floor stools and furniture.

Ron Simpson Textiles,
Tel: 0171 727 0983
Ret.; A.; N Am. India
Antique and decorative textiles. Collector and orga-
nizer of exhibitions of textiles.

Robert Stephenson,
1 Eylstan St., London SW3 3NT
Tel: 0171 584 8724
Ret.; A.O.; Anat. Pers.
Specializes in antique kilims, and decorative kilims
from the Balkans and Eastern Europe. Also cushions
and kilim-upholstered furniture.

Thames Carpet Cleaners Ltd,
48–56 Reading Road, Henley-on-Thames,
Oxon RG9 1AG
Tel: 01491 574676
Ret. Rep.; A.O.
Specialist in cleaning and restoration of Oriental rugs,
tapestries and silks.

Lynda Wrigglesworth Chinese Textiles,
34 Brook St, London W1Y 1YA
Tel: 0171 408 0177
Ret.; A.; China
Specialist dealer in antique Chinese court costumes
and textiles.

United States of America

Adraskand Inc.,
15 Ross Avenue, San Anselmo, CA 94960
Tel: 415 459 1711
Ret. Rep.; A.O.N.; Anat. Cauc. Pers. Afgh.
Sales and exhibitions of antique tribal and village rugs,
kilims and textiles. Has stock of new but traditional
Anatolian kilims.

Amatulli Importer Inc.,
568 Main Avenue, Norwalk, CT 06851
Tel: 203 849 1400
Imp. Ret. W.; A.O.N.; Anat.
A vertically integrated Oriental rug company

Amerind Art Inc.,
1304 12th Street, Santa Monica, CA 90401
Tel: 213 395 5678
Ret. A.; N Am.
Run by the private dealer and collector of Navajo
textiles Tony Berlant, co-author of *Walk in Beauty*.

Anahita Gallery,
P.O. Box 1305, Santa Monica, CA 90406
Imp.; A.O.; Afgh.
Direct importer of Central Asian textiles, kilims, art
and jewelry. Obscure collector's kilims a speciality.

R. Anavian & Sons,
942 1st Avenue, New York, NY 10022
Tel: 212 879 1234
Ret. W. Rep.; A.O.; Anat. Cauc. Pers. Afgh.
Dealers in fine Oriental rugs, kilims and antique
textiles.

Michaels Andrews Antique Oriental Rugs,
2301 Bay St #302, San Francisco, CA 94123
Tel: 415 931 5088
Ret. W.; A.; S Am. Anat. Pers.
Open by appointment.

Antique Carpet Gallery,
533 S.E. Grand Avenue, Portland, OR 97214
Tel: 503 234 1345
Ret. W. Rep.; A.O.; World
A gallery specializing in old and antique pieces, with
an emphasis on natural dyes and good condition.

The Antique & Decorative Textile Company,
254 West 73rd Street, New York, NY10023
Tel: 212 787 0090
Ret.; A.; S Am. Anat. Pers. India
Run by Frank Ames, author of *The Kashmir Shawl*. Open
by appointment.

Jeff Appleby
Rt 3, Box 470 A/,100 Cortez Place, Escondido, CA
92025
Tel: 619 480 4455
Ret.; A.; S Am. Indon.
Rare textiles to be seen by appointment.

Ariana Oriental Rugs,
211 King St, Alexandria, VA 22314
Tel: 703 683 3206
Fine antique and semi-antique rugs, textiles, kilims
and jewelry.

Asia Minor Inc.,
801 Lexington Avenue, New York, NY 10021
Tel: 212 223 2288
Imp. W; A.O.N.
Primarily kilim dealers, also selling carpets and
tapestry.

J.R. Azizollahoff,
303 Fifth Avenue, Suite 701, New York, NY 10016
Tel: 212 689 5396
Ret. W.; A.O.N.; Anat.
A dealer and consultant in mainly vegetable-dyed
Anatolian carpets and kilims.

Bellas Artes,
Canyon Road, Santa Fé, NM
Tel: 505 983 2745
Ret.; A.O.; World
An interesting gallery juxtaposing contemporary fine
arts and crafts with decorative textiles.

Berbere Imports,
144 South Robertson Boulevard, Los Angeles, CA
90048
Tel: 213 274 7064
Imp. Ret. W. Rep.; A.O.N.; Anat. Cauc. Pers. Afgh.
Importers of rugs and kilims whose distinguishing
features are truly ethnic design, colour and weave,
and large size.

Steve Berger Bolivian Weavings,
904 Irving Street #220, San Francisco, CA 94122
Tel: 415 753 0342
Ret.; A.; S Am.
A large and historic collection of Bolivian textiles may
be seen by appointment.

David Bernstein Fine Art,
737 Park Avenue, Appt 11B, New York, NY 10021
Tel: 212 794 0389
Ret.; A., S Am. Africa, Indon.

James W. Blackmon Antique Textiles,
PO Box 25, Olema, CA 94950
Tel: 415 669 7411
Imp. Ret. Rep.; A.; S Am. Africa. Anat. Pers.
Appraises, lectures on, cleans, conserves and sells
antique textiles.

Jacques Carcanagues, 21 Green Street, New York, NY
10012
Tel: 212 431 3116
Imp. Ret. W.; A.O.N.; Anat. Pers. Afgh.

Douglas Dawson Gallery,
814N Franklin, Chicago, IL 60610
Tel: 312 751 1961
Imp. W.; A.O.; World

Folklorica – NYC,
89 Fifth Avenue, New York, NY 10003
Tel: 212 255 2525
Imp. Ret.; W.; A.O.N.; S Am. Africa. Indon.
A gallery of primitive art.

Cora Ginsberg,
819 Madison Ave 1A, New York, NY 10021
Tel: 212 744 1352
Ret.; A.
Antique costumes and textiles from America and
Asia. Open by appointment.

Renate Halpern Galleries Inc.,
325 E 79th Street, New York, NY 10021
Tel: 212 988 9316
Ret.; A.O.; World
Open by appointment only.

Jonathan S. Hill Ethnic Textiles,
PO Box 40616, San Francisco, CA 94110
Tel: 415 647 9399
Imp. Ret. W.; A.O.; S Am.
Textiles of the Andes and Himalayas.

Indian Art Center,
Box 2560, Gallup, NM 87305
Tel: 505 863 6948
Ret. W.; O.N.; N Am.
South-West American Indian arts and crafts.

Interwerks,
PO Box 7417, Dallas TX 75209
Tel: 214 521 8544
W.; A.O.N.; Anat.
Direct wholesaler to interior designers and architects.

Jerrehian Brothers
25 Station Road, Haverford, PA 19041
Tel: 215 896 0900
Ret. Rep.; A.O.N.; Anat. Pers.

Stephen King Oriental Rugs,
Boston Design Center, 660 Summer St., Boston, MA
02210
Tel: 617 426 3302
W.; A.O.; Anat. Cauc. Pers. Afgh.
Sales through designers and architects of antique and
new carpets and kilims.

Kilim,
150 Thompson St, New York, NY 10012
Tel: 212 533 1677
Imp. Ret.; A.O.; Anat. Cauc. Pers.
Specialists in old and antique kilims, saddlebags,
prayer kilims, runners and tribal kilims in all sizes.

Maqam/ Dennis R. Dodds,
PO Box 4312, Graver's Lane, Philadelphia, PA 19118
Tel: 215 438 7873
Ret.; A.; Anat. Pers.
Author, lecturer and dealer in antique textiles.

Krikor Markarian,
151 West 30th St, Room 801, New York, NY 10001
Tel: 212 629 8683
W. Rep.; A.O.; Anat. Cauc. Pers.
Small and room-size antique collectable rugs and
kilims, and restoration and hand-cleaning service.

Martin & Ullman Artweave Textile Gallery,
310 Riverside Drive, New York, NY 10025
Tel: 212 864 3550
Ret. Rep. W.; A.; World
Specialists in ancient textiles who also conserve and
mount textiles. Open by appointment.

Marian Miller Kilims,
148 East 28th St., New York, NY 10016
Tel: 212 685 7746
Imp. Ret. W.; A.N.; Anat. Cauc. Pers.
Antique kilims, with a selection of new Anatolian
kilims.

Stephen A. Miller Oriental Rugs Inc.,
212 Galisteo St, Santa Fe, NM 87501
Tel: 505 983 8231
Ret. Rep.; A.O.N.; Anat. Cauc. Pers. Afgh.
Comprehensive selection in all sizes, representing
major weaving centres of the world.

Mohr Textile Arts,
125 Cedar Street, New York, NY10006
Tel: 212 227 1779
Ret.; A.O.; World (not N Am.)
Open by appointment.

Mokotoff Asian Arts,
Place des Antiquaires, Gallery #88, 125 E 57th Street,
New York, NY 10022 – 2209
Tel: 212 751 2280
Ret.; A.; Africa. India
Primarily Chinese textile dealer.

Mount Vernon Antiques,
Box 66, Rockport, Massachusetts
Tel: 508 546 2434
Ret. Rep. W.; A.; N Am.
Specializes in quilts, hooked rugs and clothing.

O'Bannon Oriental Carpets
5666 Northumberland St, Pittsburgh, PA 15217
Tel: 412 422 0300
Ret.; A.O.N.; Anat. Cauc. Pers. Afgh.
A personal interest in village rugs from Anatolia, but
try to offer the best available from all rug-producing
areas.

Obatu – Afshar Inc.,
311 West Superior, Suite 309, Chicago, IL 60610
Tel: 312 943 1189
Ret.; A.O.; Pers.
A gallery for kilims, specializing in antique and old
flatweaves from Persia.

James Opie Oriental Rugs Inc.,
214 SW Stark St, Portland, OR 97204
Tel: 503 226 0116
Ret.; A.; Pers.
South Persian weavings and kilims have long been
the speciality of this store.

Origins,
135 San Francisco Street, Santa Fe, NM 87501
Tel: 505 988 2323
Imp. Ret.; A.O.N.; World
A gallery of folk art to fantasy.

The Pillowry – New York,
132 East 61st St, New York, NY 10021
Tel: 212 308 1630
Imp. Ret. W. Rep.; A.O.; Anat. Cauc. Pers. Afgh.
A world-wide collection of kilims, rugs, needlepoint,
trappings and textiles. Specialists in work on
upholstery, hassocks and pillows.

The Pillowry Company,
9006 Melrose Avenue, West Hollywood, CA 90069
Imp. W.; A.O.; Anat. Cauc. Pers. Afgh.
A collection of flatweaves, Navajo rugs, saddlebags,
ethnic and formal textiles, and pillows.

Robertson African Arts,
36 W 22nd Street,
New York, NY 10010
Tel: 212 675 4045
Ret. W.; O.; Africa

The Rug Collectors Gallery,
2460 Fairmont Boulevard, Cleveland Heights, OH
44106
Tel: 216 721 9333
Ret.; A.O.; Anat. Cauc. Pers. Afgh.
Specialists in fine, old and antique rugs and kilims
with artistic merit.

Sakrisabz,
Penn's Market, Rt 202, Old York Road Store, No. 20,
Lahaska, Pennsylvania
Tel: 215 794 3050
Imp. Ret. W.; A.; Afgh.
Direct importers of antique kilims, textiles, brasswork
and carvings from Central Asia.

Shaver Ramsey Oriental Galleries,
2414 East Third Avenue, Denver, CO 80206
Tel: 303 320 6363
Imp. Ret.; A.O.N.; Anat. Pers. Afgh.
A vast collection of kilims, from antique, classic and
collectable, to the more modern and decorative.

Paul S. Shepard,
3026 E. Broadway, Tucson, AZ 85716
Tel: 602 326 4852
Ret. W.; N Am.
Pre-Colombian and American Indian textiles.

Mark Shilen Gallery,
201 Prince Street, New York, NY 10012
Tel: 212 777 3370
Ret.; A.O.; Anat. Pers. Afgh.
All types of tribal weavings, but strong emphasis on
kilims.

Silkroute,
3119 Fillmore St., San Francisco, CA 94123,
Tel: 415 563 4936
Imp. Ret. Rep. W.; A.O.N.; Anat. Afgh.

Southwest Textiles,
PO Box 1306, Corrales, NM 87048
Tel: 505 898 5058
Ret. W.; O.; N Am.
Navajo, Hispanic and Pueblo textiles.

Sun Bow Trading Co.,
108 Fourth St NE, Charlottesville, VA 22901
Tel: 804 293 8821
Imp. Ret. W. Rep.; Anat. Pers. Afgh.
Source acquisition of tribal and nomadic textiles and
rugs from Konya to Kashgar.

Tamor Shah,
3219 Cains Hill Place N.E., Atlanta, GA 30305
Tel: 404 261 7259
Imp. Ret. W.; A.O.; Afgh.
Fine antique and semi-antique rugs, kilims, tapestries,
embroideries, costume and lace.

John Bigelow Taylor,
162 East 92nd St, New York, NY 10128
Tel: 212 410 5300
High-quality photography of kilims, carpets, textiles
and works of art.

Mary Taylor,
99 Bank St, New York, NY 10014
Tel: 212 242 3652
Restorer of fine antique kilims.

Textile Arts Inc.,
1571 Canyon Road, Santa Fe, NM 87501
Tel: 505 983 9780
Ret. Rep.; A.; World
Specializes in museum quality textiles from around
the world. Gallery owner Mary Hunt Kahlenberg is
author of several textile books. Co-author of *Walk in
Beauty.*

Trocadero Textile Art,
1501 Connecticut Avenue, N.E.
Washington D.C. 20036
Tel: 202 328 8440
Imp. Ret. W. Rep.; A.O.N.; Anat. Pers. Afgh.
A large collection of kilims bought from source.

Turkana Gallery,
125 Cedar Street, Penthouse, New York, NY 10006
Tel: 212 732 0273/516 725 4645
Imp. Ret. Rep.; A.O.; World
Primarily a kilim dealer. Open by appointment.

Umbrello,
8607 Melrose Avenue, Los Angeles, CA 90069
Tel: 213 655 6447
and at
701 Canyon Road,
Santa Fe, NM 87501
Tel: 505 984 8566
Imp. Manu. Ret.; A.O.N.; N Am. S. Am.
A gallery for South-West American and Mexican
home furnishings. Facsimile Navajo rugs made in
Mexico a speciality.

Helene Von Rosentiel Inc.,
382 11th Street, Brooklyn, NY 11215
Tel: 718 788 7909
Rep.; A.O.N.; World

John and Suzan Wertime,
PO Box 16296, Alexandria, VA 22302
Tel: 703 379 8528
Ret.; A.; Pers.
Specialists in small, outstanding nomadic weavings
for the connoisseur and collector.

Woven Legends Inc.,
922 Pine St, Philadelphia, PA 19107
Tel: 215 922 7509
Imp. Ret. W. Rep.; A.O.N.; Anat. Cauc. Pers.
A constantly changing selection of fine antique and
modern kilims.

Glossary

abr Persian word meaning 'cloud'; a general term for ikat.

adire (Yoruba, Nigeria) Name given to the deep blue indigo resist-dyed cloth.

asasia (Ashanti, Ghana) Silk cloth for royalty and notables woven by a complex supplementary weft patterning technique on a three heddle drag loom.

bandha From Hindi (Bandh), the resist binding of yarn before weaving. Known elsewhere as ikat.

bandhani (s.), **bandhana** (pl.) From Hindi (Bandh), to tie or bind. Areas of woven cloth are resist bound before the dyeing process for patterning purposes.

batik Indonesian term for textiles patterned by the alternate waxing – to resist – and dying of cloth.

bayeta (baize) Plainwoven woollen cloth.

capixay (Guatemala) Thick woollen garment resembling a tunic.

chakla (Gujarat, India) Square dowry cloth, usually embroidered, initially used as a cover, then hung in the home as an auspicious emblem.

chapan Warm, padded robe of Central Asia.

chumpi (Quechua) Handwoven belt.

corte (Guatemala) Blanket-like wrap-around skirt.

cumpi (Quechua) The finest cloth woven in pre-Columbian times for priests and nobility.

darnia, dharaniyo Embroidered cover for piles of stored bedding, Gujarat, India.

derkee Quilted, patchwork coverlet from Gujarat, India.

dhurrie (Hindi and Urdu) Flatwoven cotton floorcover.

eye-dazzler Description given to the design composition of a textile – usually a Navajo rug, kilim or dhurrie – that is dominated by a single, central motif, shimmering with bright colour.

geringsing Double ikat, cotton cloth from Bali, from the village Tenganan Pageringsingan.

ghajeri Flatwoven rug from Central Asia made up of narrow strips (tent bands) of warp faced patterned cloth.

gul Turkish for rose. Stylized flower motif, usually octagonal, of Muslim tribal weavers – seen on carpets and flatweaves.

hanbel Flatwoven woollen rug/blanket, made by the Berber of North Africa.

heybe Turkish carrying shoulder or donkey pouch. Often with double pouches as a saddle bag. Kilim back with cicim, zilli, soumak or knotted decoration.

huipil South Mexican and Guatemalan Indian blouse made up of panels of decorated and plain cloth.

hurgin Persian donkey and saddle bag.

ikat From the stem of the Malay-Indonesian word mengikat meaning to bind, tie or wind around, 'ikat' refers to cloth patterned by the resist dye technique before weaving.

jajim (Persian) Narrow strips of warp-faced and warp-faced patterned cloth woven on a narrow ground loom, cut and sewn together to make a floorcover.

jaloor Similar in size to a juval but decorated by long tassels of wool, used as a tent hanging, as well as a storage bag.

jaspeado (Guatemala) A fabric decorated with jaspe designs. Jaspe is the resist dye and weaving technique known elsewhere as ikat.

juval Large rectangular, storage and saddle bags from Turkestan.

kantha Traditional Bengali embroidery decorated quilt.

katab Meaning 'to cut up', this is an Anglo-Indian term for appliqué technique and textiles.

kente (Ashanti, Ghana) General term for stripwoven cloth of Ghana, used as a garment wrap.

khasa Stripwoven, weft-faced patterned woollen blankets woven and used by Fulani, West Africa.

kilim (Turkish) Flatwoven rug or rug woven without a knotted pile.

kurachi Patchwork curtains or panels for Turkoman yurt decoration.

maffrash Three-panelled bedding and clothing bag of the Caucasus.

mihrab Prayer arch, Islam.

mit'a Incan form of taxation by way of personal service.

mola Kuna word for cloth. A panel of reverse appliqué cotton cloth used as a blouse decoration.

Mukkur Town in southern Afghanistan, home to many kilim-weaving gypsies the Koochi.

obraje Small factory or workshop of Spanish-colonial South America.

palepai (Sumatra) Narrow, ceremonial textile known as a ship cloth.

patola (S. patolu) Silk cloth, often saris, patterned by the complex double ikat technique from Gujarat, India.

plangi The Indonesian word meaning 'rainbow'.

pua The ceremonial blanket of the Iban people of Borneo.

q'epi Bolivian Indian bundle of ceremonial cloth.

rebozo Fringed ikat decorated shawl of Central and South America.

refajo Guatemalan Indian wrap-around skirt.

rilli (ralli) Patchwork and appliqué quilted coverlet, from Sind.

rukorsi Persian, square stove and oven flatwoven cloth.

sarong Malay tubular garment which is wrapped about the body.

serape Traditional North American Indian clothing wrap.

shamiana (Rajasthan and Gujarat) Cloth ceiling canopy.

soffrai Persian for small rug, used to denote such flatweaves as small runners or square eating cloths.

susani Derived from Persian for needle. General term for Central Asian dowry embroideries.

sutrangi Persian for flatwoven cotton floorcover.

tampan Sumatran square ceremonial textile, decorated with supplementary weft work.

tapis Sumatran richly decorated woman's sarong.

tatabin Sumatran ceremonial textile with ship cloth composition. Related to palepai.

toran (Gujarat) Auspicious/wedding decorative doorway hanging.

tzute Guatemalan all-purpose cloth.

yurt Central Asian circular tent of felt covers and willow staves structure.

Index

Page numbers in italics refer to illustration captions

ABOCCHANI *60*
abr 48; *see also* ikat
abrash 85
abstract designs *see* designs
Aceh, Sumatra 53, 106
acid-free paper 95, 96, 179; *20, 114, 138*
Aegean sea 45
Afghanistan 43, 44, 47, 48, 50, 79, 86, 87, 88; *8, 12, 23, 43, 49, 62, 63, 104, 108, 112, 134, 138, 139, 140, 166, 169, 174, 175*
Africa 37–43; *68–9, 119, 173*; Central 42, 84; *97*, North 38, 39, 50, 83, 86, 88; *16, 110, 140, 146, 168*; sub-Sahara 28, 37; West 40, 41, 42, 49, 84
Algeria 37, 38, 39; *19, 38, 68, 110*
Almohades *see* Berber
Almoravids *see* Berber
alpaca 36; *163 see also* cameloid
altiplano 34, 35, 83; *15, 70*
Americas, The 28, 30-7; North 30, 75; Central 32; South 34, 42, 75, 78, 82, 84; *57*
Anatolia 43, 44, 45, 77, 79, 86, 87, 88; *43, 44, 66, 67, 117, 136, 137, 139, 143, 144, 163, 167, 170*
Andes 34, 35, 36; *114, 165*
Andhra Pradesh 52, 88; *49*
Antioquia, Colombia 34
Antoni tribe, Timor 56
appliqué 34, 42, 47, 48, 50, 51, 80, 87, 88; *22, 51, 60, 69, 71, 100, 102, 103, 105, 111, 126, 129, 132, 144, 169, 170*
Arab peoples 37, 38, 39, 40, 46, 47, 53, 55, 82
Armenia 46, 47
asasia cloth 41
Ashanti tribe 41, 86; *38, 68 see also* Ghana
Asia 43, 48, 50, 82; *118, 140*
Asia, Central 43, 44, 46, 47, 48, 49, 75, 76, 77, 79, 83, 86, 88; *62–3, 78, 101, 106, 112, 120, 132, 140, 146, 151, 170, 172*
Asia Minor 43, 44, 79, 86; *66–7*
Assyrian peoples 44
Atlas Mountains 39, 83; *38, 68, 138*
Avar tribe, Caucasus 46
Ayacucho, Peru 36; *30*
Aydin, Anatolia 45; *43*
Aymara Indians 36, 37; *70*
Azerbaijan 46
Azuay, Ecuador 35

BABYLON 27, 49
bags 44, 48, 75, 77, 79, 83, 87; *76, 102, 108, 112, 118, 129, 130, 173, 176* coca 36; *36*
baize (bayeta) 31, 32
Bakhtiari tribe, Persia 46
Bakongo tribe *38*
Bali 33, 52, 53, 54, 56, 77, 79, 87; *53*
Balikesir, Anatolia 45; *43*
Balouch peoples 46, 47, 50, 77, 79, 83, 84; *4, 8, 63, 154, 164, 166, 168*

Balouchistan 83; *43, 49*
bandha *see* ikat
bandhani *see* tie and dye
Bangladesh *49*
Bansali caste, India 80
Bantu peoples, Africa 42
Bardiz, Anatolia 45
bark cloth *98*
basketwork motif *see* design
Batak peoples 27; *175*
batik 53, 56; *22*
batten, weaving 85
bed covers 48, 53; *144, 145*
belts 32 (chumpi 36); *140, 146*
Bengal, West, 51; *44*
Berber 38, 39, 40, 50, 83; *16, 68, 140*
Bessarabian kilims 45; *66 see also* Karabagh
Bikaner, Rajasthan *60*
birth rites 27
Black Sea *43*
blankets 30–3, 35–6, 39, 41–3, 75, 77; *14, 68–9, 71–2, 108–9, 116, 131–2, 134, 143, 165*
bobbin 86
Bokhara 48, 79, 84; *8, 21, 43, 62, 133, 145, 146*
Bolivia 34, 35, 36, 78, 88, 178; *15, 36, 70, 147, 163, 165, 172*
Bonwire, Ghana 41
Borneo 53, 56, 80; *53, 58*
Bosque Redondo 31
braid 36
Broach, India 49
brocades 30, 33, 36, 44, 88; *63, 65, 70, 87*
bsath 44
Buddhism 53, 80
bull covers *61*
buying 178
Byzantine 28, 29, 37, 38, 83

CAIRO 27
calico 28
Calicut 28
camel 37; bag 79; hair 83; cameline 83; motif 39, 43, 77; decoration *2*
cameloids 34, 35, 36, 83; *36*
capixay 33
carding 83; *44*
Carib peoples 34
carpet gripper 94–5; *140 see also* wall hangings
Carthage 38
Caspian Sea *43*
caste system, India 50, 51, 80
Cathay 47, 75
Caucasus 44, 45, 46, 77, 83, 88; *43, 65, 66, 76, 104, 108, 129, 173*
Celebes Islands *see* Sulawesi
Central Asia *see* Asia
Chad, Lake 41
chakla 80; *61, 132*
Chancay period 35, 36, 78, 89; *30*
Chavin period 35

Chiadma, Morocco 40
chief blankets (Navajo) 31, 86; *14, 72, 115*
Chile 35
chilim *see* kilim
Chimu Indians 35
China 28, 46, 47, 49, 55, 56, 75, 82, 83; *43, 106, 120*
Christianity 37, 39, 44, 75, 78, 79, 80
chumpi *see* belts
cicim 79, 87–8; *167*
cleaning of textiles 179
Colombia 32, 34, 35
Colotenango, Guatemala 70
combs, weaving 29; motif 83, 86; *82, 39*
Congo 86; *11, 15, 98, 100, 122, 126*
Coptic weaving 37, 83, 87; *20, 68*
corte 33
cotton 28, 30, 33, 34, 35, 36, 37, 39, 40, 41, 45, 46, 47, 48, 49, 50, 52, 56, 75, 80, 82, 87, 88; *44, 54, 58, 59, 60, 61, 62, 64, 65, 66, 68, 70, 100, 102, 115, 135*
cumpi (cloth) 34
curtains 44, 47, 48, 53; *12, 62, 167*
cushions 108, 113, 116, 129, 130, 132, 140, 143, 148, 176

DEATH CULT 27, 35, 78
Deccan, India *49*
derkee 88
designs, abstract 42; *70*; architectural 39; animal 48, 56; basketwork *40*; birds 79; *80*; crocodile's back 79; dazzler *61, 72*; deer 56; double-headed bird *77*; dragon *80*; eagles 48; eight-legged spider 47; eye 79; eyebrows *43, 40*; Fatima 79; figurative 39, 51; fish 39, 56; floral 48, 50, 51; *66*; forest vine *43, 40*; geometric 43, 46, 51, 88; *98*; gul 79; hand 79; human figures 56; medallion 45, 46, 47, 48; *64–7*; ram's horns 48, 79; rectilinear 42, 43; seven pillars 79; skull trees 56; smoke 79; stars and stripes 108; tortoise 43; *40, 69*
dharaniyo 80
dhurrie 47, 50, 51, 79, 80, 86; *14, 15, 48, 60, 61*; jail *29*
division of labour in weaving 40
Dogon people, Africa 27
donkey bag *21*
door hanging *22*
dowries 44, 47
draughtsman, textile design 47
dyestuffs 52, 55, 77, 84–5; natural 29, 32, 33, 34, 36, 37, 38, 40, 44; synthetic 28, 32, 33, 35, 40, 44, 45, 48, 76, 82

EAST INDIA COMPANY, Dutch 54
eating cloth 47; *46*
Ecuador 27, 29, 34, 35, 77, 78, 87, 88; *30*
Egypt 27, 37, 49; *38, 43, 68*
embroidery 28, 33, 35, 37, 39, 42, 44, 47, 48, 50, 51, 77, 78, 80, 87, 88, 89; *11, 12, 13, 17, 18, 60, 61, 67, 69, 78, 100, 101, 105, 104, 110, 111, 112, 116, 132, 146, 148, 144, 150, 151, 154*
Erzurum, Anatolia 45; *43, 67*
Europe 38, 39, 42, 43, 44, 45, 48, 49, 50, 76, 82, 83, 86; *139*
Ewe tribe 41; *14, 18, 38, 39*

'FACSIMILE' TEXTILES 178
feather textiles 36, 75; *70, 102*
felt 77
fibres, natural 29; manmade 29, 33, 35, 36, 44, 52
flax 34, 35, 82
fleece 83
floral covers 155–160; *154–76 see also* rugs
floral designs *see* designs
Flores, Indonesia 54, 56; *53, 59*
Fostat, Egypt 27, 49
framing textiles 96
Fulani tribe, West Africa 42, 86; *38, 69*
fulling, cloth process 83
funeral use of textiles 40, 42, 54, 80; *59*
furnishing textiles 53

GAFSA, Tunisia 39, 40; *38*
Garmsar, Persia 46; *13, 131*
gelim *see* kilim
Gemanstown, Pennsylvania 32; *99*

geometric motifs *see* design
Georgia, USSR 46
geringsing 56
Ghana 77, 38, 68
ghujeri 88; *63 see also* jajim and stripweave
Gibraltar, Straits of 38
ginning process 83
Greece 27, 37, 44–9, 75, 82
Guatemala 32, 33, 77, 78, 88; *18, 30, 33, 70, 77, 115, 132, 141, 144, 148, 174*
Gujarat, India 51, 52, 54, 80, 88; *12, 49, 51, 52, 60, 61, 78, 104, 118, 132, 170*
gypsy 44, 47; *108*

HAIR, GOAT 38, 43, 47; camel 47; *63*; alpaca 75, 82–3; *70*
hanbel, hambel 39, 40, 50, 77; *68, 147, 173*
hangings *see* wall hangings
hats 36, 41; *21, 140, 150, 151*
Hausa tribe, Nigeria 38
headscarves 41
Hellenistic influences 37, 47
Herat, Afghanistan 43
herati *17*
heybe *and* hurgin 77
High Pamirs *see* Pamirs
Himalayan Mountains 47
Hinduism 49, 52, 53, 79, 80; *132*
Hispanic influences 32, 34, 39
horse covers 47, 77; *62, 74*; hair 83
Huancayo, Peru 36; *30*
Huari culture 35, 78; *20, 30, 70, 78, 102, 139, 163*
huipil 33; *18*

IBAN TRIBE, Kaliman Tan, 56; *58, 148*
Iberia 28, 39
ikat 33, 35, 36, 42, 44, 47, 48, 51, 53–6, 77, 79, 80, 83, 84, 87, 88; *8, 21, 22, 50, 54, 58, 59, 62, 80, 98, 101, 104, 129, 130, 135, 145, 148, 152, 172, 176*
Incan Empire 28, 34–6, 78
India 27, 28, 47–50, 53, 55, 56, 75, 76, 78–80, 82, 83, 85–8; *12, 14, 15, 43, 48, 49, 51, 52, 60, 61, 104, 105, 111, 112, 132, 144*
Indians, American, central 32; north 30; south 34; Aymara 36–7; *70*; Aztec 32; Cara 35; Carib 34; Chancay 35, 36, 78, 88; *30*; Chavin 35; Chimu 35; Hopi 31; Huari 35, 78; *70, 78, 102, 139, 163*; Incan 34–6, 78; Kuna 34, 78; *71, 77*; Mayo 33; Mixtec 32; Nazca 35, 36, 88; *70*; Olmec 32; Paracas 35; *30, 78*; Pueblo 30, 31; Tarahumara 33; Tiahuanaco 35, 36; Toltec 32; Yaqui 33; Zapotec 32, 33; Zuni 31
Indigo dye 31, 42, 53, 56, 82, 84, 85, 88; *69, 115*
Indonesia 53, 75, 76, 79, 80, 82, 84, 85, 87, 88, 125, 127; *16, 22, 53, 58, 59, 109, 129, 130, 135, 152, 170, 176*
Indus valley 83
industrialization 28
Iraq 44; *43, 166*
Islam 27, 28, 35, 37–9, 43, 44, 46, 49, 53, 79, 80, 82; *19, 79, 113, 144*

JAJIM 88 *see also* ghujeri and stripweave
jaloor 77
jaspeado *see* ikat
Java, Indonesia 53, 55, 56; *22, 53*
Jewish influence 39, 47, 48
jute 82
juval 77; *47*

KABUL, Afghanistan 104
Kairouan, Tunisia 39
Kano, Nigeria 85
kantha 88
Kasai river, Zaire 42
katab 88
Kathiawar, Gujarat, India *60, 61*
Karabagh kilim 45; *66*
Kazak people 47
kelim *see* kilim
kente 41; *68, 119*
khasa cloth 42

Khorasan, Persia 46, 47; *43*
kilim 39, 43, 44, 46, 47, 50, 77, 79, 80, 82, 83, 86–8; *12, 17, 26, 45, 63–8, 80, 104, 108, 112, 113, 116, 117, 122, 132, 134, 136–40, 142–5, 152, 154, 161–4, 166–71, 174–6*
Kirghiz people 47, 84
knotted textiles 40, 43
Konya, Anatolia 45; *43, 66*
Koran 53, 77
Kuba people, Zaire 12, 43, 79, 87; *11, 40, 69, 97, 116, 119*
Kuba, Caucasus 46, 43, 65
Kuna Indians, Panama 34, 78, 88; *71, 77, 102*
Kurdish people 44, 46, 77, 79, 84; *43, 65, 66, 134, 137, 152, 162, 175*
Kutch, Gujarat, India *49*

LAKAI *see* Uzbek
lazy lines 87 *see also* weaving
Lebanon 44
lemba leaves 54
lighting textiles 94
linen 83 *see also* flax 37
linseed oil 83
Lio tribe, Flores 56
llama 83; *36, 57*
Lombok, Indonesia *53*
looms 50, 52, 75, 85, 86; angled 42, 85; backstrap 30, 33, 35, 54, 55; *54*; continuous warp 47; drag 77; *44*; ground 36, 38, 44, 86; *63*; harness 48; heddle, double 40 single 40, 44; hip strap 82; 85–6; *70*; horizontal 34; machine 83, 86; pulleys *119*; rigid 30; strip 40; treadle 31, 33–5, 40, 86; vertical 38, 39, 42, 86; *168*; village 48
loose covers 128

MADDER PLANT *see* dyeing
maffrash 77; *108, 129*
Mahajan caste, India 61
Maimana, Afghanistan 47, 86; *43, 63, 142, 170*
Malabar, India 28
Malatya, Anatolia 45; *43, 66*
Malaya, Malaysia 56; *53*
Mali 38, 69
Mandvi, Kutch, Gujarat 61
Manggarai tribe, Flores 56; *59*
mantle 37, 55, 56; *22, 59, 68, 70, 114*
Marrakesh, Morocco 40; *38*
Matisse, Henri 43; *97, 122*
Mayo *see* Indians
Mazar-i-Sharif, Afghanistan 47
Mediterranean Sea 27, 43, 49; *43*
Mexico 32, 33, 77, 88; *10, 11, 18, 29, 30, 71, 114, 134, 137, 140, 164, 171, 174*
mihrab 45, 79; *11, 67*
mirror work 51; *118*
mit'a 34
Mixtec *see* Indians
mola 102, 132
Moluccas Islands, Indonesia 53; *53*
Mongol peoples 27, 44
Moorish peoples 38, 39
mordants 49, 83–5
Morocco 37, 38–40; *38, 68, 104, 130, 138, 140, 146, 176*
mosque floor coverings 79; *8*
Mughal Empire 27, 47, 49, 50; *136*
muslin 48, 49, 75

NATURAL DYES *see* dyes
Navajo 31, 32, 78, 83, 84, 86, 87; *14, 18, 23, 30, 31, 71, 72, 99, 115, 164, 174*
Nazca *see* Indians
New Mexico 31; *72*
Niger river *69*
Nigeria 40, 42, 83, 84; *38, 68*
nomads 42–4, 46–8, 76, 77, 79, 83, 86, 124, 125; *26, 64, 106, 166, 174*
North-West Frontier 50, 51, 88; *8, 12, 21, 26, 49, 116*

OASIS TOWNS 47
Oaxaca, Mexico 33; *30*

obraje workshops 34, 35, 76
Olmec, Mexico 32
Orientalist art *19*
Orissa, India 51, 52, 88; *49*
Ottoman Empire 27, 37, 38, 39, 44–6, 80, 83, 88; *13, 17, 110, 132, 133, 145*

PACIFIC OCEAN 34–5
Pakistan 50, 51, 79, 83; *43, 49, 60*
Palembang, Sumatra 53
palepai *see* ship cloth
Pamir Mountains 43, 83
Panama 32, 34, 78, 88; *30, 71, 102, 132*
Paracas culture 35; *30, 78*
pardah 62
patchwork 37, 48, 77, 88; *2, 98, 104*
patola cloth 52, 54, 56, 80; *88, 104*
Pazyryk, Siberia 27
Persia 29, 37, 44, 46–9, 77, 79, 83, 87–8; *43, 46, 62, 64–6, 74, 102, 112, 113, 116, 118, 120, 129, 130, 132, 161, 162, 166, 168, 175–6*
perspex 96
Peru 27, 34–7, 75, 77–8, 83, 86–8; *10, 20, 30, 36, 70, 139, 143*
plexiglass *102, 106, 117*
ponchito 36–7; *172*
poncho 32, 35–6, 75, 86; *10, 70, 102, 115, 134*
powerloom 28
prayer mat 45, 47, 50, 79; *60*
pre-Columbian cultures 32–6, 75, 78, 86, 87, 125; *10, 11, 36, 70, 139, 147, 163*
pua 56; *58*
Pueblo *see* Indians
Punjab 51, 88; *49*

Q'EPI 37, 78; *70, 114*
Qala-i-Nau, Afghanistan 43
Qashqai tribe, Persia 44, 83; *64, 130, 161, 174*
Qazvin, Persia 46
Quechua-speaking peoples 34, 36
quilting 50, 51, 77, 80, 88; *60, 104–5, 170*

RAJASTHAN 51–2, 88; *49, 60*
raphia 40, 42–3, 82, 84, 87–8; *11, 40, 100, 103, 116, 122, 127*
rebozo 35
rectilinear designs *see* designs
Redeyef, Tunisia 39; *38*
refajo 33
religious influences 28, 51
repair 179
resist dyeing 35 *see also* tie and dye
reverse appliqué *see* appliqué
ritual use of textiles 40, 54
Rivera, Diego 32
rod and sleeve *see* wall hangings
rodillera 33
Roman Catholicism 34, 36
Rome 27–9, 38, 49
Roti, Indonesia 53
rove of fibres 84
rugs 27–8, 30, 32–5, 39–40, 43–4, 47, 51
rukorsi kilim 77
Rumania 43
rush matting 40

'S' TWIST 84
Sabah 53

saddle bags *39; 24*
saddlecloth 32, 42
Safavid Empire 27, 44, 46, 80, 83, 88
Salcaja, Guatemala 33
Saltillo, Mexico 32–3; *30*
Samarkand, USSR 47–8, 77; *43, 135*
Samur tribe, Caucusus 46
San Pedro de Caias, Peru 36
San Blas Islands, Panama 34; *30, 102*
Sarawak 53–4, 58
Sarkoy, Thrace 45
sarong 53, 55–6, 75, 80, 84, 86; *54, 59*
Sart peoples 47
sash 28, 33, 35–6; *148*
satin 44
Sava, Persia 46
Seljuk peoples 27, 44
selling 178
selvedge 41, 77, 86; *59, 62*
Senegal river 41
Senna, Persia 46, 79; *12, 17, 43, 65, 122, 168*
serape 31; *18, 29;* Mexican 33; *71, 137*; Navajo 32; *108*
sericulture 48, 83
Shakhrisyabz, USSR 48
Shamiana 60
shearing 83
shed 85–6 *see also* countershed
sheep 34, 43, 83; Andalusian churro 31
Shirvan, Caucasus 46; *65, 104*
Shivaz, Persia *43*
Shoowa tribe 42 *see also* Kuba people, Zaire
shuttle 40
Siberia 27
Sigsig, Ecuador 35
silk 28, 33–5, 37, 40–1, 44, 46, 48, 50–1, 75, 79, 80, 82–3, 84, 87–8; *58, 60–2, 67–9, 71, 101, 106, 112, 135, 145–6, 166, 170, 172, 174*
Sind (Thar Parkar) 51, 88; *12, 49, 60*
Sivas, Anatolia 45; *43, 67*
soffrai 77; *63*
Soma, Gold Coast 41
soumak 47, 79, 88; *87, 112, 173*
Spain 28, 30–2, 34, 36, 76; *70*
spindles *47, 138*
spinning wheel 36, 82–4; *29*
stitching, over- 42, 55, 88; *42;* plush 42
Sulawesi Islands, Indonesia 53, 56, 80; *53, 98*
Sumatra 52–3, 55, 75, 84, 87–8; *53, 58, 100, 101, 106, 117, 170, 172, 175*
Sumba 54, 56; *22, 53, 59, 80, 130, 134, 176*
susani 47–8, 80, 88; *62, 120, 135, 145*
sutrangi 47; *8*
symbolism 44, 78–80
Syria 44; *43, 139*

TADJIK peoples 47
talisman 27
tampan *see* ship cloth
Tamurlane 47
tapis 55, 88; *58, 172*
Tarahumara, Mexico 33
Tashkent *43, 132*
Teec Nos Pos *18*
Tehran 46
Tenganan Pageringsingan, Bali 56
Tennsift river, Morocco 40

tents 38–9; bands 77; *166;* cloth 43; hangings 48; runners 47; trappings 38
Teotitlan, Mexico 33; *30, 174*
Thar Parkar (Sind) *49*
Thrace 44; *43, 66, 113, 139, 176*
Tiahuanaco, Bolivia 35–6, 30
Timor, Indonesia 56; *53, 80*
Timurid Empire 83
Titicaca, Lake, Bolivia and Peru 35–6; *30*
Toltec peoples 32
Toradja tribes 56; *59*
toran 80; *12, 52*
Totonicapan, Guatemala 33
trade, cashcrops 34, 36, 49, 75–6; cloth European 31; textiles 27–9
tree of life 45, 79, 80; *66*
Tuareg 37; *173*
Tunisia 37–40; *38, 68, 170, 173, 176*
Turkey 29, 38, 43, 45, 76–7; *66, 132, 171*
Turkic tribes 44–7, 76, 79, 88; *62, 166, 173*
Turkoman 48, 77; *2, 12, 19, 47, 62, 113*
tzute 33

UKRAINE 43
underlay 155–6; *15, 104, 167, 173–5*
unusual use of textiles 121–8; *120, 129–51*
upholstery 127; *130, 134, 137, 142–3, 144, 149, 162, 169, 176*
Uzbek 47–8, 88; *12, 62–3, 106, 120*

VALUATION 178
vegetable dyes *see* dyes
Velcro 95 *see also* wall hangings
velvet 42, 44; *133, 146*
Veramin, Persia 46; *43*
vicuna 83, *see also* cameloid

WALL HANGINGS 41, 43–4, 47–8, 50–1, 54, 56, 77, 80, 88–96; *59, 97–119;* colour and pattern 91–2; durability 93–4; formal and informal styles 92–3; lighting 94; methods 94–6; pattern 91–2; scale 91; size and shape 90–1
warp 37, 40; striping 42, 52, 55, 83, 85–7; *63–4*
weaving: atavistic 29; double interlock 50, 87; *60, 63, 85, 87;* eccentric weft 50; plain 37, 42, 87; *70;* single interlock 50, 79, 87; *60, 61, 68, 72, 85;* slit 35, 37, 39, 46–7, 50, 79, 87; *63–7, 70, 72, 85;* strip 41–2, 47, 88; *14, 39, 41, 68–9, 100, 119;* supplementary weft techniques 55–6, 86–8; *58–9, 106, 117;* sword 85–6; traditional 29; warp-faced 36–7, 40, 47, 79, 88; *63, 70;* weft-faced 36–42, 45, 47, 50, 54, 79, 87–8; *59–60, 63, 68–9, 87, 154;*
weft 37, 52, 55, 83, 85–7; *63–4*
whorl 84
wool 31, 33–40, 42–8, 50–2, 75, 82–4, 87; *47, 63–9, 71–2, 138, 165, 174*

YAQUI, *see* Indians
yarn 48, 77, 84
Yoruk peoples, Anatolia 44–5
Yurt 47–8, 123–4

'Z' TWIST 84
Zagroz Mountains, Persia 46
Zaire 37, 42, 79, 88; *38, 69, 97, 103*
Zapotec peoples, Mexico 32–3
Zarand, Persia 46; *43, 64*
zilli 79, 87–8